DIARY OF A TRAIN-SPOTTER

Volume 2
1960-68

Nostalgic recollections of visits to locomotive
depots, workshops, railway stations and
scrapyards

Michael G. Harvey

Silver Link Publishing Ltd

The author (left) standing beside his close friend Eddie Rooke; we had met up with two of our former Portsmouth train-spotting pals of the early 1960's, Frank Allen (second from right) and Trevor Robson. The setting is Norchard station on the Dean Forest Railway at Lydney, Gloucestershire. *Trevor Radway (Chairman of the Dean Forest Railway Co)*

ACKNOWLEDGEMENTS

My appreciation is directed to the following persons, who in some way or other have contributed their services towards the compilation of this book:

Frank Allen; Colin Asprey; Don Aylward; John Barker; John Barrowdale; Basil Batten; Alan Bell; David Bird; David Bodenham; Alfred Coffin; the late Tony Collett; Phil Cooper; the late David Copus; Colin Cromwell; A. D. Davies; Ron Davies; Jim Davidson; Roy Davidson; Tom H. J. Dethridge; Roger Emptage; Peter Esgate; Ted Gamblin; David Greenfield; Norman Hampshere; Phil Harding; John Harris; Tony Holley; Terry Hunt; Tony Ingram; G. E. 'Jim' Jackson; Gerald A. Jacobs; Ron Jelley; Bill Jenkins; John Jones; Timothy Julnes; John Kinchen; Jack Knowler; Jim 'Jimpy' Lawrence; Ernie Middleton; Bruce R. Oliver; Dave Pallett; Trevor Robson; Eddie Rooke; John Scutt; A. Shepperd; Bob Smith; John Spence; Jack Stillwell; Michael Street; Andrew Sutherland; Pete Walsh; Bob Whitney; Doug Willis; Dave Woolley; and Mike Yerbury.

If I have omitted anyone, please accept my apologies.

Special thanks also go to: Ian Allan Publishing Ltd; British Railways Board; Carreras Limited; Hull Museum of Transport; Isle of Wight Steam Railway; Merchant Navy Locomotive Preservation Society Ltd; National Tramway Museum, Crich; *The News*, Portsmouth (formerly *The Evening News*); Portsmouth Football Company Limited; and Swindon Railway Museum.

A very special 'thank you' goes to my close friend Eddie Rooke for his knowledge and assistance in helping me to compile this book - and to the late David Copus, to whom Volume 1 of *Diary of a Train-spotter* was dedicated, for his memories and all the good times we shared, which have been contained within these pages.

Finally, a sincere thank you to Andrew Prescott, a working colleague of Eddie Rooke at NatWest Bank, who undertook to put all of the relevant text on to computer disk at very short notice.

British Library Cataloguing in Publication Data

A catalogue record for this book is available from the British Library.

ISBN 1 85794 054 7

Remember that trespassing on the railway is both illegal and dangerous.

Silver Link Publishing Ltd
Unit 5
Home Farm Close
Church Street
Wadenhoe
Peterborough PE8 5TE
Tel/fax (01832) 720440

Printed and bound in Great Britain

CONTENTS

INTRODUCTION

Diary of a Train-spotter Volume 2, relating to the years 1960 to 1968, fulfils my life-long ambition of completing the final pieces of the nostalgic recollections and escapades of myself and my close friends in the days when steam trains ruled the rails on the British Railways system. It recalls the halcyon days when steam locomotives and their numbers were pursued up and down the country by train-spotters of all ages, prior to the coming of the anorak and long before television and video took a firm grip on most people's leisure-time.

The publisher described Volume 1, covering the years 1955 to 1959, as 'something completely different'. Train-spotters of the 1950s and 1960s, together with numerous other age groups, who like me travelled all over the British Isles to jot down train numbers and maybe capture that rare photograph, will, I hope, find reading Volume 2 not only once again 'something completely different', but also unique in that no other publisher has ever attempted a book that delves in such detail into the life and times of a train-spotter in the days of steam.

I had, by the early 1960s, taken hundreds of railway photographs and many appear in this book, together with a selection from my close friends; as in Volume 1, these are all original and contemporary. On a personal note, the sales of Volume 1 have given me the springboard on which to launch this book, as the response from the general public, societies, friends and relatives and the local press and radio have proved most encouraging - a 'plug' by DJ Steve Wright on Radio One certainly promoted much interest!

Also through the sales of Volume 1 I have been joyously re-united with many of my former railway friends whom I had given up for 'lost', and at the same time have been introduced to new friends both young and old, all of whom share the same passion for steam and rail travel in days gone by.

This book, being in the format of a diary, naturally 'reads on' from Volume 1, and its layout is basically the same in that it caters not only for railway enthusiasts but also highlights numerous other leisure-time activities of the 1960s, such as football, pop music, cinema, buses and walking.

To sum up, this book is intended to bring a tinge of nostalgia to its readers and portray a vivid and imaginative insight into our travels and adventures - even someone of 'non-railway' interest might find its text somewhat intriguing, and at times quite amusing, to say the least!

Train-spotters like myself who spent their entire teenage years in pursuit of steam were a breed apart, and anyone who is remotely interested in railways or steam trains of a bygone era should now read on. . . I'm sure you'll be glad you did!

All the visits by rail described in this book start either from Fratton, Portsmouth & Southsea or Portsmouth Harbour stations. Other visits were made by scooter or car, and these started from Eddie Rooke's parents' house in Fratton.

All the photographs in the book were, unless otherwise stated, taken by the author. Some of the line drawings and maps are also by the author, and give only a rough indication and are not necessarily to scale.

To help anyone not familiar with pre-decimal currency, I include the following conversion table from pounds, shillings and pence (£ s d):

2½ old pennies (d) = 1p	2/6d (2s 6d) = 12½p
6d = 2½p	10s = 50p
1 shilling (s) = 5p	20s = £1

Thus '35 shillings' is the equivalent of £1 15s 0d, or £1.75; '21 shillings' is £1.05; '12/3d' is approximately 61p, and so on. Of course, the value or 'buying power' of the equivalent amount of money was much higher in the 1960s!

1960

SHEFFIELD, SWANSEA AND BLACKPOOL EXCURSIONS

SHEFFIELD FOOTBALL EXCURSION

SATURDAY 9 JANUARY

This football excursion was run for the FA Cup Third Round match between Sheffield United and Portsmouth. I travelled with David Copus, Bill Jenkins, David Greenfield and Jack Knowler, and the return fare was 35 shillings (£1 15s).

The party met prior to departure, which was at 7.30 am from the Harbour station. We were steam-hauled as far as Basingstoke, travelling via Botley and Eastleigh by 'Lord Nelson' 4-6-0 No 30862 *Lord Collingwood*; 'King Arthur' Class 4-6-0 No 30800 *Sir Meleaus de Lile* was used as a 'banker' between the Harbour and Portsmouth & Southsea High Level. The train consisted of a set of 12 carriages in Southern green livery, including a Restaurant Car.

On these Sunday excursions it was common practice, if we desired, to collect a card table from the guard's compartment, which would be used to keep our Ian Allan *ABCs*, spotters' books, etc, at easy reach. The occasional game of cards would also take place.

No fewer than 52 steam locomotives were noted between Fratton and the Oxford area. It was sad to note, on passing Eastleigh Works scrapyard, 'King Arthur' No 30774 *Sir Gaheris* awaiting its turn to be cut up.

Lord Collingwood was taken off at Basingstoke, and we were then steam-hauled as far as Leicester by Class '4900' ('Hall') 4-6-0 No 5962 *Wantage Hall*.

BANBURY, WOODFORD HALSE AND RUGBY AREAS			
Steam locomotives:			
1473	3801	4919	4987
5912	5921	6001	6311
7234	7314	7324	44397
45419	48444	60908	61285
61438	61454	63838	90365
90475	90504	90518	90701
Diesel locomotives:			
12072	D3066	D3106	

Wantage Hall was taken off at Leicester and we were then steam-hauled on the final stage of the excursion to Sheffield by Standard Class '5' 4-6-0 No 73053.

A further 48 steam locomotives were noted between Rugby and Sheffield, travelling via Leicester, Annesley and Staveley - indeed, there was a very wide variety of classes, including LMS tanks, Class 'A4' 'Pacifics', Class 'B1' 4-6-0s, numerous Class 'O1' and 'O4' 2-8-0s and a fair number of Class 'WD' 2-8-0s and Class '9F' 2-10-0s. Seven electric locomotives were also noted: 26002, 26029,

26032, 26038, 26048, 26054 and 27000.

It was a very cold afternoon as we made our first ever visit to Sheffield; the sun just managed to shine briefly. We were quite surprised to note that trams were still being used in this city, one of the last in Great Britain to use this form of public transport. The tram system was to be abandoned in October of 1960.

Darnall was a straight shed with ten through roads and two other roads blocked off where minor repairs were undertaken. Nos 62660-9 were 'D11' ('Director') Class 4-4-0s, introduced in 1920. An elegant two-cylinder design with large side windows to the cab, most of the Class (11) were named after battlefields of the First World War, such as *Somme* and *Jutland*. They had exceptionally large driving wheels of 6 ft 9 in diameter. All were 'in store' except No 62662 *Prince of Wales*, which was in working order.

Leaving the shed we then caught a bus to Brammal Lane to see the FA Cup match - it was not a very good game if you happened to be a Portsmouth supporter, as we lost 3-0! The attendance was

We noted no fewer than 11 Class '9F' 2-10-0 freight locomotives between Banbury and Sheffield, Nos 92012, 92033, 92074, 92076, 92087, 92090, 92092, 92095, 92137 (pictured), 92222 and 92233.

SHEFFIELD (DARNALL) DEPOT

Steam locomotives:
60029   61027   61033   61041   61051   61094   61111   61139   61150   61151   61154   61162   61169
61181   61183   61249   61313   61315   61318   61361   61379   61728   61747   61760   61761   61847
62660   62662   62664   62666   62667   62669   63599   63658   63661   63685   63695   63734   63742
63783   63821   63850   63881   63966   64329   64373   64387   64441   64443   64445   64447   64736
64746   64804   69258   69296   73010   90668

Diesel locomotives:
D208   13325   D3663   D3701

62 locomotives on shed

19,528. After the game we caught a bus to Grimesthorpe to visit the depot; this location was also known as Brightside.

Grimesthorpe had a strange layout: the shed consisted of a single roundhouse building, but just outside there was another open-air turntable with 12 radiating roads. Behind the roundhouse was an eight-road works supplied by a traverser from two lines, one from the roundhouse and one from the open turntable. This was probably the only layout of this kind on BR. Undergoing repairs in the works were Standard Class '5' 4-6-0s Nos 73000 and 73073, together with two 0-6-0 diesel shunters.

A RIDE ON A TRAM

On leaving Grimesthorpe we walked for almost a mile in the direction of our next depot, Millhouses. We then chanced to catch a tram which showed a 'Millhouses' destination blind, and were thrilled to travel on the upper deck - it was a very bumpy journey and an experience none of our party would forget.

Although the tram number was not recorded, I do recall that it was painted cream with broad bands of blue. It was one of the 'Standard' types build in the Queens Road Works at Sheffield in 1934. It was a straight-sided metal-body car with upholstered seating for 24 in the lower saloon and 37 on the top deck, and carried the insignia 'STD' on its upper deck panels. The cost of the single journey was not recorded, but from information received the cost in 1958 would have been about sixpence to Millhouses.

One of the 'Standard' trams, No 189, has been preserved at the National Tramway Museum at Crich, Matlock, Derbyshire, who kindly supplied these details, and to whom I am most grateful.

Millhouses depot was adjacent to the railway station, and was an eight-road block-ended depot. Class 'B1' 4-6-0 No 61240 *Harry Hinchcliffe* was displaying the slogan 'UP THE BORO' chalked across the smokebox door in very large capital letters, having obviously been employed on a Middlesbrough Football Excursion, whose team were paired against the other Sheffield club, Wednesday.

We travelled by tram from Millhouses to Sheffield Victoria station, where we purchased some food and drink from the station buffet prior to catching the return excursion to Portsmouth.

SHEFFIELD (GRIMESTHORPE) DEPOT

Steam locomotives:
42904   43174   43203   43234
43406   43431   43637   43669
43749   43800   44039   44087
44265   44437   44457   44941
45040   46450   47513   47624
47636   48144   48178   48189
48322   48407   48519   48642
48733   73000   73073   78025

Diesel locomotives:
D3251   13253   13288   D3662

36 locomotives on shed

MILLHOUSES DEPOT

Steam locomotives:
40907   42116   42857   44857
44919   45239   45566   45570
45576   45656   45664   60885
60945   61240   61409   73048
73054   73065   78023

19 locomotives on shed

It is of note when comparing steam/diesel ratios that at this date BR had approximately 17,833 steam locomotives in stock compared to approximately 700 diesel, gas-turbine and petrol types, and only 71 electric locomotives - these figures were to change rapidly by 1965.

SHEFFIELD, LEICESTER AND BANBURY AREAS

Steam locomotives:
40167 60960 61051 61124
61154 61162 61164 61982
67799 90538

Electric locomotives:
26022 26037 26052 26056
27002 27003 27005

David Copus decided during the return journey that another visit to the Sheffield depots should be made, possibly taking in other depots in this area. The accompanying permit proves that he 'kept his word', and a visit took place on 29 May 1960. It is of interest that the name of his school railway enthusiasts' club, to which he belonged (and which originally started off as a model railway club), should be displayed at the foot of the permit, as by this date it had now become a sizeable train-spotters'

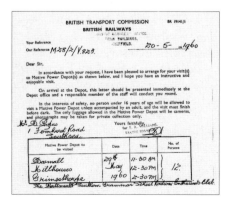

club with a very enthusiastic following! I did not participate in this particular trip, but David had no trouble in gathering up the required party number.

As this book unfolds, the reader will no doubt realise that following the fortunes of Portsmouth Football Club was probably our number two pastime after train-spotting; together with our interest in the pop music scene, it totally consumed all our leisure-time.

David Copus was an avid 'Pompey' supporter and it was he that instigated the printing of 5,000 gummed labels bearing the slogan 'PLAY UP POMPEY' - as you can imagine, these stickers were placed at random on the football excursions, and this Sheffield trip was no exception. Prime targets were the football ground, public transport and even in the gents at Brammal Lane!

As you read through these pages you'll find that these stickers even found their way to such locations as Blackpool Tower and the far north of Scotland!

SWANSEA

SATURDAY 23 JANUARY

Although this was not an official football excursion to see the league match, Swansea v Portsmouth at the Vetch Field, we nevertheless travelled by purchasing child special day excursion tickets from the Co-op travel agents in Fratton Road on the day prior to our trip, and dated 23 JA 60. The return fare was 30 shillings (£1 10s). It had been decided several weeks beforehand to make this trip and at the same time incorporate visits to engine sheds in the Swansea area. I was accompanied on this trip by Eddie Rooke, David Copus, Terry Hunt, Mike Yerbury, Trevor Robson, Timothy Julnes and Dave Woolley. Our day began at Fratton station at 6.20 am - the party gathered just as it had started to rain. Departure was on the 6.37 am electric unit Waterloo train as far as Guildford.

As with all early morning starts, an alarm clock was an essential item to enable me to wake up in plenty of time for breakfast and to make the 10-minute walk to Fratton station, but on the majority of these early starts I need not

have bothered, as my mother was always awake before me and made sure that I had everything packed in my haversack for the day.

Fratton-allocated Class 'U' 2-6-0 No 31637 hauled our train between Guildford and Reading South, arrival time at this terminus station being 8.30 am. The 68-minute wait for our connecting train, an express from London (Paddington) to Swansea, on the platform at the General station produced no fewer than 30 steam locomotives at Reading South and General.

We were steam-hauled to Swansea (High Street) by 'Castle' Class 4-6-0 No 4099 *Kilgerran Castle*, an 87E (Landore)-allocated engine.

READING SOUTH

6353	30549	31631	31636
31861	31867	31871	32469
33008	76028		

READING GENERAL

2212	2872	3723	4670
4930	4963	4973	6102
6103	6112	6150	6324
6654	7032	7906	7909
8430	9447	31635	76019

Even a fleeting glimpse of Swindon Works and its area on passing proved to be interesting train-spotting, with numerous types of steam classes to be seen. From information learned on a later visit, we found that Swindon's massive workforce included at one time women, whose job it was to french polish the carriage doors!

These Class '5700' 0-6-0 pannier tanks were to be seen on this trip at virtually every depot, goods yard, station and siding, in both directions, between Reading and Swansea. In fact we noted 50 in all - No 3754 is pictured.

PASSING SWINDON WORKS AND SCRAPYARD

Steam locomotives:

1024	1502	2842	2847
2883	2893	3739	3863
4081	4697	4902	5035
5059	5160	5164	5380
5991	6025	6167	6601
6839	6909	7031	7301
8419	8427	8445	8455
9721	48430	73001	

Diesel locomotives:

D603	D815	D3195	D3504
D3751	15100		

We were kept very busy between Bristol and Cardiff, as steam locomotives of many WR classes were noted; they included Class '2800' 2-8-0s employed on coal trains, many pannier tanks and side tanks of the 2-6-2 wheel arrangement, and of course main-line steam locomotives such as Nos 4097 *Kenilworth Castle*, 5084 *Reading Abbey* and 7021 *Haverfordwest Castle*, together with 'Britannia' Class 4-6-2 Nos 70018 *Flying Dutchman* and 70022 *Tornado*. Only nine diesel shunters were noted.

On emerging from the Severn Tunnel, the weather, which up to this point had been steady rain, had now become pouring rain! Eight steam engines, all of a saddle-tank design, were noted in sidings near Bridgend; they were painted dark red, and most probably owned by the National Coal Board. All appeared to be in working order. There had been a minor derailment of some wagons at the east end of Bridgend station, so we approached with caution and were diverted via a loop line.

On arrival at Swansea we purchased special cheap day return tickets to Llanelly, for our first shed visit of the day. We were greeted at the station by an enormous downpour, the signal for our party to don their plastic macs! We were steam-hauled between Swansea and Llanelly by 'Castle' Class 4-6-0 No 5016 *Montgomery Castle*.

We made the 15-minute walk from Llanelly station to the engine shed and were quite relieved to enter the large building, which consisted of a double roundhouse and single-road repair shop, as it provided us with shelter from the rain.

For this trip highlights of the 'on shed' lists of locomotives at both Llanelly and Landore have been included in text form, as Eddie and I were to make visits to these depots at a later date, and complete lists will be given there.

LLANELLY DEPOT (87F)
It was quite a busy scene as we entered the depot yard with numerous steam locomotives moving on and off shed. Although we had a permit for this and other depots on the trip, we did not go through the formalities of producing it at the foreman's office - this would have taken up valuable time! Our party of eight split up into groups of two, and although we noted the shed foreman lurk-

BRIDGEND, NEATH AND SWANSEA AREAS

Steam locomotives:

1101	1102	1103	1104	1105	1106	1141	1142	1143	1144	3644	3701	3768
3785	4107	4121	4207	4232	4266	4282	4293	4653	4923	5014	6652	6851
6953	6999	7006	7207	7739	7765	7798	8416	8490	8748	8784	8788	8794
9448	9457	9609	9637	9777	9792							

Diesel locomotives:

D3352 D3353 D3356 D3431 D3432 D3433 D3434 D3436 D3438 D3754 D3759 D3827

Nos 1101-1106 were Class '1101' tanks (complete class noted) - introduced 1926 and used for dock shunting. Nos 1141-1144 were Class 'SHT' (Swansea Harbour Trust) saddle-tanks, introduced on various dates 1905 to 1911. Both classes noted on passing Neath.

ing, we needed some smart foot-work to dodge his attention! 'On shed' were 51 steam locomotives and four 0-6-0 diesel shunters. The steam included no fewer than 20 pannier tanks, six 2-8-0 tanks, two LMS Class '4' 2-6-4 tanks, Nos 42305 and 42390, together with seven Class '8F' 2-8-0s. It was pleasing to note several 'Hall' Class 4-6-0s in excellent condition, Nos 5903 *Keele Hall* and 5909 *Newton Hall*; others of the same Class were Nos 5931 and 6912. Three 'Grange' Class 4-6-0s were 'in steam', Nos 6810 *Blakemere Grange* (87F), 6827 *Llanfrechfa Grange* and 6853 *Morehampton Grange*.

Leaving the depot we walked to Landore, a predominantly main-line shed. The building consisted of two separate four-road sheds, one with a single-road repair shop built on to its side.

LANDORE DEPOT (87E)
This depot produced an 'all-steam' total of 34 locomotives. Nos 4074, 4093, 5004, 5007, 5013, 5041, 5051, 5077, 5080 and 7028 were all main-line 'Castle' Class 4-6-0s, and as far as we could make out they were all in working order. Other 4-6-0s, in the form of 'Halls' and 'Modified Halls', were noted, Nos 4923, 5927, 5990, 6933 and 6999. Class '5600' 0-6-2 tank No 6680 was undergoing minor repairs in the repair shop.

Our next visit was to Swansea East Dock, and our mode of transport was double-decker bus. By now we had resigned ourselves to the incessant downpour!

East Dock was a small, neat three-road shed without a turntable. It was while walking around this depot that Dave Woolley tripped over a signal wire and came crashing down in the rain puddles and coal dust. He picked himself up and attempted

SWANSEA EAST DOCK DEPOT

Steam locomotives:

1151	1152	2220	3641
3661	4225	5210	5232
5616	6613	6616	6738
7203	7215	7248	8423
8431	8444	8476	9431
9489	9744		

22 locomotives on shed

Nos 1151 and 1152 were Class 'PM' 0-4-0 saddle-tanks. Introduced 1907. Peckett design for P&M (Powlesland & Mason) Contractor. Weight 33 tons 10 cwt. Only two in class.

to clean himself - thereafter we nicknamed him as 'tripping' Woolley!

It was early evening as our party of eight made its way through the rain-swept streets of Swansea, the walk taking us 30 minutes via some very hilly roads, Tennant Road and Castle Street, to Swansea (High Street) station. We were very relieved to reach the station, not only to rest our legs, but to dry out our severely dampened clothes.

Eddie Rooke, together with several others who still had a little energy left and seemed oblivious to the rain, decided that, if they hurried, they could just manage to visit Danygraig depot (87C) and get back in time for the return train to London. This unusual stone-built depot surprisingly contained a four-road engine shed, a single-road repair shop and a three-road carriage and wagon repair shop. Unfortunately, however, my friends were not to know that the shed had closed to steam locomotives less than three weeks earlier, and as a result there were only

DANYGRAIG DEPOT

Diesel locomotives:
D3753 D3755 D3761 D3762
D3826 D3828 D3830 D3831

8 locomotives on shed

eight diesel shunters of the standard 0-6-0 type 'on shed' - this was obviously the reason why we had seen all of the Class '1101' and 'SHT' tanks away from their home shed, at Neath, no doubt en route to Swindon for scrapping. For information purposes the shed list is shown.

We did not have time to see the football match, but no one seemed to mind, as we had visited three depots and noted some interesting tank engines that were native to that area. The Portsmouth team that played and drew 1-1, with scorer Harry Harris (a Welshman), was: Beattie, Gunter, Dickinson, Howells, Snowdon, Carter, White, Saunders, Hayward, Harris and Cutler. Attendance was 12,000.

My friends returned from Danygraig just in time to board the London-bound train, which was steam-hauled by two 'Castle' Class 4-6-0s, Nos 5077 *Fairey Battle* and 4073 *Caerphilly Castle*, stopping only at principal stations. The total weight of both engines was 253 tons, and this was, to my knowledge, the first time that I had been double-headed by 'Castles'.

We were steam-hauled between Reading South and Guildford by Standard Class '4' 2-6-0 No 76054. On reaching Guildford we transferred to an electric unit train to Portsmouth for the final stage of the journey - needless to say, it had rained all day!

BIRMINGHAM

SUNDAY 13 MARCH

Return fare for this Portsmouth Harbour to Wolverhampton refreshment car excursion was 21 shillings. To give the reader some indication of fares at this date, other destinations on this train were Reading (7 shillings), Oxford (12/3d) and Banbury (15/3d).

I walked via Canal Walk to the Harbour station where I had arranged to meet my travelling companion Mike Yerbury. Departure time was 10.12 am, I was on the train, the guard was blowing his whistle and Mike had not appeared - then he suddenly came dashing up the platform, boarding the train virtually seconds before it moved off!

We took with us a used permit from David Copus; it showed five engine sheds in the Birmingham area, some of which we intended to visit. We were steam-hauled as far as Eastleigh, travelling via Botley, by Standard Class '5' 4-6-0 No 73116. On arrival at Eastleigh 'West Country' Class 4-6-2 No 34045 *Ottery St Mary* took over. No 30096, a Class 'B4' 0-4-0 tank, was noted on passing Winchester.

The 'West Country' was taken off at Basingstoke and we were then steam-hauled by 'Hall' 4-6-0 No 4984 *Albrighton Hall* - this engine continued to Birmingham. Our route took us via Reading West, Didcot, Oxford and Banbury to Birmingham. During this section we noted 43 steam locomotives, these included a sprinkling of LMS and 'Standards' and a diesel railcar (W20) together with numerous WR types ranging from pannier tanks to 'Halls', 'Granges' and 'Castles'.

Leaving Snow Hill station, we quickly boarded a 3A bus to Sheepcote Street, where we alight-

We noted a Class 'WD' 2-8-0 freight locomotive, No 90313, employed on a pw train near Banbury. It is of note that over 700 of this class were built and that they were allocated over a wide area of Great Britain, although they rarely ventured on to the Southern Region. We noted Nos 90268, 90312, 90482 and 90544 'on line'. No 90722 of this class is pictured.

MONUMENT LANE DEPOT

Steam locomotives:

40108	40936	41168	42267
42950	43822	44444	44490
44506	44683	44686	44711
44746	44807	45034	45071
47474	47494	47561	58135
58185	58220	58271	

23 locomotives on shed

At this date No 44444 was the sole five-figure repeated number on BR (steam).

ed and walked to Monument Lane depot entrance, a six-track 'dead end' straight shed.

We then caught a No 41 bus from Navigation Street to Mary Vale Road for our second depot of the visit, Bournville, close to the Worcester & Birmingham Canal. The rain was pouring down as we entered the depot gate, and we were glad to get some cover in the brick-built roundhouse. All the locomotives at this location were stored,

BOURNVILLE DEPOT

Steam locomotives:

40439	40443	40511	40568
43490	43675	43693	43858
44084	44227	44406	44515

12 locomotives on shed

waiting to go to Derby Works - many were labelled 'DERBY'.

We then caught a bus to the city centre, where we changed to another bus to Stratford Road, the nearest stop for our next depot, Tyseley.

TYSELEY DEPOT (84E)

Tyseley depot consisted of two roundhouses and a substantial 12-road repair shop served by a traverser. We noted 57 locomotives 'on shed', of which 51 were steam. Numerous GWR classes were noted, including pannier tanks, 2-6-2 side tanks, Class '2800' 2-8-0s, 4-6-0 passenger types included six 'Halls', three 'Granges' and one 'Castle'; the latter, No 5012 *Berry Pomeroy Castle* (81F), proved to be 'special' for us as we were allowed permission to 'cab' it. LMS types included 'Black Five' No 45249 and four Stanier-designed Class '8F' 2-8-0s. 'Standards' noted were Nos 75000, 75005 and 75006, together with one very grimy-looking Class 'WD' 2-8-0, No 90691, which we noted carried a 84C (Banbury) shed-plate. To conclude, three 0-6-0 diesel shunters were noted, and three GWR diesel rail-cars, Nos W13, W14 and W17.

We continued by bus towards the city centre for our final depot of the visit, Saltley. It was now dark but the rain had finally stopped. We entered the shed via Duddeston Mill Road.

It seemed that we were oblivious

SALTLEY DEPOT

21 A

Steam locomotives:

42764	42799	42823	42825	42829	42857	42890	43013	43017	43033	43036	43041	43046
43214	43263	43309	43359	43389	43453	43482	43507	43521	43523	43583	43594	43599
43620	43644	43673	43680	43687	43911	43932	43948	43949	43951	43963	43986	44092
44137	44143	44151	44165	44179	44184	44211	44213	44260	44516	44540	44571	44580
44583	44585	44660	44663	44690	44775	44776	44804	44812	44813	44818	44841	44888
44919	44965	44981	45040	45268	45280	45447	45607	45610	48037	48060	48105	48123
48141	48153	48193	48201	48204	48342	48351	48359	48388	48523	48647	58138	58143
75042	90112	90719	92052	92057	92138	92139	92152	92155	92165			

Diesel locomotives:

12040	12041	12043	12044	12060	12061	12062	12066	13167	13248	13250

112 locomotives on shed

to the dangers and hazards of engine shed visiting, especially when they took place after the hours of daylight; lurking dangers such as inspection pits, moving locomotives and dimly-lit shed buildings with tools and equipment scattered about. We obviously did take extra care in these conditions; in fact, at Saltley we needed the use of a torch to obtain some of the engine numbers. It was lucky for us that the shed foreman did not appear, as no doubt he would have had a few choice words to say to us! Saltley was a very large, spread out depot, consisting of three roundhouses. Being a Sunday, it was crammed tight with predominantly freight and mixed-traffic locomotives. We were glad to complete our visit safely, then catch a bus to Snow Hill station. We purchased cups of hot tea and some biscuits prior to boarding the return Wolverhampton excursion at 8.10 pm.

BRISTOL, SEVERN TUNNEL JUNCTION, NEWPORT AND CARDIFF

SUNDAY 12 JUNE

The advertised excursion from Portsmouth Harbour to Cardiff was due to depart at 10 am, but we had decided several weeks before to make an early start, as we had planned to visit a total of six engine sheds. We obtained a return Reduced Fare Party Ticket from Fratton to Cardiff for 10/6d. Some of the party purchased tickets from the Co-op Travel Agent in Fratton Road prior to this trip. An application form is reproduced here.

Our party of 12 began our day by catching the 7.41 am diesel unit train to Salisbury, travelling via Fareham, Southampton Central and Romsey. On arrival at Salisbury we transferred to another train, a diesel multiple unit (DMU), and travelled at the front end; these trains allowed maximum window viewing.

On arrival at Bristol (Stapleton Road) we set off on the long walk to Barrow Road shed. It was raining quite heavily, and the majority of us wore plastic macs and caps.

One of the forms issued, which was used by several of our party on this trip.

The walk, made at a brisk pace, took us about 15 minutes through the almost deserted back streets. We entered the shed by means of a not-too-high wall at the rear, but I ripped my mac as I fell from the top of the wet, slippery wall, catching it on a buffer. I was wedged between the buffer and the wall, but soon freed myself! Others also experienced difficulty. Entering this way saved us a 5-minute walk to the main gate, from which a footbridge led to the centre of the depot yard; if we had entered via this bridge we would have certainly been asked to show our permit to the foreman on arrival in the normal way, but this took time and we had a very tight schedule to keep for the day ahead!

We all managed to note every locomotive 'on shed' without being questioned. This was achieved by the party splitting up into groups of three, which gave us less chance of being seen by officials; a party of 12 going round together would certainly have attracted some attention, even on a Sunday! Afterwards we gathered outside the depot to compare our lists, although the pouring rain made it difficult for us to jot down the numbers.

Despite the adverse weather conditions we continued spiritedly by making the 15-minute walk to our next depot, St Philip's Marsh. The reader will no doubt realise that at this date train-spotters had not yet become familiar with the anorak, normal clothing in adverse

weather being the black plastic mac, a standard inclusion in our haversack on many trips. Whenever a visit to this depot took place it was always completed in minimum time as there always seemed to be an evil-smelling aroma in the area, perhaps from a public rubbish tip!

We then walked to Bath Road shed, entering via the rear entrance.

Departure from Temple Meads was by DMU train to Severn Tunnel Junction, via Lawrence Hill and Stapleton Road. From information received from a railwayman while travelling from Bristol, we learned that the Severn Tunnel was the longest main-line tunnel in Great Britain, running for 4¼ miles beneath the estuary of

BRISTOL (BARROW ROAD) DEPOT

Steam locomotives:

6323	6346	6376	8725	40098	40501	41207	41208	41304	42771	42827	43194	43263
43444	43855	43911	44045	44135	44167	44209	44264	44269	44296	44411	44466	44534
44553	44560	44666	44775	44776	44825	44828	44888	44918	45280	45577	45621	45656
45660	47544	47552	47678	48101	48388	51217	51218	73003	73015	73156	73168	75002
75004	75021	75027										

Diesel locomotives:
13182   13256   D3806

58 locomotives on shed

BRISTOL (ST PHILIP'S MARSH) DEPOT

Steam locomotives:

2213	2215	2244	2292	2865	3218	3632	3643	3650	3665	3765	3773	3784
3795	3837	3862	4102	4131	4284	4297	4655	4660	4688	4945	4948	4949
4963	4975	4980	5337	5376	5771	5924	6312	6327	6356	6378	6630	6670
6671	6681	6807	6834	6957	7729	7749	8746	8790	9438	9601	9651	9729
46517	48404	48434	48436	90697	92203							

Diesel locomotives:
13000   D3001   D3183   D3185   D3257   D3503   D3504   D3508   D3805   D0226

68 locomotives on shed

BRISTOL (BATH ROAD) DEPOT

Steam locomotives:

1028	1410	1412	3440	3604	3677	3748	4077	4083	4129	4706	4922	5049
5065	5073	5078	5096	5104	5529	5561	5949	5967	6324	6363	6847	6981
6982	7003	7034	8486	8741	9481	9623	9626	41202	41240	41249	82007	82009
82030	82035	82037	82038	82040	82042	82044						

46 locomotives on shed

Nos 3604, 4706, 5104, 6847, 8486 (83F, Truro) and 82007 were all undergoing minor repair in the adjoining depot works. This was an 'all steam' depot.

---

the River Severn. It took 13 years to build, starting in 1873 and completed in 1886.

On arrival, our route from the station to the engine shed was via the end of the station platform; this was not the official direction as given in the *Locomotive Shed Directory*, but it did save us 5 minutes walking time!

SEVERN TUNNEL JUNCTION DEPOT (86E)

This depot was situated in virtually open countryside and comprised six roads and a separate single-road repair shop, together with a turntable. There were 51 'on shed', of which 48 were steam, the majority being tank designs, many used as 'bankers' assisting heavy freight trains through the nearby Severn Tunnel. The only non-tank locomotives were Nos 2231, 2261, 4989, 5311, 5972, 6345, 6362, 6369, 6386, 6843, 90516, 90685 and 92216.

We then travelled by DMU train to Newport (High Street) for our next depot of the visit, Ebbw Junction.

My only previous visit to Ebbw Junction had been on Sunday 28 April 1957. As we only had a very limited time to visit this depot and return to catch a train to Cardiff, we decided between ourselves to travel there by taxi, so the party of

BETWEEN SEVERN TUNNEL JUNCTION AND NEWPORT

Steam locomotives:

3694	4119	4671	5037
5191	7322	9619	9662

12 split up and travelled in two taxis, six in each. The driver of our taxi was concerned about being overloaded, but we persuaded him to carry on with the journey. I was in the leading taxi and gave the driver directions to the depot. On arrival I instructed him to drive past the gateman at speed; the latter looked at the two taxis in amazement, obviously wanting to see our permit. We *did* have a permit, but we were in a hurry and we had no time for such formalities! This memorable taxi journey worked out at a cost of 1 shilling each.

NEWPORT (EBBW JUNCTION) DEPOT (86A)

The depot produced everything that we expected, with 100 'on shed' of which 96 were steam! Classes ranged considerably from 0-6-0 pannier tanks to 2-8-0 freight types, 2-8-2 tanks, LMS tanks, 'WD' 2-8-0s and '9F' 2-10-0s; of the latter we noted Nos 92000, 92001, 92202, 92215, 92225,

92230, 92242, 92248, 92249 and 92250. Under repair in the depot works were Nos 2889, 5602, 5612, 5656, 7220 and 8766. Withdrawn and 'stored' on the 'dead line' at the rear of shed were Nos 2227, 2832, 5155 and 6325.

Leaving the shed, the party of 12 ran past the gateman's hut, who shouted out to us and frantically waved his arms, but we accelerated past him! We couldn't stop - we had seen a bus with a 'NEWPORT STATION' destination waiting on the opposite side of the road to the depot gate. A quick dash was made and we were aboard. We obviously had not planned to visit the nearby Newport (Pill) depot (86B), a location where only tank engines were allocated, as on our arrival by bus we quickly entered High Street station and within 4 minutes had departed on a DMU for Cardiff! This gives some indication of our hectic timetable! At this date the noting of DMUs was on the increase.

The 10-minute walk from Cardiff General to the shed was made at a brisk pace - we did not have a permit, so we decided to split up into groups of three and meet outside the main gate afterwards. My previous visit to Canton shed had been on Sunday 18 August 1957.

CARDIFF (CANTON) DEPOT (86C)

This was 'all steam' - in fact 90 were 'on shed'. Many GW side tanks and pannier tanks were crammed into the depot with a fair number of 'Hall', 'Grange' and 'Castle' Class 4-6-0 main-line types. We noted seven 'Britannia' Class 4-6-2s, Nos 70016, 70018, 70022, 70024, 70026, 70027 and 70029. Also of note were five Class '9F' 2-10-0s of which one, No 92220, was named *Evening Star* - this was the final steam locomotive built by British Railways.

The return excursion to

Portsmouth departed at 5.10 pm from Cardiff General. We were steam-hauled between Cardiff and

One of the official permits taken on this trip. A separate permit to visit Newport (Ebbw Junction) was also taken, but we did not have permission to visit Cardiff (Canton), although we did! David Copus, whose name appears, had the responsibility of organising the majority of permits whenever a trip like this was made. The right-hand column states '16 persons', being the number David probably envisaged at the date he sent off for the permits.

Salisbury by 'Hall' Class 4-6-0 No 4947 *Nanhoran Hall* (82B).
With a total of six engine sheds visited and over 450 steam noted, it had been a most enjoyable yet tiring day.

LONDON

WEDNESDAY 27 JULY

The finer details of this trip have been omitted, together with the complete 'on shed' lists of locomotives (except Finsbury Park); some locomotives have been highlighted at the end of the depot visit. As on all London trips, the schedule was hectic and involved a tremendous amount of travelling by tube, bus and on foot. An early start was made, catching the 5.32 am workmen's train from Fratton to London. I travelled with a party of five that included David Copus.

STEWARTS LANE DEPOT (73A)

37 steam, 4 diesel and 5 electric locomotives (total 46) were noted on shed. Three 'Schools' Class 4-4-0s were seen, Nos 30921 *Shrewsbury*, 30922 *Marlborough* and 30923 *Bradfield*.

We then travelled to Finsbury Park diesel depot; this was my first visit. *Deltic* was the forerunner of the D9000 series. While at the depot we noted Class 'A4' 4-6-2 No 60017 *Silver Fox* passing with a passenger train for King's Cross.

• FP •

FINSBURY PARK DEPOT

Diesel locomotives:
'Deltic' D208   D209   D2018
12101   D3693   D3705   D3706
D3710   D3712   D5587   D5590
D5591   D5602   D5606   D5610
D5909   D8021   D8045

19 locomotives on shed

HORNSEY DEPOT (34B)

44 steam and 6 diesel (50) locomotives were on shed. No fewer than 40 steam were tanks, of which 34 were Class 'J50' 0-6-0s.

STRATFORD DEPOT (30A)

126 steam and 85 diesel (211) locomotives were on shed; there also 16 'E' prefix DMUs. An unusual visitor noted was SR Class 'Q1' 0-6-0 No 33013 (70B). A 'Britannia' 4-6-2 was noted, No 70002 *Geoffrey Chaucer*.

OLD OAK COMMON DEPOT (81A)

119 steam and 14 diesel (133) locomotives were on shed. A grand total of 21 'Castle' Class

4-6-0s was noted. Strangely, no 'King' Class 4-6-0s were present.

WILLESDEN DEPOT (1A)

96 steam and 13 diesel (109) locomotives were on shed. Of note was Carlisle (Upperby) 'Princess Coronation' Class 4-6-2 No 46256 *Sir William A. Stanier FRS*.

NEASDEN DEPOT (14D)

44 steam and 2 diesel (46) locomotives were on shed. The driver of Class '9F' 2-10-0 No 92021 let us 'cab' his engine.

CRICKLEWOOD DEPOT (14A)

50 steam and 13 diesel (63) locomotives were on shed. Six Class '9F' 2-10-0s were noted, Nos 92018, 92027, 92081, 92105, 92124 and 92129.

CAMDEN DEPOT (1B)

37 steam and 19 diesel (56) locomotives were on shed. Two 'Britannia' Class 4-6-2s were noted, Nos 70046 (un-named) and 70049 *Solway Firth*.

KENTISH TOWN DEPOT (14B)

55 steam and 4 diesel (59) locomotives were on shed. ER Class 'B1' 4-6-0 No 61041 of Sheffield (Darnall) was a surprise noting.

HITHER GREEN DEPOT (73C)

22 steam and 17 diesel (39) loco-motives were on shed. Four Class 'C' 0-6-0s of 1900 vintage were all 'in steam' - Nos 31268, 31287, 31686 and 31689.

To sum up, no fewer than 765 locomotives were noted on this trip, of which 637 were steam.

BRIGHTON

SUNDAY 31 JULY

Bill Jenkins accompanied me on the 1.58 pm electric unit train from Fratton to Brighton on this Bank Holiday weekend. The return fare was 7/6d. On passing Havant we noted Class 'A1X' 0-6-0 tank No 32661 awaiting its departure with the Hayling Island branch train, which we noted was very well patronised.

Right This view of Brighton Depot yard shows two main-line steam locomotives, 'Schools' Class 4-4-0 No 30917 *Ardingly* and 'Battle of Britain' 4-6-2 No 34055 *Fighter Pilot*. On the extreme right is Class 'K' 2-6-0 No 32351. The terminus station roof forms part of the background.

Above The familiar view that greeted train-spotters as they made their way up the steep Terminus Road that runs parallel from the station to the depot entrance.

 75 A

BRIGHTON DEPOT

Steam locomotives:
30049 30051 30056 30328 30377 30501 30545 30900 30901 30902 30917 30919 31322
31410 31411 31522 31530 31543 31556 31776 31866 31890 31891 31902 32338 32339
32343 32347 32351 32418 32449 32475 32479 32495 32503 32512 32578 32580 32662
34008 34048 34055 34103 44916 45037 45089 76017 80013 80032 80033 80081 80144
80145 80146 80152 80153

Diesel locomotives:
D2281 D2282 D3094 D3217 D3219 D3220

62 locomotives on shed

Nos 32479 and 32495 were ex-Fratton-allocated Class 'E4' 0-6-2 tanks.

'Black Five' 4-6-0 No 45037 and Class 'N' 2-6-0 No 31410.

over the wall at the top of Terminus Road with their binoculars trained on the locomotives below; perhaps they did not have a permit and only got as far as the office window! Luckily, on this visit we managed to 'dodge' the foreman and fully complete our visit.

Of particular note on this summer Sunday visit was the sight of three LMS 'Black Five' 4-6-0s 'on shed'. All three had been employed on excursions from the Midlands: No 44916 (1A) had come from Bletchley, No 45037 from Rugby and No 45089 from Tring. Other excursions had arrived that day from Oxford and Gillingham (Kent), the information on these coming from notice boards displayed at Brighton station. Engines 'in store' at the shed were Class 'L' 4-4-0 No 31776 and Class 'E6' 0-6-2 tank No 32418.

It was most difficult to gain entry to this depot without a permit, as one needed to pass the foreman's office window via a narrow passageway. Having no permit, Bill and I decided to 'duck' as we passed the window, making sure that we kept quiet, but Bill, being a bit clumsy, bumped into me and I lost my balance; somehow I refrained from a few choice words and, picking myself up, we continued our entry. I had always wondered why numerous train-spotters stood peering

SOUTHERN REGION RAILROVER

SATURDAY 6 TO FRIDAY 12 AUGUST

This trip was along the same lines as my 1959 Railrover, as described in some detail in Volume 1. My companions for the seven-day escapade were two local train-spotting pals, Bill Jenkins and Jim Lawrence.

The locomotive depots and other installations were visited in the following order:

TILBURY (33B) (an additional fare of 7d was paid to catch the ferry from Gravesend to Tilbury); RAMSGATE (73G); DOVER (73H); ASHFORD (73F); HORSHAM (75D); THREE BRIDGES

A map showing the area in which you could travel on the Railrover ticket for a period of seven consecutive days.

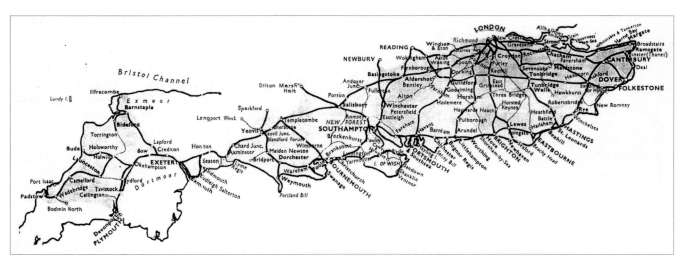

Rebuilt 'Battle of Britain' Class 4-6-2 passenger locomotive No 34088 *213 Squadron*, in excellent condition, was photographed near Dover (Marine) station. As can be seen, it had been employed on the 'Golden Arrow' boat train from London (Victoria). This famous named express first ran in 1929, having taken over from a service that began in 1925 named the 'Flèche D'Or' ('Arrow of Gold'), which linked Paris with Calais, the complete journey from London to Paris taking about 6½ hours. Note the flags of both Great Britain and France displayed on the buffer beam.

(75E); REDHILL (75B); TUNBRIDGE WELLS WEST (75F); TONBRIDGE (73J); READING (SOUTH); READING (81D); SLOUGH (81B) (as this was on the Western Region we purchased tickets from Reading General, being steam-hauled by 'Castle' Class 4-6-0 No 5098 *Clifford Castle*); FELTHAM (70B); STEWARTS LANE (73A); BRICKLAYERS ARMS (73B); KING'S CROSS (34A); NORWOOD JUNCTION (75C); TEMPLECOMBE (82G); BOURNEMOUTH (71B); and ASHFORD WORKS.

We visited LIVERPOOL STREET STATION during the evening rush-hour, and noted no

fewer than 48 locomotives, a spotting rate of one every 90 seconds.

We then went on to EXMOUTH JUNCTION (72A); EXETER (83C); TAUNTON (83B) (successfully 'bunked' at 2.40 am!); PLYMOUTH (FRIARY) (83H); WADEBRIDGE (72F); and OKEHAMPTON. We were steam-hauled between Okehampton and Exeter by Class 'T9' 4-4-0 No 30313, and on passing the one-road engine shed at Meldon Quarry we noted Class

'O2' 0-4-4 tank No 30199.

DOVER (73H) was visited for a second time, then NEASDEN (14D); WILLESDEN (1A); OLD OAK COMMON (81A); and KING'S CROSS (34A), also visited for a second time.

Estimated miles travelled during the week was 2,030. Bearing in mind that the ticket cost £6 10s, the total mileage worked out at roughly 7½d (3p) for every 10 miles travelled - just compare this to the cost of travel on British Rail today!

LONDON AND WATFORD

TUESDAY 6 SEPTEMBER

I travelled alone on the 8.34 am from Fratton to Waterloo, and the first visit was to Nine Elms shed (70A). My main interest in this depot was the large numbers of ex-Eastern Section steam engines that were either stored or working from here. One tank in particular, a

Class 'H' 0-4-4 No 31328, was one of the two that I needed to spot to enable me to have noted *all* SR steam locomotives. The other, Class 'M7' 0-4-4 tank No 30253, was allocated to Barnstaple Junction.

I was halted by the gateman as I entered Nine Elms shed. I had no permit, so explained to him that I was one of the party from 'Jim' Jackson's Southampton Group whom I knew were visiting here on this day! 'The remainder of the party are on their way,' I told him. The idea of travelling 'solo' did not bother me, but I did miss the company of my companions.

I then caught a bus, alighting near Waterloo, from where I made my way by tube train to Euston and then by DMU to Watford. This was a brick-built, six-track

Class 'E4' 0-6-2 tank No 32473 in the yard at Nine Elms. In later years it was to be preserved and used on the Bluebell Railway in Sussex.

NINE ELMS DEPOT

Steam locomotives:

4634	4672	4692	4698	9770	30035	30039	30245	30321	30457	30489	30498	30521
30694	30699	30763	30781	30800	30803	30840	30910	31145	31271	31326	31328	31481
31495	31505	31617	31634	31753	31754	31756	31760	31766	31768	31771	31783	31786
31787	31789	32473	32498	32506	33038	34006	34009	34016	34017	34028	34090	35003
35004	35008	35014	35015	35019	35020	35028	73083	73084	73088	73112		

63 locomotives on shed

WATFORD DEPOT

Steam locomotives:

40672	41223	42097	42098
43325	44440	44838	48374
48449			

9 locomotives on shed

EUSTON TO WATFORD AND RETURN

Steam locomotives:

40049	40659	42095	42104
42234	42351	42367	42368
42478	42604	44442	44451
44866	44870	45147	45222
45284	45307	45331	45352
45434	45439	45674	46144
46146	46203	46228	46229
46243	46431	46472	47307
47668	48195	48422	48518
48630	48665	92156	

Diesel locomotives:

D5	D7	D8	D218
D268	D290	10201	12075
12078	D3017	D3018	D3050
D5015	D5016	D5018	D5019
D5084	D8000	D8003	D8037

dead-end shed, and was at the date of this visit in quite good condition, but the sight of only nine 'on shed' was disappointing.

On my return journey to Euston I was hauled by one of the Bulleid-designed diesels, No 10202 - this main-line passenger type, together with No 10201 (see accompanying list) were introduced in 1951. A later version, No 10203, slightly modernised, was introduced in 1954.

Returning to the city I then visited St Pancras, King's Cross, Liverpool Street and Broad Street stations prior to a visit to Willesden depot (1A), where I noted 58 steam and nine diesel locomotives. Of note here was Class 'WD' 2-8-0

No 90637 carrying a 55E (Normanton) shed-plate.

Steam of note at King's Cross station included Nos 60003 and 60029, and main-line diesel *Deltic*. While at Liverpool Street, for a 30-minute visit, I noted five 'Britannia' 4-6-2s, including No 70000 *Britannia*. Briefly looking in at Broad Street, four diesels were noted. I noted Class 'Q1' 0-6-0 No 33012 on a goods at Hampstead as I travelled by DMU between Broad Street and Willesden Junction.

Class '8F' 2-8-0 No 48518 (1A) enters Watford station with a freight bound for London. Watford depot is in the background.

BLACKPOOL ILLUMINA-TIONS EXCURSION

FRIDAY 9 TO SUNDAY 11 SEPTEMBER

I travelled with David Copus, Mike Yerbury and Jim Lawrence together with numerous other younger rail enthusiasts from the Portsmouth area on this Special Restaurant Car excursion. The trip gave local railway enthusiasts a very good opportunity to visit locomotive depots in the Blackpool area, and at the same time a chance to see the Illuminations, visit the famous Tower and indulge in the numerous amusement arcades and pintables that occupied most of the sea-front. If time allowed, we had made plans to take a ride on a tram and have a paddle in the Irish Sea!

BLACKPOOL ILLUMINATIONS 1960.			
SPECIAL RESTAURANT CAR EXCURSION TO BLACKPOOL NORTH. FRIDAY NIGHT 9th. SEPTEMBER. RETURNING SUNDAY MORNING 11th. SEPTEMBER.			

The notice as advertised at local stations giving all details of excursion.

FRIDAY 9 SEPTEMBER (Day 1)

The excursion consisted of five-coach set No 430 in SR green livery. An excursion was also being run from Bournemouth to

Those were the days! This was one of the author's favourite modes of transport in Portsmouth - here we see two City of Portsmouth Corporation trolleybuses at the Hard (the stop adjacent to the Harbour station) in 1960, Nos 269 (RV 9120) and 313 (ERV 938). The Blackpool excursion began for me with a ride on one of these buses from Fratton Bridge to the Guildhall Square. *John Kinchen*

Blackpool North, departing at about the same time, and the Bournemouth carriages were to join up with ours at Eastleigh. The 2nd Class adult fare was 43 shillings (£2 3s).

Departure was on time at 10.25 pm. We were steam-hauled as far as Basingstoke by 'West Country' 4-6-2 No 34018 *Axminster* (I asked the driver of this locomotive if I could 'cab' it shortly before its departure, and he agreed). Bulleid-designed 'Battle of Britain' Class 4-6-2 No 34074 *46 Squadron* was used as a 'banker' between Portsmouth Harbour and Portsmouth & Southsea (High Level). A 10-minute stop was made at Eastleigh to pick up the Bournemouth carriages, making a total of 11, then we continued via Winchester City to Basingstoke, where No 34018 came off. We were then steam-hauled by 'Hall' Class 4-6-0 No 6926 *Holkham Hall*. The change-over gave us

time to step on to the platform and get some fresh air.

SATURDAY 10 SEPTEMBER (Day 2)

The route through the night from Reading West was via Oxford, Banbury, Wolverhampton, Crewe and Preston to Blackpool North. Many steam engines were noted both working and resting in sidings, depot yards and stations as we sped on our way. It was a very clear and mild night, and overhead lighting in the large sidings and other illumination in depot and station areas enabled us to note many of the numbers. We noted no fewer than 32 steam locomotives between Oxford and Crewe, including Class 'V2' 2-6-2 No

BETWEEN WARRINGTON (BANK HALL) AND PRESTON

Steam locomotives:
42439 42607 42635 42934 44374 44525 44544 44709 44730 44761 44905 44907 44947
45094 45244 45271 45316 45408 45503 45600 45700 46110 46235 47319 47392 47413
47603 47657 47669 47671 49025 49422 49438 49449 49451 56032 58120 78033 78040
90257 90423 90667

Diesel locomotives:
D2 D220 12022 D3369 D3371 D3581 D3795 D3834 D3836

No 56032 was a Class '0F' 0-4-0 saddle-tank of 1885 vintage. It had at this date been taken into Departmental Stock, but still retained its BR number.

BETWEEN PRESTON AND BLACKPOOL (NORTH)

Steam locomotives:
40099 40174 40183 41261 42447 42867 42963 44737 45174 45189 45212 45220 45350
45442 45512 45643 58177 90317

60810 and 'Jubilee' No 45586 *Mysore* as we passed Gresty Lane shed.

On arrival at Crewe the 'Hall' was taken off and we had a 10-minute wait until Class '5' ('Black Five') 4-6-0 No 44683 took over. Our arrival at Blackpool North station was much delayed; the expected time of arrival was 6.32 am, but we did not arrive until 8.25 am, only 5 minutes before our planned departure for Manchester - from Blackpool Central! Our party of three decided we could make it, but only at the expense of a taxi, so this we did immediately, arriving at Blackpool Central just in time to board the train. The

guard was blowing his whistle as we scrambled into the carriage. It had originally been intended to get some breakfast and hot drinks on arrival at the North station, but the lateness of our arrival prevented this, and we were left to finish off some sandwiches, biscuits and the remains of a bottle of fizzy drink. We were steam-hauled between Blackpool Central and Manchester (Victoria) by Class '5' 4-6-0 No 45354.

We had purchased special 'child' cheap day return tickets from Blackpool to Preston, but we intended to travel to Manchester, quite some distance beyond Preston! At Manchester (Victoria)

station one of us left the platform and paid a 'child' single excess fare from Preston, then purchased platform tickets for the others; following a short wait at the station they made their exit!

We had decided that we would travel around Manchester by taxi to visit the sheds, as this would be much quicker than the bus journeys originally planned. After enquiring at three taxi ranks to find a reasonable 'all-in' fare, we eventually agreed with a driver to pay £1 10s. We gave the driver instructions and directions, taken from *The British Locomotive Shed Directory*, of the areas we wanted to visit; he was quite familiar with

BETWEEN BLACKPOOL AND MANCHESTER

Steam locomotives:
40091 40164 40166 42158 42297 42299 42473 42546 42565 42568 42621 42625 42631
42662 42673 42899 42946 44714 44733 44744 44874 44945 44950 45013 45058 45101
45303 45305 45349 45526 45535 45577 45617 45631 45661 46419 46484 46485 47293
47579 49592 49662 51498 52543 70045 75015 75047 90316 90523 90535

No 51498 was a Class '2F' 0-6-0 saddle-tank, introduced in 1891, a rebuild of an engine introduced in 1877.

the routes as he told us that he had taken many other train-spotters to these locations before. The three of us each paid 10 shillings prior to setting off. This was to be the start of a mammoth taxi journey!

Our first depot of the visit was Agecroft, which would have meant a 25-minute bus journey, but using a taxi it was less than 15 minutes. It was an eight-road straight shed; four of the roads had no roof. 0-4-0 and 0-6-0 saddle tanks were in evidence; dating from the late 1890s, the majority were still in active daily use.

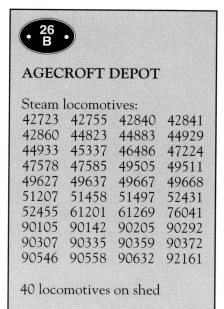

26 B

AGECROFT DEPOT

Steam locomotives:

42723	42755	42840	42841
42860	44823	44883	44929
44933	45337	46486	47224
47578	47585	49505	49511
49627	49637	49667	49668
51207	51458	51497	52431
52455	61201	61269	76041
90105	90142	90205	90292
90307	90335	90359	90372
90546	90558	90632	92161

40 locomotives on shed

We then continued by the waiting taxi to our next depot, Patricroft. This was an L-shaped shed, consisting of two straight sheds, both being block-ended. One shed had ten roads, the other eight. There was a large coaling plant and a turntable.

We then continued by the waiting taxi to our third depot, Trafford Park. This was a 19-road straight depot with a block end. It was in a run-down state, with roofing over five of the roads having been removed. It had two turntables in the yard.

The taxi then took us to

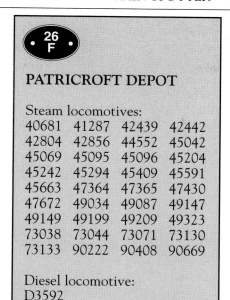

26 F

PATRICROFT DEPOT

Steam locomotives:

40681	41287	42439	42442
42804	42856	44552	45042
45069	45095	45096	45204
45242	45294	45409	45591
45663	47364	47365	47430
47672	49034	49087	49147
49149	49199	49209	49323
73038	73044	73071	73130
73133	90222	90408	90669

Diesel locomotive:
D3592

37 locomotives on shed

Every depot we visited on this trip, except Gorton and Wigan, had a 'Black Five' on shed. Designed by William Stanier, a total of 842 of these very versatile engines were built. This 4-6-0 was the forerunner of the Standard Class '5' 4-6-0. No 44770 is pictured.

9 E

TRAFFORD PARK DEPOT

Steam locomotives:

40009	40017	40018	40055
40056	40088	40141	40208
42319	42428	42469	42479
42676	42969	43211	43580
44088	44566	44717	45239
45654	48273	70004	70015
70032	70042	76086	

27 locomotives on shed

Newton Heath, but as it arrived at the shed entrance it developed a puncture! The driver said that he would repair it while we were visiting the depot.

NEWTON HEATH DEPOT (26A)

Unfortunately, on stepping into the shed entrance we met the shed foreman who asked us for our permit - we didn't have one. At that moment I was suddenly violently sick at the feet of the foreman - I'm sure he did not appreciate my vomit splattering all over his shoes! However, I could not avoid my actions and it was most embarrassing to say the least! The effects of the long taxi rides coupled with a lack of a decent meal probably contributed. The foreman stared in amazement at me, and when my travelling companions asked him if we could please visit the depot, he gave us a very stubborn 'No'. He then walked off at great speed and was heard muttering something about train-spotters with no permits, etc.

Luckily, from the point where all this happened, we did manage to note a few locomotive numbers - including three steam, Nos 42621 and 45320, 'Jubilee' Class 4-6-0 45700 *Amethyst*, and one 0-6-0 diesel shunter, D3589 - but we were unable to see the numbers of the old Lancashire & Yorkshire locomotives that were visible in the background. Newton Heath, the original main depot of the L&YR, was an enormous 21-road straight shed with a turntable at each end of the yard.

It had certainly been a most unusual shed visit, but undaunted by this setback and having recovered sufficiently from my ordeal - and the taxi driver having changed the wheel - we continued to our fifth depot, Gorton. This was a 22-road block-ended straight shed with a turntable. Coaling facilities were located quite some

GORTON DEPOT

Steam locomotives:
41702	42373	42374	42472
42748	42760	42873	43330
43399	43499	43721	44025
44114	44284	61198	63575
63585	63600	63603	63649
63686	63743	63767	63816
63848	63915	64324	64341
64359	64375	64440	64743
64744	64875	69307	90064
90189	90311	90624	90698
92108	92124		

42 locomotives on shed

distance from the shed. A locomotive and wagon works was also situated nearby, but we did not make a visit.

We then continued by the waiting taxi to our sixth depot, Longsight. This depot consisted of a two-ended shed of unusual design, made up of two block-ended straight sheds back-to-back. The north shed had eight roads, and the south 12. A turntable was sited at the north end of the sheds. We did not realise this on our visit, as we had not met such a lay-out previously, and consequently we found out afterwards that we had only visited the south shed! We did not bother to return and complete our visit.

The taxi driver then returned us to our starting point at Manchester (Victoria) station forecourt. We thanked him for his services, and before continuing our visits by rail visited the station buffet, where we purchased food, drink and aspirins - the latter to help combat the after-effects of my earlier sickness. While resting for 10 minutes we reflected on our most eventful taxi journey; having glanced at

LONGSIGHT DEPOT

Steam locomotives:
42333	42337	42369	42539
42772	42923	42924	42930
43306	43832	44250	44780
45644	45680	46135	47341
47528	48275	48465	49281
70046			

Diesel locomotives:
D1	12099	D3765	D3768
D3772	D5080	D5083	

Electric locomotives:
E2001	E3002	E3007	E3037
E3038	E3040	E3047	E3048

36 locomotives noted

the mileometer, we had covered 32 miles! It was now back to the train, and we were steam-hauled by Standard Class '4' 4-6-0 No 75017 to Wigan.

BETWEEN MANCHESTER AND WIGAN

Steam locomotives:
40015	40671	42297	42311
42458	42473	42494	42548
42614	42647	42733	42865
42901	44693	44729	44751
44781	44971	45048	45108
45553	45645	45661	46411
46485	47574	47578	49402
51494	61161	61298	90415

No 51494, noted on the way, was a Lancashire & Yorkshire re-built Class '2F' 0-6-0 saddle-tank of 1891 vintage. Withdrawn from BR official lists several years prior to this noting, it was used by a private company, probably as a stationary boiler, but still retaining its former BR number.

ON PASSING LOWER INCE SCRAPYARD

Steam locomotives:
40061 43388 43674 51412
51414 51515

Nos 51412/4 and 51515 were 0-6-0 saddle tanks introduced in 1891. There were many other steam engines at this location awaiting their fate.

On arrival at Wigan station we made the 30-minute walk to Springs Branch (Wigan). We chanced to smell the aroma of a home-made bakery, where we stopped off and purchased large bags of freshly baked Eccles cakes and jam doughnuts, which we ate as we walked.

Springs Branch was a 16 lane block end straight shed. At the date of this visit it was in a very dilapidated condition.

Leaving the depot we then walked to our next depot, Wigan, a wooden-built shed consisting of 14 roads. At one time all roads in this straight shed were covered, but on this visit only three remained partially covered, a sure sign of its demise.

A brief ride was then taken on a Wigan Transport double-decker

WIGAN DEPOT

Steam locomotives:
41206	42299	42475	42554
42557	42631	42640	42642
42644	42715	42731	42733
42821	42864	43952	44221
44225	44464	44486	49007
49150	78040	78060	78061
78062	78063	78064	90327
90527	90552		

30 locomotives on shed

SPRINGS BRANCH (WIGAN) DEPOT

Steam locomotives:

42303	42317	42462	42471	42564	42572	42606	42825	42965	43189	44069	44280	44386
44438	44708	44714	44842	44907	44983	45026	45109	45135	45185	45286	45314	45408
45431	45600	45638	46428	46448	47270	47281	47659	47669	48416	48895	48915	48942
49008	49020	49023	49025	49129	49139	49141	49154	49191	49381	49422	49449	49451
58120	58123	65157	65198	90147	90173	90257	90507	90509	90574	90667	90686	

Diesel locomotive:
D3851

65 locomotives on shed

Above Class '7F' 0-8-0 No 49139 (8F) 'on shed' at Springs Branch (Wigan). This Class was known as 'Austin Sevens'.

Right Class 'J10' 0-6-0 No 65198, also at Springs Branch. This design was first introduced in 1896.

bus, taking us to the station for a fare of 2d. We then caught a train to Bolton, a 12-road block-ended straight shed.

A MINI-FORTUNE!

While crossing the main road outside Bolton (Trinity Street) railway station I had the unbelievable good fortune to literally 'pick up' from the centre of the road a sum of money - three £1 notes and one 10-shilling note! I just did not believe my luck - the money had obviously been lying in the road for only a short while. It was scooped up instantly and deposited in my pocket. We didn't stop to look back, but continued immedi-

BOLTON DEPOT

Steam locomotives:

40062	40063	40065	42207
42289	42444	42563	42626
42652	42656	42703	42770
42820	43002	44000	44190
44205	44456	44499	44545
44950	45339	47440	49592
49662	51408	51498	52182
52345	52393	52415	52443
52523	73064	84013	84014
84019	90267	90641	90729

40 locomotives on shed

ately into the station. It was agreed that the money would be shared between us, and as we were visiting Blackpool promenade later in the day, it could be used to purchase food and drink, while any remaining cash would be gambled on the 'one-armed bandits' and pin-tables that abound along the promenade. In 1960 this amount of money, in the hands of teenagers, must have seemed like a 'mini-fortune' - it may seem ridiculous, but in 1960 it would probably have bought a railway ticket between London and Scotland!

I and my travelling companions, David Copus, Mike Yerbury and Jim Lawrence, were now in very good spirits - we were looking for-

Standing forlorn in Bolton shed yard is Class '3F' 0-6-0 No 52345. This Class was introduced in 1889, and at this date No 52345 was classed as a 'Service' locomotive, although it still retained its British Railways number.

ward to our next visits and to the end of the day with a 'binge' on the seafront. We had to look at the money again while on the way to Preston, just to make sure that they were really genuine notes!

On arrival at Preston we made the 15-minute walk from the station to the depot, a straight shed with 15 roads and a block end. It had varying lengths of roof cover-ing, and limited yard and siding space. Of note here was Kitson-designed 0-4-0 saddle-tank No 47008, introduced as late as 1953.

Our next depot of the visit was Lostock Hall, but having missed the train from Preston we decided to travel the 8 miles by taxi. This eight-road block-ended shed was destined to become one of the final three steam sheds on BR, and consequently accumulated more steam in its later years than during its normal working life.

We then returned to Preston station by the waiting taxi, sharing the fare equally, and caught a train to Blackpool. It was early evening and we were beginning to feel the effects of a hectic days' travelling, but it was far from over - we still had the two Blackpool depots to visit, then off to the promenade to purchase an extra-large helping of fish and chips with some of the money that I had found at Bolton.

On arrival at Blackpool North we again travelled by taxi to Blackpool depot; it was only a short journey but by this time we had become somewhat drawn to this ideal means of travel. Perhaps the sharing of the fares made it preferable to buses. The depot, situated near the Central station, consisted of an eight-road straight shed with a block end and a turntable. Of note was the total of no fewer than 16 'Black Five' 4-6-0s.

BLACKPOOL DEPOT

Steam locomotives:

40091	40166	42638	42789
44680	44731	44732	44733
44737	44759	44766	44769
44776	44779	44832	45215
45318	45436	45442	45464
45559	45580	45653	45655
45705	46154	46419	61893
73127			

29 locomotives on shed

24 K

PRESTON DEPOT

Steam locomotives:

40118	40183	42403	42606
42710	44730	44807	45013
45021	45054	45094	45140
45182	45189	45244	45411
45415	45425	45428	45542
45577	45633	45735	46126
46136	46161	46167	47008
47293	47360	47472	58177
58182	61161	84017	90212

36 locomotives on shed

24 C

LOSTOCK HALL DEPOT

Steam locomotives:

40192	42187	42433	42434
42481	42634	42661	42707
42976	44778	44874	44878
49447	52429	78044	90271
90295	90357	90367	90541
90556	90564	90584	90658
90675	90689	90720	

Diesel locomotives:
D3172 D3780 D3783 D3846

31 locomotives on shed

We then walked to our final depot (the 13th of the day), Blackpool North. This was a small straight shed with four roads, and was mostly used to accommodate summer excursion traffic. At this date it was a sub-depot of Blackpool.

It was now late evening and we had until 1.05 am on Sunday morning to enjoy the pleasures of Blackpool before the return

BLACKPOOL NORTH DEPOT

Steam locomotives:
40099 40174 42206 42455
42657 44683 44913 45066
45077 45102 45198 45256
45387 45512

14 locomotives on shed

excursion departed for Portsmouth. We immediately made our way towards the promenade, our first objective being food. We each purchased large portions of haddock and chips, the chips costing 2 shillings, which must have been quite a feast, as we normally purchased sixpenny or 1 shilling bags! We then viewed the famous 500-foot Tower, which is part of the town's very large amusement centre and can be seen from many miles around. We did not actually

ascend to the top but stood and marvelled at it from its base. After numerous visits to the amusement arcades and pin-tables, we took a ride for 4d on one of the famous Blackpool trams.

As mentioned earlier, 'PLAY UP POMPEY' gummed stickers were taken by David Copus on football excursions, but it did not stop there - they were distributed on many railway visits! Holidaymakers at Blackpool must have been mystified when they saw these stickers prominently displayed on Blackpool Tower!

One of our final duties was a paddle in the Irish Sea; unfortunately the tide was out, and it seemed an endless walk to reach the bliss of paddling our feet in the warm sea - they certainly needed refreshing after a long days' walking. We splashed water over our faces and hands and came back to the promenade feeling fresh and revitalised.

We returned to the waiting

return excursion carriages at about midnight, found an empty compartment and fell asleep! It is worth pointing out that our taxi journeys during the day totalled over 50 miles!

SUNDAY 11 SEPTEMBER (Day 3)

We were awoken by the jolt of the carriage as the return excursion departed from Blackpool North exactly on time at 1.05 am. The return journey varied slightly from the outward one in that we travelled via Crewe, Worcester, Evesham and Didcot, this being due to engineering works on the line.

The same 'Hall' Class locomotive that hauled the forward excursion between Basingstoke and Crewe, No 6926 *Holkham Hall*, was used on the corresponding section of the return journey. Arrival time at Fratton station was 9.45 am - just 6 minutes late.

EASTLEIGH

MONDAY 26 DECEMBER

Engines noted in Eastleigh shed yard were: 2240, 5950, 7928, 9770, 30029, 30096, 30357, 30707, 30860, 31735, 32350, 32650, 32678, 92205 and 92206. The Works produced 35 locomotives, of which 32 were steam; of note was preserved Adams 4-4-0 No 563.

The Works visit was possible as I knew of a party of enthusiasts visiting, and I joined them at the main gate. Steam locomotives noted in the Works were: 563, 4610, 30451, 30499, 30540, 30585, 30770, 30796, 30841, 30850, 34022, 34024, 34056, 34072, 34080, 34095, 35001, 35006, 41300, 73083, 73113, 73114, 75068, 76025, 80017,

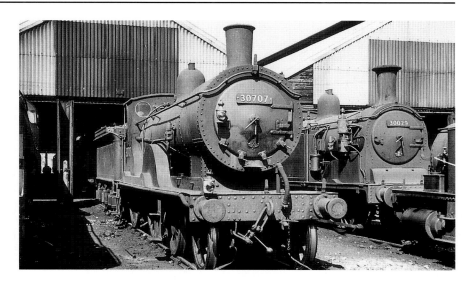

Eastleigh Depot yard: Class 'T9' ('Greyhound') 4-4-0 No 30707 (71A) was, at this date, the sole representative of this Class working east of Exeter, but 1961 saw 'T9' No 30120 in use, prior to being side-lined for preservation. I noted it on 9 July 1961 on Eastleigh shed yard 'dead line'. On the right is Class 'M7' 0-4-4 tank No 30029 (71A), and just visible (far right) is part of Class 'B4' 0-4-0 tank No 30096 (71A).
Courtesy of Merchant Navy Locomotive Preservation Society Limited

80138, 80141, 80144, 80146, 82012, 82013 and 82022. One

diesel and two electric locomotives were also present.

ADDITIONAL HIGHLIGHTS OF 1960

LONDON: SUNDAY 17 APRIL - Yet another start by bus due to engineering works on the line at Hilsea. We had a Southdown double-decker, which departed 18 minutes late, and travelled via Goldsmith Avenue and the Eastern Road to Havant, where we joined the waiting electric unit train. As on previous bus journeys, the train guard, who travelled on the bus, gave a blast on his whistle to start the bus off!

WILLESDEN (1A) - 110 'on shed', of which 30 were Class '8F' 2-8-0s!

OLD OAK COMMON (81A) - Two working 'preserved' steam locomotives were seen in the roundhouse: Caledonian Railway 4-4-2 No 123 and GWR 4-4-0 No 3440 *City of Truro*. This visit produced no fewer than 128 'on shed',

'Castle' Class 4-6-0s Nos 7017 *G. J. Churchward* and 7018 *Drysllwyn Castle*, coupled together, the latter fitted with a double chimney, move off Old Oak Common Depot. For those into the finer details of photography, this was taken with a 'Coronet' and timing was $\frac{1}{100}$ second. *John Harris*

of which only eight were diesels. Steam engines undergoing repair in the works were Nos 4075, 4992, 5071, 5094, 6013, 6108 and 6119. Steam activity in the yard was highlighted by the movement of two 'Castles' blowing their whistles prior to moving off shed. Luckily a photograph of them was captured by one of our party of 12 train-spotters as the engines moved away.

NEASDEN (14D) - Standard Class '4' 4-6-0 No 75061 was noted hauling an excursion train from Bedford to Bognor Regis past Neasden depot; when it reached its destination it travelled 'light' to Fratton for coal and water, then returned to pick up the return excursion. These facts were passed to me from reliable enthusiasts at Fratton. The engine was from Leicester depot.

CAMDEN (1B) - Of note here was the decline in steam power compared to a visit only eight months previously - 30 August 1959 saw 63 steam and four diesel, but on 17 April 1960 we saw 30 steam and 25 diesels.

NINE ELMS (70A) - No fewer than five Class '5700' 0-6-0 pannier tanks were 'on shed', Nos 4634, 4672, 4681, 4698 and 9770, these replacing the ageing 'M7' 0-4-4 tanks, although on this visit we saw Nos 30039 (ex-70F), 30241, 30245, 30248 and 30249 still in working use.

EXETER: SUNDAY 17 JULY - I went on a rail/coach trip to the West Country with my father, visiting Buckfast Abbey and Widecombe-in-the-Moor. The fare was 26/3d.

EXETER DEPOT (83C) was visited, and I had the distinction of being ejected by the foreman, but not before I had noted 21 steam, which included 'Grange' No 6866 *Morfa Grange* in ex-works condition. We were steam-hauled between Fratton and Salisbury by Class 'U' 2-6-0 No 31800, and from Salisbury to Exeter by 'West Country' Class 4-6-2 No 34099 *Lynton*.

Steam noted 'on line' on this visit: 1024, 4930, 5234, 30315, 30453, 30719, 30825, 30830, 30832, 30956, 34015, 34024, 34030, 34032, 34035, 34050, 34054, 34057, 34059, 34095, 34096, 76008, 76027, 76054, 82010, 82019 and 82024.

SR RAILROVER: 10 AUGUST - While travelling the crowded tube train with Jim Lawrence and Bill Jenkins, Jim, as mentioned in Volume 1, began counting aloud the number of 'domes' (bald heads)! He stood behind a 'City gent' who was wearing a bowler hat, and was heard to say 'Raise your hat, sir'. On this particular day the gent duly obliged and to our amazement revealed a 'complete dome'! 'Dome-spotting' on tube trains

was originally suggested by Jim and David Copus, and it did not take too long to spread to our fellow train-spotters whenever they used this type of transport. On leaving the train we would deposit a sheet of paper on a seat displaying in large capital letters wording such as 'TEN DOMES' - those passengers who occupied our seats must have been quite puzzled by their presence! It certainly helped to alleviate any boredom associated with tube travel, especially on the longer journeys!

THE PORTSMOUTH AREA DURING 1960

As mentioned previously, we local train-spotters had many other varied leisure-time interests and activities, including football, 'live' shows, cinema, walking and the occasional girlfriend - television had not really got a hold and videos were unheard of!

In 1960 we had a varied choice of cinemas in Portsmouth in which to see our favourite films. More often than not we would attend a comedy or a black and white thriller together; a group of five or six of us would be quite common, and these visits would normally take place once or twice a month. In those days you got two films, a short feature film and the usual 'Pathe News' together with all the forthcoming films - real value for money!

I recollect seeing *Pillow Talk*, starring Rock Hudson and Doris Day, at the Gaumont in Bradford Junction, Southsea, and later in the year, just a few yards down the road from the Gaumont, I had the pleasure of a 'live' show at The Kings Theatre starring 'skiffle king' Lonnie Donegan; one of the supporting acts was the country duo Miki and Griff.

FRATTON (70F): SUNDAY 24 JANUARY - Steam locomotives of note were Class 'G6' 0-6-0 tank No 30349 and 'Schools' 4-4-0 No 30910 *Merchant Taylors* (stored).

FOOTBALL EXCURSIONS: FEBRUARY AND MARCH - Class 'N15' 'King Arthur' 4-6-0 No 30453 *King Arthur* (72B) was in ex-works condition employed on a Bristol Rovers football excursion. 'West Country' 4-6-2 No 34095 *Brentor* took out the football special to Plymouth.

SOME WESTERN REGION STEAM LOCOMOTIVES NOTED AT FRATTON
SATURDAY 23 JULY - Nos 5965 *Woollas Hall* and 6861 *Crynant Grange*.
SUNDAY 24 JULY - No 5930 *Hannington Hall*.
THURSDAY 28 JULY - No 7324 (81E).
WEDNESDAY 5 AUGUST - No 5944 *Ickenham Hall* came in with the headboard 'MIDLANDS HOLIDAY EXCURSION'.
SUNDAY 21 AUGUST - Excursions with large black and white route indicators appeared: Nos 5914 *Ripon Hall* on 'X12' and 6926 *Holkham Hall* on 'X15', from Gloucester and Wolverhampton respectively. Many others followed, especially on Sunday excursions to Portsmouth Harbour.
THURSDAY 8 SEPTEMBER - 0-6-0 pannier tank No 4616 appeared 'on shed'.
SATURDAY 24 SEPTEMBER - No 5977 *Beckford Hall* brought in a Norwich football excursion.

This diminutive Class 'P' 0-6-0 tank, No 31556 (75A), a Wainwright SECR design for push-and-pull working, introduced in 1909, was a very rare class to be seen at Fratton depot, and was photographed in the yard in August 1960. It was thought to have been sent to Fratton from its home depot of Brighton for trials on the Hayling Island branch line. Weighing only 5 cwt heavier than the Class 'A1X' 0-6-0 tanks, which worked this branch, it was obviously intended to work with or replace one of the 'A1Xs', but its proposed use did not materialise and it was returned to Brighton depot.
John Spence

SOME OBSERVED WORKINGS IN PORTSMOUTH -

Class 'T9' 4-4-0 No 30707 (71A) on a parcels train.

The 7.30 am Portsmouth Harbour to Reading General was usually double-headed, and on one occasion I saw 'Schools' 4-4-0 No 30908 *Westminster* with Standard Class '4' 2-6-0 No 76064 (71A).

SUNDAY 28 AUGUST - Standard Class '4' 2-6-0 No 76017 was employed on the 8.22 pm to Waterloo via Eastleigh and Basingstoke.

A most unusual sight was Class 'WD' 2-8-0 No 90261 (ex-Banbury, but at this time shedded at Feltham) employed on the 12.15 pm passenger train from Portsmouth & Southsea to Plymouth, which it took as far as Fareham.

A diesel-hauled excursion arrived behind No D5583 (Ilford to Portsmouth Harbour), while another rare visitor was electric locomotive No E5011, also terminating at the Harbour with an excursion.

FRATTON: CHRISTMAS DAY -

Fratton Depot had officially closed in November 1960, but it remained open for purposes of coaling-up and servicing of locomotives. Engines at this date were being transferred to other depots, staff were sent to Eastleigh and some were made redundant. The depot dated from the 1890s and had a complete roundhouse with a total of 25 roads. As already mentioned in earlier pages, the fascination of steam had led me to apply for a job at the depot. I had gathered much knowledge about it and had always admired its fine building and interesting layout. It was indeed sad to learn of its closure, and a gradual 'run-down' would result in demolition.

No 4689 was a Class '5700' 0-6-0 pannier tank allocated to Weymouth (71G), a rare visitor to Fratton, probably employed on

FRATTON DEPOT

Steam locomotives:

4689	30133	30546	30549
31410	31622	31623	31638
31757	31790	31793	32338
32640	32661	73084	73110
80067			

Diesel locomotives:

D3011	D3665	D3666	15236

21 locomotives on shed

Christmas parcels traffic. At about this date another pannier, in the 97XX series, was noted on the 'Dockyard Goods'.

FRATTON DEPOT LOSES ITS ALLOCATION

Although the Class 'A1X' 0-6-0 'Terriers' used on the Hayling Island branch line had been re-allocated to Eastleigh, they were still to be seen occasionally at Fratton shed during 1960. Otherwise Fratton shed had lost its allocation of steam by about February or March of 1960, the locomotives going to other depots such as Eastleigh, Guildford, Three Bridges, Brighton and Norwood Junction. One of my favourite tanks allocated to Fratton

was Class 'E1' 0-6-0 No 32694 - it was turned out in a very smart condition on Thursday 7 January, as it was making its final run on the daily Fratton goods sidings with the Dockyard goods. I well remember the many times that I would make a stop at Somers Road Bridge when cycling to work in Blackfriars Road just to see the 'Dockyard Goods', a regular duty for No 32694. Other tanks had been employed on this duty in previous years, including Class 'O2' 0-4-4 No 30207 and Class 'E1' 0-6-0s Nos 32138 and 32139. Following its move from Fratton, No 32694 was allocated to Southampton Docks shed (71I).

HILSEA GAS WORKS

On Friday 10 June I made an afternoon visit to one of Portsmouth's less well-known locations.

The saddle-tank illustrated was painted green, but its condition was somewhat faded. It had rusted considerably. Its works plate read 'ANDREW BARCLAY SONS & CO LIMITED, CALEDONIA WORKS, No 1398. 1915. KILMARNOCK'. At a later date the locomotive was moved to Eastleigh Works, towed by a 'Lord Nelson' Class 4-6-0.

This 0-4-0 outside-cylinder saddle tank had been left on an isolated siding at Hilsea Gas Works for well over a year, prior to this photograph being taken.

STEAM 'ON SHED' AT FRATTON

Some of my favourite photographs taken during 1960 . . .

Fratton Depot, viewed here from Goldsmith Avenue, housed a 50-foot turntable, and was the only complete roundhouse on the SR. The van (right) displays the words 'TO WORK BETWEEN PORTSMOUTH HARBOUR AND FRATTON ONLY'.

There's plenty of steam being released in this photograph of Class 'A1X' 0-6-0 tank No 32640 at the main-line end of the yard. Fratton East signal box is on the left and behind this can be seen the rear of houses in Walmer Road. The location of the former 'Sooty Footbridge' was to the right of the signal box. February 1960.

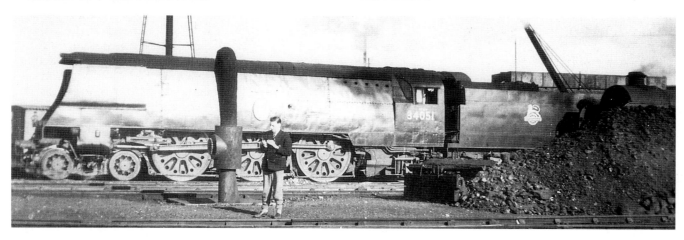

Above Bulleid-designed 'Battle of Britain' Class 4-6-2 No 34051 *Winston Churchill* in the shed yard being coaled up, having taken over a Cardiff General to Portsmouth train at Salisbury. Local railway enthusiast Eddie Rooke is in the foreground, jotting down some numbers - he is complete with cycle clips, as he nearly always cycled to the depot from his home at Sandringham Road, Fratton.

Right A rear view of Standard Class '4' 2-6-4 tank No 80067 and Class 'K' 2-6-0 No 32337 (70F) being coaled-up by steam crane DS200.

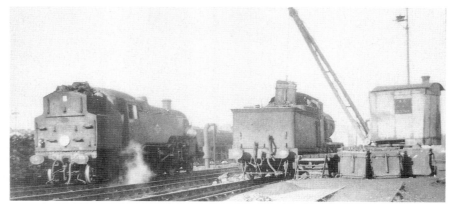

It was re-conditioned in the works, painted red and was put to work in a gas works on the Southampton Terminus line. It was eventually purchased privately in 1967 and operated on the East Somerset Railway at Cranmore, near Shepton Mallet.

The gas works had its own brick-built one-road engine shed, which was located at the southern end of the main-line sidings.

A fire at Fratton station? Nothing too serious, but the fire brigade were called on a summer Saturday afternoon in 1960. The vehicle is a Dennis, registration GRV 952.

Steam at Fratton: 'Schools' Class 4-4-0 No 30905 *Tonbridge* gets quickly away from Platform 2. Prior to the 'direct' Portsmouth to Waterloo line being electrified by the third rail in 1937, the 'Schools' were one of the main types used on this route. Saturday 14 May.

Steam engines worked at this location, usually a Peckett 0-4-0 saddle-tank. Fratton-allocated tanks would also be noted at this gas works along with a very distinctive red diesel, *Fleet No 1139*.

PORTSMOUTH & SOUTHSEA STATION

LOW LEVEL: At this date the Low Level station was in constant daily use. Platforms 1 and 2 were used for local steam and 'Hampshire' diesel unit trains to Southampton, Eastleigh and Andover Junction, while platforms 3 and 4 were usually occupied by the familiar 2-BIL and 2-HAL electric unit stopping trains for the Waterloo and Brighton lines. Platform 5 was often the starting point for the steam-hauled through trains to Cardiff.

HIGH LEVEL: The High Level platforms consist of a single covered island platform, its faces numbered 6 and 7. At this date the electric unit trains serving Waterloo, Victoria and Brighton used these platforms. Platform 7 was for Portsmouth Harbour and platform 6 was for all northbound trains. A large sign in Southern Green with white lettering told arriving passengers to 'ALIGHT AT THE NEXT STATION FOR ISLE OF WIGHT AND GOSPORT FERRIES'. Local enthusiasts always knew the High Level as the 'pigeon house' - the sight of these birds in the roof rafters was always a feature of this structure, until replaced in later years.

No information would be complete without a mention of the dockyard line. A single line, midway along platform 6 curved away northwards and followed the edge of Victoria Park. There were level crossings at both Edinburgh Road and Alfred Road before the line entered the dockyard.

COSHAM STATION SIDINGS

The early 1960s saw much activity in the sidings on the north side of the station. These sidings (four in all) were a part of Erith & Co's builders yard. Steam engines would bring wagons of bricks into these sidings and off-load them into the yard; these trains would consist of 46 wagons per day, six days per week, and this practice

Above A general view of the terminus platforms 1 to 5 at Portsmouth & Southsea. The covered high level platforms 6 and 7 are on the extreme left, No 7 being used for trains to the Harbour station. The station had opened in 1866 and at this date had seen little modernisation. The steam locomotive departing from platform 2 is Class 'S15' 4-6-0 No 30506 (70B) with the 12.15 pm to Plymouth (which it would take as far as Fareham, where this train would join up with another train from Brighton). In later years No 30506 was destined to be preserved and used on the Mid Hants Railway (Watercress Line). The photograph was taken from 'Jacob's Ladder', the nickname given to the large footbridge that spans these tracks. The signal box (right) is now demolished.

Right The 12.15 pm Portsmouth & Southsea (Low Level) to Plymouth, steam-hauled as far as Fareham, was a turn that produced a varied selection of classes, including a 'WD' 2-8-0, 'S15' 4-6-0s, 'C2X' 0-6-0s, 'T9' 4-4-0s and Standard Class '4' 2-6-0s. Here we see Class 'M7' 0-4-4 tank No 30030 (71A) on this turn, emerging from under Fratton Bridge. *John Harris*

continued for many years as the bricks and other materials were being used in the construction of huge housing estates at both Leigh Park and Paulsgrove. I remember that a steam crane (from Horsham) would often be seen working in this yard. At about this date an old-type crane, mounted on a base, was located in the yard, but its use was very rarely witnessed, and it was removed in the mid-1960s. Fleets of lorries would convey the bricks and materials from the yard to both Leigh Park and Paulsgrove.

ENTERTAINED FOR SIXPENCE!

Prior to 1960 I have some fond memories of the Savoy (ABC) cinema in Commercial Road, as it was here that I and my cousin David, and sometimes other friends, attended the 'Saturday Club' for an admission charge of sixpence.

The morning started off with the playing of the 'Club tune', with which all the children sang along as they read the words from the screen; this followed the organist's arrival with the famous 'Compton Wonder Organ' rising from out of the depths! We were mystified, especially when we heard it for the first time, and couldn't understand why it was not visible!

The manager would always appear during the interval and quite often would arrange a competition for the boys and girls; this would consist of making models or painting a picture. In one such competition I won first prize for making a model railway locomotive! Winners were proudly presented on stage, usually with a small gift or complimentary 'Saturday Club' tickets.

MODEL RAILWAYS . . . A RAILWAY OF MY OWN

I had from the age of seven always been in possession of a train-set, firstly clockwork, then later OO gauge electric, and wherever my parents resided I would inevitably have a layout, albeit on a very small scale, somewhere in the house. It was not until later years, when I married, that I had the chance to set up my own layout - in the garden shed - and ironically the shed backed on to Cosham railway station. I spent many happy hours there perfecting my OO gauge layout, scenery and buildings, and all this with the sound of the 'real' railway in the background.

It was a perfect location: accompanied by my two cats and a second-hand piano (purchased for £5), on which I had taken lessons many years ago, I would, after 'playing trains', end up with a few tunes!

My friend David Copus, also being a model railway fanatic in the 1960s, had his layout in a bedroom.

Eddie and I would visit him and view the layout following a visit to Fratton shed, this being ideal as his house was opposite the shed entrance. Not only were our interests now involved in model railways, but also football, pop music and girlfriends. All these interests seemed to blend together - for example, when visiting Fratton Park to see 'Pompey' play we would also visit Tony Collett's shop in Winter Road and ponder over purchasing the latest model railway locomotives or buildings, including those superb card and plastic models that Tony designed himself.

It was a bit of a wrench when we moved house, as transferring the layout was not easy, but eventually it was set up in my loft. My late father helped me in constructing OO gauge buildings and accessories in his spare time. Although not a completely working layout today, I am still somewhat proud of the results achieved over a period of many years owning my own railway, if only in model form.

Some of the author's OO gauge engines. Far right is one of the Tony Collett-designed wagons, as described in the text.

1961

PETER-BOROUGH ARRIVALS

SATURDAY 7 JANUARY

Prior to attending the football match at the nearby Fratton Park, I visited Fratton station area to photograph incoming excursion trains bringing football supporters from Peterborough for the FA Cup Third Round match against Portsmouth.

Out of the 13 steam locomotives noted at Fratton station,

seven were employed on football excursions from Peterborough, these being Nos 4921, 6927 (headcode 'X56'), 6970 ('X57'), 34017, 34020, 34037 and 34045. Another 'West Country' Class 4-6-2, No 34105 *Swanage*, arrived at platform 3 displaying a large nameboard on its smokebox door with the words 'WESTBURY PANTO EXCURSION'. The passengers on this excursion were mostly children, off no doubt to sample the pantomime at the

nearby Kings Theatre in Albert Road, Southsea.

It had indeed been a very busy Saturday at Fratton station with the 'specials' and all the normal workings, one of which was the daily Reading General to Portsmouth & Southsea train; this arrived at 11.32 am behind 'Hall' Class 4-6-0 No 7906 *Fron Hall* (81D).

If you were a Portsmouth football fan, the result of this FA Cup match was disappointing . . . they lost 2-1! The team that turned out

---

FRATTON STATION

Steam locomotives:

4921	6927	6970	7906
31633	34017	34020	34037
34045	34105	75076	76006
76053			

Above right Un-rebuilt 'West Country' Class 4-6-2 No 34020 *Seaton* arrives at platform 3. The headcode (above the buffer-beam) reads '983'. Eastern Region carriages were used.

Right With another train-load of Peterborough football supporters having been emptied, 'Hall' Class 4-6-0 No 4921 *Eaton Hall* takes the empty carriages towards Portsmouth & Southsea station. An engine from Fratton shed would then couple on to the rear of the carriages and bring them back to Fratton goods sidings. Sometimes football excursion carriages would be put in the single siding, adjacent to the up main line, between Fratton Bridge and Somers Road Bridge.

on that day was: Beattie, Rutter, Dickinson, Howells, Gunter, H. Harris, Priscott, Chapman, White, Blackburn and A. Wilson. Alex Wilson scored and the attendance was 27,533, obviously boosted by the seven excursions from Peterborough. 'Pompey', which I had supported since the 1948-49 season, were not only out of the Cup, but that season (1960-61) ended with them being relegated to Division 3!

LEAMINGTON SPA, BANBURY, OXFORD AND READING

SUNDAY 2 APRIL

It was Easter Sunday, and this trip was incorporated in the Wolverhampton excursion, which departed from Portsmouth Harbour station. A party, in excess of 12, travelled - some of those who accompanied me were Eddie Rooke, David Copus, Jim Lawrence, Bill Jenkins, Terry Hunt and David Bodenham (home on Forces leave).

We were steam-hauled from Portsmouth by Standard Class '4' 2-6-0 No 76068, and the carriage set was No 791. No 76068 was replaced by 'West Country' Class 4-6-2 No 34046 *Braunton* at Eastleigh. At this date Basingstoke had 14 steam locomotives in its depot allocation, including Class 'G6' 0-6-0 tank No 30258.

A second change of motive power was made at Basingstoke; No 34046 came off and we were then steam-hauled by 'Hall' Class 4-6-0 No 5910 *Park Hall*, travelling via Reading West, Didcot and Oxford to Leamington Spa.

On arrival at Leamington Spa

DIDCOT AND OXFORD AREAS

Steam locomotives:

4649	4982	4994	5351
5988	5989	6168	6363
6911	7023	7220	7328
7404	7908	8494	9404
9455	48269	73035	75001
75008	90693	92224	

Diesel locomotive:
D3964

Diesel railcar:
W26

---

station we made the 15-minute walk to the shed, as directed in *The British Locomotive Shed Directory*. This was a four-road straight shed with a turntable.

---

84 D

LEAMINGTON SPA DEPOT

Steam locomotives:

2256	2267	3619	3631
4112	4118	4171	4176
5089	5101	5177	5184
5194	5318	5966	6933
6976	7734	7808	8100
40085	41285	42566	48045
48320			

Diesel locomotives:
D3975 D3985

27 locomotives on shed

Pannier tank No 7734 had been withdrawn from service.

We were then steam-hauled to Banbury by 'King' Class No 6017 *King Edward IV*. On arrival at the station we made the 5-minute walk to the shed. This was my first visit to this location, which con-

---

sisted of a four-road shed with a separate single-road repair shop, being distinctive by its two ash shelters on either side of the coaling stage at the front of the shed.

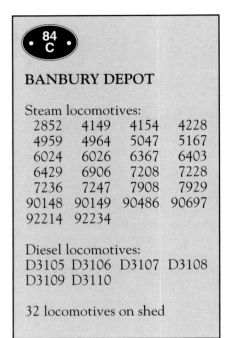

84 C

BANBURY DEPOT

Steam locomotives:

2852	4149	4154	4228
4959	4964	5047	5167
6024	6026	6367	6403
6429	6906	7208	7228
7236	7247	7908	7929
90148	90149	90486	90697
92214	92234		

Diesel locomotives:
D3105 D3106 D3107 D3108
D3109 D3110

32 locomotives on shed

We were then steam-hauled (much to our surprise) by an Eastern Region Class 'B1' 4-6-0 No 61078 to Oxford. This engine was allocated to Woodford Halse (2F).

We were steam-hauled between Oxford and Reading General by 'Modified Hall' 4-6-0 No 6970 *Whaddon Hall*.

READING DEPOT (81D)

Here we noted 44 steam locomotives and five 0-6-0 diesel shunters 'on shed'. Reading, like the previous depots visited on this Sunday, had minimal locomotive movements. Types were quite varied: pannier tanks, Class '6100' side tanks, 2-8-0 freight engines, the usual 'Hall' Class 4-6-0s and three Class '9F' 2-10-0s.

We then walked to Reading West, and after a short wait we boarded the return Wolverhampton excursion, arriving back in Portsmouth at about 1 am (Monday).

OXFORD DEPOT

Steam locomotives:
1442	1444	1450	2894	3861	4085	4125	4148	4649	4979	4982	5034	5933
5947	5957	6106	6123	6129	6138	6150	6154	6927	6956	7008	7209	7239
7404	7445	7760	7900	7921	9455	9653	9654	61880	75000	75001	75008	75021
75038	92224	92240										

Diesel locomotives:
D3760 D3959 D3963 D3964 D3971

47 locomotives on shed

The party of train-spotters who travelled on this excursion performed or witnessed one of the many silly antics which, by now, had become commonplace on Sunday excursions, this particular one being termed as 'Doing a Bog Roll'! The procedure would be for two of us to enter the end toilet of the last carriage; a full toilet roll would then be dangled over the open toilet, with two fingers acting as a roller. One of us would hold the paper while the other would flush the toilet. The toilet roll would then unwind and rapidly disappear down the toilet of the speeding train, until it had completely unrolled.

This action would usually take place when the train was on a curve. If all went to plan, we would quickly look out of the end carriage window and observe a complete white BR toilet roll resting between the tracks! British Railways track workers must have been mystified when they came across the scene!

EASTLEIGH

SATURDAY 13 MAY

I went on this trip with Peter Esgate of the Grosvenor Press, Southsea. He was a keen photographer, and our aim was to take photographs at Eastleigh depot. Peter was not a train-spotter, but nevertheless I persuaded him that this subject would be a new experience for him.

We were steam-hauled by Standard Class '4' 4-6-0 No 75076 between Portsmouth & Southsea and Eastleigh, travelling via Botley. On passing Fratton shed we noted Service locomotive No DS680, a Class 'A1' 0-6-0 tank allocated to Lancing Carriage & Wagon Works, Sussex. It had recently undergone minor repairs on the depot crane, which were now complete; it had been rumoured that the locomotive was to be used on the Hayling Island branch line.

On passing Eastleigh Works scrapyard we noted two steam in the process of being cut up for scrap: Class 'M7' 0-4-4 tank No 30479 and Class 'T9' 4-4-0 No 30707 (both 71A).

The accompanying Eastleigh list comprises roughly half of those 'on shed'.

EASTLEIGH DEPOT

Steam locomotives:
3671	30050	30059	30102	30104	30117	30124	30200	30287	30306	30316	30338	30357
30457	30532	30584	30695	30788	30790	30839	30851	30855	30913	32646	32661	33020
33021	33023	34074	41306	41310	73041	73052	73082	73088	75003	75076	90630	92007
92205	92206	92231										

42 locomotives noted

CAMERA ON EASTLEIGH - MAY TO OCTOBER

Following the photographic visit to Eastleigh with Peter Esgate, I decided to make further such visits during 1961. The selection of photographs that follow were all captured between May and October of that year.

Top left One of the Eastleigh-allocated Class 'Lord Nelson' 4-6-0s, No 30855 *Robert Blake*, waits in the yard.

Middle left Ex-Eastern Section Class 'D1' 4-4-0 No 31145 had been sent here for scrapping.

Bottom left Ex-Llandudno Junction-allocated LMS Class '2' 2-6-2 tank No 41238 had just come out of Eastleigh Works. It had been re-shedded to 72A, Exmouth Junction.

Top right Ex-works condition Class 'Q' 0-6-0 No 30532 (71A) awaits running-in duties. Behind its tender is Standard Class '5' 4-6-0 No 73088 *Joyous Gard*.

Middle right Drummond-designed Class 'M7' 0-4-4 tank No 30111 (71B) 'on shed' in ex-works condition.

Bottom right On the Works yard scrap line an un-identified Class 'M7' 0-4-4 tank (its number painted over) awaits its call to the scrapyard; its smokebox door has been left wide open.

Eastleigh-allocated Class 'T9' 4-4-0 No 30120, all cleaned up, awaits its next duty at the airport end of the yard. It is being kept company by Class 'E4' 0-6-2 tank No 32510 (71A). Several months later No 30120 was relegated to the 'dead line' prior to being restored for preservation - it subsequently came out of Eastleigh Works painted apple green and numbered 120, and was used extensively on specials during the twilight of steam on the SR before eventually finding its way to the Bluebell Railway via the Mid Hants (Watercress Line) and Swanage railways. *Ted Gamblin*

'KING ARTHUR' CLASS 4-6-0s 'DEAD' AND 'ALIVE'

'Live' in the depot yard is 30798 *Sir Hectimere*. Class 'S15' No 30501 is on the right.

'Dead' in the scrapyard is 30799 *Sir Ironside*. Definitely *no* reprieve!

TANK ENGINES HIGHLIGHTED

Right Class 'O2' 0-4-4 No 30223. Behind it is Class 'A1X' 0-6-0 No 32661.

Below Class 'C14' 0-4-0 No 30588. Introduced in 1923, it was a Urie rebuild of a Drummond steam railmotor 2-2-0, originally introduced in 1906.

Below right Class 'E2' 0-6-0 No 32107 (ex-Southampton Docks, 71I).

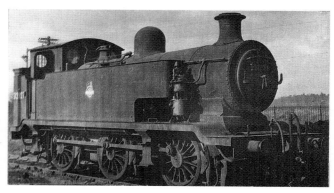

WESTERN REGION RAILROVER

FRIDAY 26 MAY TO FRIDAY 2 JUNE

I went on this Railrover with my close friend Eddie Rooke and Tony 'Inky' Ingram. Permits to visit most of the depots had been applied for and received three weeks prior to our departure. Eddie and I planned our week ahead with precision, visiting the information office at Portsmouth & Southsea station frequently to check on times and routes; we had also purchased a Western Region timetable. As this was a Western Region ticket we decided to start our journey from London (Paddington), this being the ideal starting point as we had planned to travel overnight by sleeper to South Wales.

The adventure started at 6.30 pm on the Friday evening as I left my parents' house at Fratton. This could be termed as my 'greatest adventure' involving train travel, visiting numerous cities and towns, many of which I had never seen before.

I met up with Eddie and we walked to Portsmouth & Southsea station, where we were joined by our travelling companion Tony Ingram - he told us that we had been offered overnight accommodation on Saturday at his relatives' house in Swansea. We had previously checked that we had everything we needed for the week ahead: items such as camera, timetable, *Shed Directory*, notebooks, pens, transistor radio, plastic mac, not forgetting some food and drink and obviously enough money. I wore my usual brown 'Tuf' shoes; having been purchased in 1958, these must have done some miles!

We purchased single tickets to Waterloo; departure from High Level was at 7.24 pm.

Steam locomotives noted at Clapham Junction were Nos 4672, 4698 and 44051. On arrival at Waterloo we caught a tube train to Paddington where we collected our Western Region Railrover tickets; we had been informed by return of post that they were ready to collect.

With time on our hands before our departure from Paddington, we decided to visit Old Oak Common shed (81A) - however, we got no further than the main gate when we were confronted by the foreman. We had no permit as this shed was not on our list! Leaving the entrance we chanced to see a trolleybus with an 'ACTON' destination - this we boarded and planned a quick visit to the pin-tables at Acton funfair. On leaving the funfair we had to run to catch the bus to Paddington; clambering to the upper deck as the bus moved off, Eddie was heard to shout out loud a very rude word, as he had tripped as he ascended the stairs! We arrived at Paddington at 11.30 pm.

Departure from Paddington was on the 12.45 am sleeper train to Pembroke, south-west Wales. It is

The map displayed in the folder advertising the Railrover.

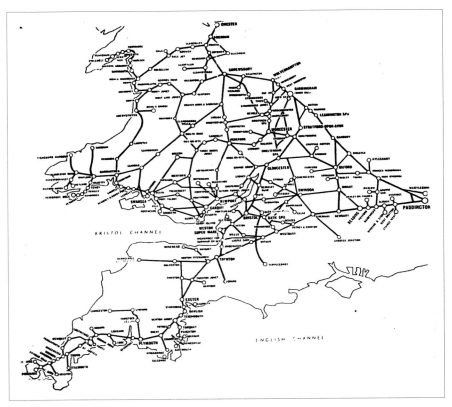

of note that, about this date, BR had 467 sleeper cars in service! We were steam-hauled by 'Castle' Class 4-6-0 No 5023 *Brecon Castle*.

SATURDAY 27 MAY (Day 1)

It was exactly 6 am when we awoke. Looking out of the window, we found that we were near Newport - the sleeper car attendant then supplied us with hot cups of tea and an assortment of biscuits. Much activity was noted, especially in the numerous marshalling yards and sidings, and this is reflected in the accompanying list of 60 locomotives, of which only ten were main-line types.

On arrival at Carmarthen station at 7.05 am we made the

---

87 G

CARMARTHEN DEPOT

Steam locomotives:

4935	4962	5030	5039
5249	5357	5549	5938
5956	5961	6316	6329
6650	6662	6822	7312
7321	7334	7402	7407
7440	7820	7823	9632
90529			

25 locomotives on shed

A general view of Carmarthen station: the locomotive is 'Hall' Class 4-6-0 No 6918 *Sandon Hall* (87E, Landore). Note the silver buffers - this was a feature of many Landore engines.

5-minute walk to the depot. It was a brick-built, six-road straight shed with a block end. A two-road lifting shop was also observed.

Returning to the station we caught the 7.55 am train to Goodwick, via Whitland. Our arrival at Goodwick was on time at exactly 9.35 am - we made the 5-minute walk to the depot. All the engines in the accompanying list except No 3206 were allocated to this depot. At the date of this visit, it had 15 steam locomotives in its allocation, consisting of eight pannier tanks, five 'Halls' and two '2251' 0-6-0s. The building was a brick-built, two-road dead-end shed.

---

87 J

GOODWICK DEPOT

Steam locomotives:

3206	3637	4677	5905
5908	5928	9602	9666
9677			

9 locomotives on shed

I'm not sure if our route to Fishguard Harbour station was official, but it took us along the side of the railway tracks. In the station we noted Nos 9645, 9666 and 9760. We then caught a train to

---

BETWEEN NEWPORT AND CARMARTHEN VIA CARDIFF AND SWANSEA

Steam locomotives:

1607	2845	2892	3678	3747	3768	3785	3834	3836	4106	4236	4274	4289
4293	4682	5017	5062	5078	5203	5225	5239	5604	5656	5661	5905	5991
6688	6829	6918	6936	7211	7439	7753	7903	8407	8416	8467	8488	8497
8760	9452	9473	9606	9637	9744	9761	9777	42182	70020	90579		

Diesel locomotives:

13354	D3355	13356	D3360	D3399	D3427	D3431	D3824	D4001	D4002

Goodwick depot: The locomotives are 'Hall' Class 4-6-0s Nos 5928 *Haddon Hall* and 5908 *Moreton Hall*, with pannier tank No 9677.

Clarbeston Road. On arrival there at 11.01 am we changed trains and departed at 11.10 am for Whitland.

Our arrival at Whitland was 11.30 am. It took less than 5 minutes to walk to the shed, which at this date was, together with Cardigan, Milford Haven and Pembroke Dock, a sub-depot of Neyland (87H). The shed was a corrugated, one-road through shed without a turntable. It certainly looked as if it had seen better days, judging by its external view! All the engines at this depot on this visit were tank designs.

Returning to the station, we

caught the 12.41 pm train to Bridgend. We were steam-hauled by 'Manor' Class 4-6-0 No 7825 *Lechlade Manor*. On arrival at Bridgend we alighted and changed to a DMU to Tondu, where we arrived on time at 4.01 pm. We then made the few minutes walk to Tondu shed, which consisted of a large single roundhouse-type building with two extended roundhouse tracks serving as a repair area.

On returning to Tondu station

we continued as per the timetable, catching a DMU to Bridgend, where we changed again and caught the 4.58 pm to Cardiff General. Our route then took us through the Welsh valleys on the 5.45 pm DMU to Abercynon, via Radyr and Pontypridd. Arrival at Abercynon was at 6.26 pm and the shed was entered via the side of the platform, not the official entrance! It was a very neat two-road shed, constructed of corrugated materials. It had no turntable.

BETWEEN CARDIFF AND ABERCYNON

Steam locomotives:
5635   5643   5665   6647
9622

Diesel locomotives:
13259   D3430   D3431   D3606

 88 E

ABERCYNON DEPOT

Steam locomotives:
1612   1641   1663   3707
3730   3734   3783   5601
5617   5630   5641   5680
5682   5686   5699   6410
7744   8730   8735   9728

20 locomotives on shed.

Every locomotive was a tank design.

WHITLAND DEPOT

Steam locomotives:
1613   1666   1669   4107
4159   4573   5520   5550
6148   6680   8738   9681
9779

13 locomotives on shed

 88 H

TONDU DEPOT

Steam locomotives:
3668   3690   3738   4108
4121   4144   4218   4243
4251   4263   4269   4274
4675   5208   5629   6408
6673   6676   7732   7736
7753   7786   8453   8710
8712   8721   8748   9609
9649   9738

30 locomotives on shed.

Every locomotive was a tank design.

Having visited the depot we returned to the station and caught the 7.14 pm train to Radyr. It was late evening as we made our way along the cinder footpath to the depot, a long, four-road straight shed and, unlike many of the smaller sheds in the area, with a turntable. Its location was in close proximity to the River Taff. All locomotives, except No 3804,

Abercynon depot: Class '6400' 0-6-0 pannier tank No 6410.

were tank designs. Noted in the vicinity of the depot was 0-6-0 diesel No PWM651, a service locomotive (88B).

We then returned to the station and caught a train to Cardiff. We were then steam-hauled from the General station to Swansea by 'King' Class No 6019 *King Henry V* on the 'Red Dragon' express from Paddington. Departure was at 9.15 pm. It must have been about 11 pm as we arrived at Swansea.

The first day of the Railrover had run as planned, and we were feeling quite exhausted after trav-

BETWEEN CARDIFF AND SWANSEA
Steam locomotives:
3781   5923   6872   6936
45303   48338   90573

elling many miles and visiting six locomotive depots. On leaving the station at Swansea we made our way to 'Inky's' relatives' house at Llanelly. On our arrival we were made welcome and given cups of tea. We had a short summing-up of the depots and places we had visited before we went upstairs to the bedroom. We were extremely

tired, but still managed to listen to Radio Luxembourg on Eddie Rooke's transistor radio for almost an hour. Sleep overcame us about midnight. I think we must have been very tired, for when we awoke we were laying at different angles; 'Inky' was on the floor, Eddie had his feet at the head of the bed and my first recollection of the morning was looking down towards the foot of the bed to see my mud-splattered brown 'Tuf' shoes still firmly laced to my feet!

SUNDAY 28 MAY (Day 2)

All three of us were well awake by 6 am, and we did not take too long to get dressed as we were almost fully clothed when we fell asleep! We were given a breakfast of bacon, eggs and bread and butter. After thanking 'Inky's' relatives for our stay and food, we left the house and made our way to the first depot of the day, Llanelly. We stopped a milkman and purchased pints of milk, which we drank from the bottles as we walked to the depot. It was a cold, sunny morning with some mist.

Departure from Llanelly station was on the 8.44 am to Swansea (High Street), and we were steam-hauled by 'Castle' Class 4-6-0 No 4094 *Dynevor Castle*. Arrival time at Swansea was 9.15 am - we then walked to Landore depot.

On leaving Landore we chanced

RADYR DEPOT

88 B

Steam locomotives:

1447	3401	3402	3404	3405	3406	3407	3408	3409	3672	3681	3705	3804
5633	5635	5648	5652	5663	5669	5683	5697	6434	6603	6606	6608	6612
6614	6626	6633	6647	6648	6665	6682	6684	7205	7242	7252	8420	8438
8439	8469	8470	8478	8749								

44 locomotives on shed

LLANELLY DEPOT

Steam locomotives:

1606	1607	1614	1615	1643	3698	3719	3761	3771	3812	4241	4242	4298
4676	5209	5223	5602	5656	5692	6310	6633	6810	6818	6832	6837	7235
7307	7745	8467	8474	8477	9485	9621	9744	42385	42388	48172	48309	48400
48470	48707	48730	48735	48737	48739	48768	73021	73023	73036	90179	90529	92210

Diesel locomotives:

13352　13353　13354　13355　13356　13357　D3358　D3360

60 locomotives on shed

Pannier tank No 3698 was being repaired in the depot works, together with Class '7200' 2-8-2 tank No 7235.

LANDORE DEPOT

Steam locomotives:

3678	3701	3768	3785	3797	3836	4076	4078	4099	4106	5004	5016	5056
5074	5078	5091	5673	6680	6688	6695	6912	6917	6918	7001	7020	7021
7024	7902	7903	8789	8794	9416	9637	9715	9761	42182	42305	42387	42394
70025	70029											

41 locomotives on shed

Llanelly depot: LMS Fowler-design Class '4' 2-6-4 tanks Nos 42385 and 42388. Note the sunglasses being worn by Eddie and 'Inky'!

Landore depot: Awaiting its next duty alongside the coaling plant is Old Oak Common-allocated 'Castle' Class 4-6-0 No 7024 *Powis Castle*.

to hitch a lift to our next depot, Upper Bank - this was a very small engine shed situated on top of a high strip of land overlooking a wide river (hence the name). It was a stone-built shed with two roads. On approaching we noticed that the shed doors were closed, but we entered through a small

hatch door. This depot was a sub-depot of Swansea (Victoria), which at the date of this visit had probably been closed. On shed were ten pannier tanks, Nos 6700/38/55/7/62/4/5/7/77 and 78.

Immediately upon completing our visit, a railwayman came along and locked the small hatch door

by which we had gained entrance. We then travelled by United Welsh bus to the next depot, Swansea East Dock.

Our next shed visit was Duffryn Yard; we travelled by bus from Swansea. This brick-built shed consisted of six roads with a dead end. It had a single-road repair shop.

NEATH DEPOT

Steam locomotives:

1152	1645	3741	3743
3766	3832	3838	4134
4254	4255	4621	4927
4943	5222	5239	5616
5720	6641	7212	8102
8104	8418	8439	8732
8760	8784	8788	9442
9446	9448	9452	9473
9478	9734	9783	

Diesel locomotive:
D3432

36 locomotives on shed

All except Nos 3832, 4927 and 4943 were tank designs.

NEATH (N&B) DEPOT

Steam locomotives:

3757	3774	4653	5761
5773	7799	8715	9627
9750	9786		

10 locomotives on shed

All locomotives were Class '5700' 0-6-0 pannier tanks.

SWANSEA EAST DOCK DEPOT

Steam locomotives:

1151	1338	2851	3604
3641	3648	3661	4132
4232	4271	4650	5210
5211	5253	5609	5623
5628	5675	6613	7215
7216	8414	8431	8475
8483	8488	8750	8774
8798	9441	9489	9625
73094			

33 locomotives on shed

Swansea East Dock depot: Diminutive 'Cardiff Railway' Class 0-4-0 saddle-tank No 1338. Compare its size to the wagon on the right - its weight is only 25 tons 10 cwt and its driving wheels are 3 ft 2½ in. Note also the letters 'BR' chalked on its side. This Kitson design, introduced in 1898, was for use on the Cardiff Railway.

We then visited Neath (Neath & Brecon - N&B) depot; this, together with Glyn Neath, was a sub-depot of Neath (87A). The N&B depot was a two-road brick-built shed with thick wooden doors; being a Sunday, we were lucky to find them unlocked. This depot was also known as Neath Riverside, as it was in close proximity to the Tennant Canal.

The short walk was then made to the main depot, Neath, a double roundhouse with a carriage and wagon repair shop.

Our next visit was to Barry. We caught the 5.24 pm DMU, which displayed the destination 'BARRY ISLAND'. Our first location was Woodham Brothers' scrapyard, which was about 5 minutes walk

DUFFRYN YARD DEPOT

Steam locomotives:

2867	3642	3688	3718	3762	3791	3818	4250	4256	4257	4286	4296	4299
4640	4684	4695	5204	5216	5228	5230	5232	5246	5251	5254	5260	5670
5770	5787	6620	6649	6686	6691	7248	7318	8416	8482	8490	8724	8772
9454	9456	9457	9617	9634	9671	9736	9742	9766	9785	9799	92242	

51 locomotives on shed

All except Nos 2867, 3818 and 92242 were tanks.

Nine of the condemned tanks at Woodham's. From the right, they are Nos 5552, 5557, 5794, 9468, 7722, 5558, 9462, 5510 and 8419. Some of the tanks had arrived 'dead' being towed, while others had arrived under their own steam and were left in the yard with coal, water and sandboxes intact. Brass number-plates had been removed, together with shed-plates and various cab fittings. Some had their coupling rods removed.

BARRY SCRAPYARD

Steam locomotives:

5407	5422	5510	5552
5557	5558	5794	7712
7722	7723	7725	7758
8419	9445	9449	9462
9468	9491	9492	9499

20 locomotives noted

---

from Barry Town station. This was my first visit to this yard; we did not have a permit. All the locomotives and wagons there had been withdrawn from BR service and were waiting to be cut up.

BARRY DEPOT (88C)
Here we noted 30 steam 'on shed', of which 29 were WR tank designs, the exception being Class '4300' 2-6-0 No 6365 (85B).

CARDIFF (CANTON) DEPOT (88A)
Moving on to Cardiff, we visited Canton (previously coded 86C). A grand total of 90 'all steam' was noted, which included five 'King' Class 4-6-0s, Nos 6003/18/19/23 and 28. This depot had 12 'Britannia' Class 4-6-2s in its allocation, and on this visit we noted six, Nos 70016/18/22/24/26 and 28; also noted was Class '9F' 2-10-0 No 92220 *Evening Star*. Class '4200' 2-8-0 tank No 4207 (88A) was awaiting disposal.

We then continued to Newport (High Street) station, noting Class '4300' 2-6-0 No 7307 employed on a pw train near Cardiff (General). Arrival time at Newport was 8.50 pm.

NEWPORT (EBBW JUNCTION) DEPOT (86A)
We next caught a double-decker bus to Ebbw Junction and were rewarded with the sight of a shed crammed with predominantly Western Region steam. In fact 87 were noted, together with 12 Class '9F' 2-10-0s, nine Class 'WD' 2-8-0s and one LMS 2-8-0; to make up the total of 116 'on shed' there were just seven 0-6-0 diesel shunters.

Under repair in the spacious depot works were Nos 4253, 5206, 5219, 6813, 6827, 7028, 7240, 7249 and 7736. Withdrawn from service and 'stored' at the rear of the depot were Nos 4265, 6325, 7219, 7232 and 9494.

Our walk to Newport (Pill) Depot took us through some allotments; this was a short cut to the depot, which served a large dockland area.

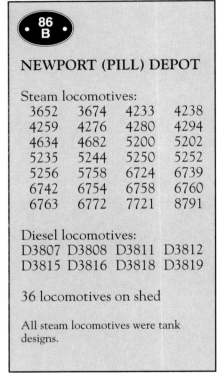

NEWPORT (PILL) DEPOT

Steam locomotives:

3652	3674	4233	4238
4259	4276	4280	4294
4634	4682	5200	5202
5235	5244	5250	5252
5256	5758	6724	6739
6742	6754	6758	6760
6763	6772	7721	8791

Diesel locomotives:
D3807 D3808 D3811 D3812
D3815 D3816 D3818 D3819

36 locomotives on shed

All steam locomotives were tank designs.

It was late evening as we made the 30-minute walk from the docks to the city centre. We stopped at a small cafe where we purchased bags of hot doughnuts and flavoured milk shakes, which Eddie and I consumed together with bars of chocolate, which we termed as our main meal of the day. 'Inky' was not too impressed with our menu and wanted to stop and sit down for a meal. We explained to him that we were running to a very strict timetable and that stops for food could result in us missing our train!

86 E — SEVERN TUNNEL JUNCTION DEPOT

Steam locomotives:

2231	2232	2292	2872	2873	2876	2877	2892	3786	3803	3805	3822	3834
3835	3843	3848	3852	3864	4102	4119	4127	4131	4136	4166	4289	4297
4558	5203	5212	5224	5234	5236	5262	5336	5620	6125	6158	6331	6338
6369	6379	6384	6386	6412	6430	6642	6666	6672	6936	7206	7228	7308
7322	7403	48471	90579	90630								

Diesel locomotives:
D3102 D3103 D3104 D3188 D3190

62 locomotives on shed

Class '4500' 2-6-2 tank No 4558 was in ex-works condition.

We caught a train from Newport to Severn Tunnel Junction, which would be the final depot visit on the second day of our Railrover. Entrance to the depot was via the end of the station platform. It was 10 pm as we entered the yard.

We had planned to use Cardiff General station as an overnight base, so adjourned to a large waiting room, but the presence of several tramps gave us little chance of any sleep.

MONDAY 29 MAY (Day 3)

The tramps were ordered out by station staff at 1 am, so we then had a chance to 'get our heads down'. However, station staff approached us just after 1 am and asked what we were doing. We explained that we were on a seven-day Railrover and were waiting here for the arrival of the 4.45 am train to Treherbert - which we were - and after showing our tickets we were allowed to stay where we were. Sleep overcame us eventually, but we were awake soon after 4 am.

We departed for Treherbert at exactly 4.45 am - we travelled on a DMU via Radyr. Our journey of about 1 hr 40 mins gave us another chance to get our heads down. Treherbert was a corrugated-built, four-road dead-end shed with a turntable.

88 F — TREHERBERT DEPOT

Steam locomotives:

5600	5646	5665	5668
5688	5691	5693	5694
6108	8482		

10 locomotives on shed

We then returned to Cardiff, departing from Queen Street station on a DMU for Caerphilly.

On arrival at Caerphilly we

ON WAY TO CAERPHILLY

Steam locomotives:

3406	3407	3409	5601
5611	5614	6647	6684
8478			

Diesel locomotives:
D3603 D3607

stopped to glance at the impressive castle, the largest in Wales, towering high above the town; it is one of the finest examples of combined land and water defences. We made the 20-minute walk to Caerphilly Locomotive Works, the largest repair shop in South Wales. The majority of the locomotives that were sent to this location were tanks and mixed-traffic types from the Welsh valleys. We arrived at about 8.35 am and showed our permit to the gateman; he introduced us to a guide, who accompanied us around the works (there were other enthusiasts visiting at the same time). This was my first visit.

CAERPHILLY WORKS

Steam locomotives:

1421	2277	3403	3636
3646	3654	3680	4145
4151	4156	4569	5214
5243	5681	5683	5964
6139	6319	6337	6347
6364	6394	6608	6932
7245	7332	8420	8471
9431	9444	9483	9493
9654	9748	75001	

35 locomotives in works

An unexpected 'cop' was Class '6100' 2-6-2 tank No 6139 (81E), formerly at Tyseley; I 'cleared' the Class with this number.

We returned to Cardiff General station, from where we walked to Canton depot. We didn't visit the depot, but remained for 30 minutes on the footbridge that spanned the entire depot yard and noted the following steam locomotives: Nos 3809, 3846, 4268, 4270, 5218, 5657, 5972, 6326, 6345, 6424, 6909, 6943, 6962, 92217 and 92246. Returning to the station, we caught a DMU to Merthyr.

On arrival at Merthyr we were greeted with a very heavy shower of rain. All three of us donned our plastic macs and put on our sunglasses - we slung our haversacks over our backs and made the brisk 5-minute walk to the shed entrance. The reason for the disguise was that we did not have a permit. As the foreman approached us we assumed a French accent - he obviously thought we were foreigners and could not converse! We walked past him, and he was heard mumbling something about visitors from overseas not understanding - anyway, we achieved our aim and the depot was visited. Eddie's brief knowledge of French from his school days obviously had some bearing on the situation!

Merthyr was a brick-built, three-road shed with a turntable.

Soon after visiting Merthyr depot the rain eased off and gave way to bright sunshine. We walked to Quakers Yard (Low Level) station and checked the departure time of the next train to Aberdare; we were told that it departed from the High Level station at 1.58 pm - it was now 1.50 pm. On transferring to the High Level platform we found the station deserted, except for one porter on the opposite platform who was busy sweeping the platform. I called across to him, 'Is the next train for Aberdare'? He continued sweeping the platform. I put the question a second time, but he still carried on sweeping. After several more requests, still with no response, we all shouted together, 'Is the next train for Aberdare, Taffy?' The porter stopped sweeping the platform, turned, looked towards us and replied with a deafening one-word answer, 'Yes!!!' A moment later the train arrived at the station.

On arrival at Aberdare we made the 10-minute walk via the goods yard and a cinder path to the

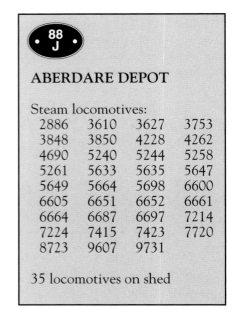

88 J

ABERDARE DEPOT

Steam locomotives:

2886	3610	3627	3753
3848	3850	4228	4262
4690	5240	5244	5258
5261	5633	5635	5647
5649	5664	5698	6600
6605	6651	6652	6661
6664	6687	6697	7214
7224	7415	7423	7720
8723	9607	9731	

35 locomotives on shed

Quakers Yard (High Level): Class '5600' 0-6-2 tank No 6628 taking on water before its departure with the 1.58 pm to Aberdare. Eddie Rooke watches the activity from the carriage.

88 D

MERTHYR DEPOT

Steam locomotives:

4632	4633	4635	5624
5626	5644	5661	6416
6433	6436	9618	9638
9676	9747	9776	

15 locomotives on shed

All were tank designs.

depot. This depot was a brick-built roundhouse with a two-road repair shop.

The next shed visit was Aberbeeg - our timetable was running as planned. We were steam-hauled between Aberdare and Aberbeeg by Class '5100' 2-6-2 tank No 4146, then made the 10-minute walk to the depot. It was a four-road straight shed with quite a long yard.

Names and locations of privately owned steam locomotives noted in South Wales

Name	Location
Tynecoed	Llwynypia
Victoria and *Weldless*	Main line near Swansea
Herbert and one unidentified	Merthyr Vale
Lion No 2	Aberaman
Menelaus	Newbridge
One unidentified	Cwmbach
Two unidentified*	Mountain Ash

* *Sir Gomer*, *Sir John* and *Llantanam Abbey* were all allocated there.

86F ABERBEEG DEPOT

Steam locomotives:
3664	4246	4247	4285
4627	4685	4688	5257
7755	7798	8417	8436
8444	8498	8499	8786
9460	9682		

18 locomotives on shed

Class '9400' 0-6-0 pannier tank No 8417 was withdrawn from service. All were tank designs.

We next travelled by bus to Pontypool, our route taking us along the A467 and A462 main roads via Crumlin. We purchased single tickets.

Our departure from Pontypool for Hereford was by DMU.

Our visits to the South Wales areas had now been completed; the next areas of the trip were to be Mid and North Wales, the West Midlands and South West England.

During our travels in the Welsh valleys we had noted numerous privately owned saddle-tank steam locomotives at such locations as collieries, steel works and gas works; their numbers were difficult to obtain, but I did manage to record most of their names, and they are listed in the table above.

On arrival at Hereford we made the 15-minute walk to the shed; at this date it carried the ex-Cardiff (Canton) code. It was a stone-built straight shed with eight roads, some of which led into a fair sized five-road repair shop.

It was late evening as we left the shed, so we purchased large portions of fish and chips, eating them as we walked to Hereford station. We also purchased some lemonade and crisps. Sitting on a platform seat we had time to reflect on the day's events before catching the overnight train to Shrewsbury.

86C HEREFORD DEPOT

Steam locomotives:
1445	1455	1617	1657
1662	2241	2249	2295
2851	3201	4115	4659
4678	4913	4990	5985
5996	6348	7309	7418
8781	8787	45726	48420
73090	78004		

26 locomotives on shed

86G PONTYPOOL ROAD DEPOT

Steam locomotives:
2859	2861	2896	3640	3685	3703	3708	3729	3779	3815	3826	3829	3833
3849	4135	4169	4600	4639	4642	4668	4916	4926	4937	5330	5679	5756
5775	5789	5920	6115	6370	6621	6634	6641	6664	6675	6677	6685	6686
6802	6840	6867	6946	7210	7213	7220	7227	7241	7246	7771	7796	8495
8707	8709	8716	9730	9796	9797	48320	75028					

60 locomotives on shed

When we eventually boarded the train, just before midnight, we found it increasingly difficult to get any rest as our compartment door was being constantly opened and closed by passengers looking for vacant seats. It became colder as the night progressed, and there was no train heating.

TUESDAY 30 MAY
(Day 4)

We were awakened by the abrupt halting of our train - I looked out of the misted carriage window to see that we had arrived at Shrewsbury. It was a very cold morning. The first priority was to visit the refreshment room and get a hot drink, but we found that it had not yet opened, so we purchased cartons of cold milk from the station vending machine. The station clock showed 7.30 am. After a short wait we caught a train to Chester General.

On our arrival at Chester we noted about five trains awaiting their departures - it was a very busy rush-hour scene.

CROES NEWYDD DEPOT

Steam locomotives:

1660	2866	3630	3760
4617	4645	4683	6306
6610	6611	6615	7314
7409	7431	7443	7828
9752	9793	64930	

19 locomotives on shed

No 64930 was a Class 'J39' 0-6-0 freight type allocated to Gorton, Manchester (9G).

WELLINGTON (SALOP) DEPOT

Steam locomotives:

3744	4120	4158	4178
7341	9636	9639	41201
41204	41231	41241	41900

12 locomotives on shed

No 41900 was a Class '2P' 0-4-4 tank, push-pull fitted, allocated to Gloucester (Barnwood).

depot was a brick-built, three-road shed with one through road. It had no turntable.

We then moved on to Wolverhampton, where we changed trains at the Low Level station and travelled to Aberystwyth via Shrewsbury, Welshpool, Moat Lane Junction and Machynlleth.

BETWEEN WOLVERHAMPTON AND ABERYSTWYTH

Steam locomotives:

1022	2204	2214	2286
4605	4910	4944	4974
5606	5965	6663	6851
6915	6916	7803	7809
7814	7821	7915	8426
9630	9657	9741	46504
46508	46522	46527	48470
48478	82032		

Diesel locomotives:
PWM654   D3752   D3757

No PWM654, an 0-6-0, was a Service locomotive used at Hookagate Sleeper Depot.

Shrewsbury station: Awaiting its departure from Platform 4 is 'County' Class 4-6-0 No 1022 *County of Northampton*. Note the LNWR signals.

CHESTER GENERAL
(30-minute stop)

Steam locomotives:

1013	5399	42198	42454
42463	42482	42493	42538
42608	42677	42973	44359
44659	44739	45055	45446
45638	48188	75014	76077

We were then steam-hauled between Chester and Wrexham by 'Hall' Class 4-6-0 No 4949 *Packwood Hall*. At Wrexham we walked to Croes Newydd shed, which took about 10 minutes. It was a brick-built roundhouse with a single-road repair shop leading off the turntable.

We then caught a train to Wellington (Salop), where the

PASSING MOAT LANE DEPOT

Steam locomotives:
46508   46522   46527

Moat Lane depot was a small wooden-built, two-road shed with a turntable.

We made the five minute walk from Aberystwyth station to the depot, which at this date was a sub-depot of Machynlleth. It was a brick-built, two-road through shed.

ABERYSTWYTH DEPOT

Steam locomotives:

2260	5180	7405	7406
7428	7802	7803	7810
7815	7818	7823	7827

12 locomotives on shed

We then walked to the nearby Vale of Rheidol depot, which was Britain's only narrow gauge railway operated by BR - the gauge was 1 ft 11½ in. The depot consisted of two bays within a wood and corrugated iron shed; entrance was via Park Avenue.

ABERYSTWYTH (VALE OF RHEIDOL) DEPOT

Steam locomotives:
7   8   9

3 locomotives on shed

We were steam-hauled between Aberystwyth and Machynlleth by 'Manor' Class 4-6-0 No 7815 *Fritwell Manor*. Our arrival was timed for 6 pm.

DOVEY JUNCTION STATION

This large, spread-out junction station, set amongst the salt marshes of the Dovey estuary where the counties of Montgomery, Merioneth and Cardigan met, was unique in that it had *no* road access! It was intended solely for passenger exchange. There was a signal box standing in a marsh at the head of a broad estuary; the only way to reach it was to follow a mile-long duck-hunters' track through the reeds! The station was often flooded from the nearby River Dovey and passengers could be delayed by heavy seas! Salmon could be netted within a few yards of the platform. The contractor responsible for the building of the station was Thomas Savin of Llwynymaen. One steam locomotive noted at Dovey Junction station, No 78006.

On our arrival at Machynlleth we made the 5-minute walk from the east-end of the station yard to the depot, which was a stone-built, three-road shed with two through roads.

We talked to the foreman of this three-lane depot, asking him various questions about the locomotives allocated there; he was very helpful in giving us the numbers

MACHYNLLETH DEPOT

Steam locomotives:

2217	2222	2233	2239
2286	2294	3213	6395
7405	7815	7822	75026
78000	78002	78005	78006
82000	82006	82036	

19 locomotives on shed

and classes. He also told us several stories about locomotives that had been there in the past. He had much praise for the 'Manor' Class locomotives, saying that they were the best steam locomotives he had ever handled, very reliable and always easy to drive, but they were getting worn out and would no

Machynlleth depot: In the yard is Class '4300' 2-6-0 No 6395 (89C) and behind its tender is Class '2251' 0-6-0 No 2233 (89C). My two travelling companions, Eddie and 'Inky', are lurking in the yard (left). All 18 of the engines at this depot were in use - these included no fewer than seven Class '2251' 0-6-0s. We remember with some significance the rugged background to the depot yard, being set beneath a sheer rock face - possibly an ideal scene for model railway enthusiasts.

doubt be withdrawn from service in favour of diesels.

We then caught a DMU to Oswestry. Only two steam locomotives were noted on the way, Nos 46513 and 46526.

It was 9.10 pm as our train arrived at Oswestry station and, much to the delight of our fellow companion 'Inky', we actually found that our hectic schedule had allowed us time for a stop for food! This we did at a small cafe near the station where we purchased meals consisting of sausage, egg and chips to be washed down with piping hot cups of tea. Following this unplanned luxury we made our way, just a short walk, to the depot entrance. It consisted of six roads with one through road.

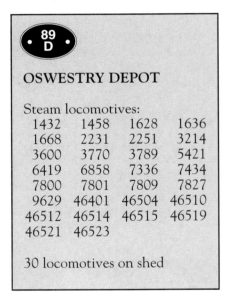

89 D

OSWESTRY DEPOT

Steam locomotives:

1432	1458	1628	1636
1668	2231	2251	3214
3600	3770	3789	5421
6419	6858	7336	7434
7800	7801	7809	7827
9629	46401	46504	46510
46512	46514	46515	46519
46521	46523		

30 locomotives on shed

To gain access to the locomotive works we crossed a very deserted main line. We had no permit for our visit and it was starting to get dark, but we chanced to spot a railwayman nearby, and asked him politely if we could have a look inside the works. He replied, 'Yes - but make it quick as I am about to lock up!'

The railwayman waited for us to go, then locked the doors. After thanking him, we walked to the station where, after a short wait,

OSWESTRY WORKS

Steam locomotives:

822	823	1438	9017
9631	78003		

6 locomotives in works

Nos 822/3 were 0-6-0 tanks introduced in 1902. Designed for Cambrian Railways, Welshpool & Llanfair section (2 ft 6 in gauge). Named *The Earl* and *The Countess* respectively.

No 9017 was a Class '9000' ('Dukedog') 4-4-0 - a Collett rebuild incorporating 'Duke' Class boiler and 'Bulldog' Class frames. No 9017 was to be preserved on the Bluebell Railway in later years.

we caught an overnight train to Birmingham (New Street). We were once again glad to get some sleep as we had experienced yet another full day of travelling and our feet were beginning to ache. This train journey afforded us ample time for a general wash and tidy up as we all no doubt must have had an odour problem after so much travelling! Washing one's feet in the basin of a toilet on a moving train was not easy, but when it was eventually achieved we found it most refreshing - the use of soap and hot water certainly helped to revitalise us!

WEDNESDAY 31 MAY (Day 5)

We awoke somewhere near Birmingham in the very early hours of the morning. The train compartment was warm and the carriage windows were misted. Soon we came to a halt at New Street station - the station clock showed 2.15 am and we were still in need of sleep. We adjourned to the waiting room, which we found full of people either waiting for trains or just finding somewhere to

sleep for the night! We left the waiting room at 3.30 am - after very little sleep - and walked around the city streets to get some fresh air and stretch our aching legs. It was a cold, grey morning and the sun had not yet appeared. The only sign of life was Birmingham City Corporation men watering the street gutters.

BIRMINGHAM (NEW STREET)

Steam locomotives:

3673	5919	5927	5950
6609	6907	7210	

Diesel locomotives:

D225	D333	D3191	D3840
D3974	D3985	D5026	

All were noted between 2.15 am and 4.40 am.

Departure from Birmingham (New Street) was at 4.40 am, our destination Shrewsbury. We eventually dozed off, and bright sunshine greeted us at Shrewsbury station, with its most impressive façade in the Tudor Gothic style, built in the mid-1880s. We made a brisk walk to the engine shed, entering the gate at 7.50 am. The very tall LNWR signal box that was quite close to the station was an impressive sight in the early morning sunshine. Shrewsbury depot was a roundhouse with two straight sheds consisting of eight and nine roads.

Returning to the station, we caught a train to Wolverhampton (Low Level) - our arrival time was 10.30 am. The next depots visited were Stafford Road (84A), Oxley (84B) and Bushbury (21C).

A most evil smell always greeted us whenever we visited Bushbury depot; needless to say, we didn't hang around too long!

We then visited Stafford Road Works, entering via the rear gate in Gorsebrooke Road as we did not

SHREWSBURY DEPOT

Steam locomotives:

1017	1022	1025	2204	2276	2807	3400	3602	3769	3815	4175	4623	4946
5038	5059	5065	5942	5968	5991	6374	6901	6915	6922	7015	7025	7330
7821	8449	9472	45188	45190	45257	45283	45298	48354	48419	48438	48474	48478
48724	48762	48768	73025	73034	73092	73096	82005	82032				

48 locomotives on shed

WOLVERHAMPTON (STAFFORD ROAD) DEPOT

Steam locomotives:

1009	3778	3792	4918
4982	5019	5032	5047
5063	5088	5089	5183
5977	5983	6005	6006
6008	6011	6014	6418
6926	7019	8452	8498
9470			

25 locomotives on shed

OXLEY DEPOT

Steam locomotives:

2818	2856	2888	3788
3813	4906	5322	5606
5985	6645	6839	6857
6862	6907	6925	6930
6980	7308	7339	8428
8464	9474	9484	9739
9746	9792	90148	92228

Diesel locomotives:
D3027 D3037 D3038 D3757
D3978 D4012

34 locomotives on shed

BUSHBURY DEPOT

Steam locomotives:

40129	44004	45071	45418
45439	46114	48502	49452
58124			

9 locomotives on shed

The previous code of this depot was 3B.

Stafford Road Works yard: The frame and wheels of Standard Class '5' 4-6-0 No 73037 are under major repair. 'Inky' stands on the buffer-beam. As can be seen from the accompanying list, a varied selection of classes were noted here.

WOLVERHAMPTON (STAFFORD ROAD) WORKS

Steam locomotives:

1011	1442	2249	2855
3208	3210	3683	3749
4110	4160	4168	4172
4290	4703	4910	5101
5420	5671	5690	6013
6304	6668	6975	7251
7253	8403	8714	9412
9430	9670	9674	9778
73027	73037	75021	

Diesel locomotive:
D3752

36 locomotives in works

TYSELEY DEPOT

Steam locomotives:

2898	3831	3839	3860	3865	4105	4111	4114	4126	4140	4155	4167	4648
5174	5192	5651	5658	5955	5965	6101	6144	6335	6618	6853	6861	6942
6950	6992	7236	7426	7912	8109	8713	9724	9733	9798	48009	48514	75003
75024												

Diesel locomotives:
D3950 D3952 D3969

43 locomotives on shed

Class '5100' 2-6-2 tank No 5192 was 'stored'; Class '5600' 0-6-2 tank No 5651 and Class '7200' 2-8-2 tank No 7236 were in the depot workshop.

have a permit. My only previous visit to this location had been on 29 March 1959.

On our way back to the Low Level station we smelt the aroma of freshly baked bread, so we stopped at a small bakery and purchased bags of piping hot doughnuts, eating them as we walked to the station.

Our next visit was to Tyseley; departure was at midday. We travelled by DMU, and on the way we noted 15 steam, including a freight hauled by grimy Class '7F' 0-8-0 No 49114 (21B, Bescot).

Our next visit was to Stourbridge depot, which consisted of two separate buildings and a roundhouse. A four-road shed was originally used to house GWR diesel railcars. There was also a single-road repair shop adjoining the roundhouse. In all, a most complex arrangement of buildings! This location was formerly known as Stourbridge Junction.

Our Railrover continued with a walk to the Junction station where we caught a train to Kidderminster, where we made the 15-minute walk to the depot. This was a two-road, steel-framed shed with corrugated sheeting. Its offices were brick-built and adjoined the shed building.

STOURBRIDGE DEPOT

Steam locomotives:

3658	3830	4104	4161
4173	4687	4696	5187
5190	5944	5972	6609
6644	6646	6663	6667
6692	6832	6906	7341
7432	7441	7806	7816
7817	7824	8742	8792
8797	9624	9767	48415
48417	48448		

Diesel locomotives:
D3192 D3982 D3996

37 locomotives on shed

NOTED ON THE WAY

Steam locomotives:

| 3601 | 4175 | 5151 | 7025 |
| 48477 | 82008 | 82032 | |

Diesel railcars:
W24   W26   W30

Returning to the station we caught a train to Worcester. It was

KIDDERMINSTER DEPOT

Steam locomotives:

| 4129 | 4147 | 4153 | 4641 |
| 5245 | 6314 | 6353 | 6388 |

Diesel locomotives:
D3981 D3990

Diesel railcars:
W21   W25   W31

13 locomotives on shed

now early evening and the sun was setting as we travelled by DMU through some delightful countryside. On arrival at Shrub Hill station we made the 5-minute walk to the depot, which was a brick-built depot consisting of two separate sheds, one of three roads and one of four, with several sidings between them.

Worcester Works was situated opposite the depot yard, but on the opposite side of the main line. We did not visit the works, but we did note four locomotives awaiting attention in the yard, Nos 3207, 7005, 7819 and PWM650, the lat-

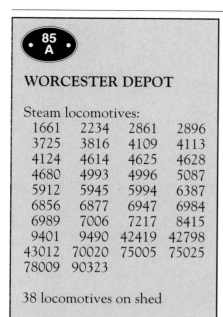

WORCESTER DEPOT

85
A

Steam locomotives:

1661	2234	2861	2896
3725	3816	4109	4113
4124	4614	4625	4628
4680	4993	4996	5087
5912	5945	5994	6387
6856	6877	6947	6984
6989	7006	7217	8415
9401	9490	42419	42798
43012	70020	75005	75025
78009	90323		

38 locomotives on shed

ter being a Service 0-6-0 diesel. The locomotive works was, in fact, part of a carriage and wagon repair complex. The works was unusual in that although it could accommodate pannier and side tanks, it was too small for tender engines, and tenders had to be left outside!

It was now late evening, and we managed to find some time for brief relaxation in the waiting room of Worcester (Shrub Hill) station. It had been yet another day of much travelling, walking and depot visiting, resulting in us being nearly exhausted; but we did have the luxury of a rest to reflect back on the day's activities. Eddie Rooke's timetable had gone to plan and we were now looking forward to completing the final two days of our seven-day adventure as we awaited the arrival of an overnight stopping train to London (Paddington). The weather had been bright and sunny, and the day at Worcester ended typically in a blaze of orange sky as the setting sun slowly disappeared.

The relationship of Eddie Rooke and I with our companion 'Inky' had by now become somewhat 'frayed', so he decided to go it alone for the remainder of the

week - Eddie gave him details of our timetable in case he decided to rejoin us at a later point. I think that our food menu, which in the main consisted of bags of greasy chips, doughnuts and ice lollies together with helpings of chocolate bars and milk from vending machines, did not agree with him!

The waiting room at Worcester became our 'base' where Eddie and I had our tea; this consisted of half-pound bags of cherries and bars of chocolate washed down with cups of British Railways tea! Cherries were Eddie's favourite fruit and numerous bags were devoured during this Railrover. We found the quiet of the waiting room an ideal location to underline our 'cops' in our Ian Allan *ABC Combined Volumes*; we also repeated the 'cops' in the Ian Allan *Loco Shed Book*, Spring 1961 edition. The latter, at this date, could be purchased for 2/6d.

BETWEEN WORCESTER AND HEREFORD

Steam locomotives:

4148	5095	5226	6126
6381	6948	42421	44780
45257			

THURSDAY 1 JUNE
(Day 6)

The overnight train from Worcester, which was diesel-hauled, arrived at Paddington at 8.45 am, 45 minutes late, but it did not affect our timetable as we had allowed 1¼ hours at Paddington. We adjourned to the 'wash and brush up' for a much needed tidy up, followed by a visit to the station buffet where we purchased sandwiches, cups of tea and jam doughnuts, which we took on the train to Bristol. Our departure was at 9.15 am, and we were diesel-hauled by a 'Warship' Class.

PASSING SWINDON WORKS

Steam locomotives:

1501	1502	1509	1634
2516	3657	3705	3758
5922	6841	8433	

We changed at Bristol (Temple Meads), then travelled to Gloucester.

BETWEEN BRISTOL AND GLOUCESTER

Steam locomotives:

2289	3665	3842	4607
5640	5958	6376	6937
6959	7429	8793	9720
42769	43049	44160	44203
44213	44296	44466	44523
44557	44558	44569	44919
45416	45577	45640	45682
45685	47417	48415	48460
48639	48769	73015	

Diesel locomotives:

D833	D3002	13186	D3989

On arrival at Gloucester we walked to the depot. On my previous visit this was known as Gloucester, but the words 'Horton Road' had been added to its title.

We then visited the ex-LMS shed, Gloucester (Barnwood), then caught a train to Lydney.

On our arrival at Lydney Junction station we walked to the depot, which took us about 5 minutes. This depot was situated on the south side of the Severn & Wye line, between Lydney Town and Junction stations, and was a sub-depot of Gloucester (Horton Road). It was a brick-built, three-road dead-end shed, with a single-road repair shop.

On leaving the shed we chanced to see a pub and decided

GLOUCESTER (HORTON ROAD) DEPOT

Steam locomotives:

1424	1473	1630	2253
2288	3203	3775	3845
3863	4100	4123	5007
5017	5035	5071	5173
6330	6341	6345	6437
6696	6806	6900	6985
7003	7013	7243	7805
7926	8404	8717	8729
9464	9471	92222	

Diesel locomotives:
D2137 D3990

37 locomotives on shed

GLOUCESTER (BARNWOOD) DEPOT

Steam locomotives:

6348	7756	7788	40540
41535	42897	43521	43620
43680	43853	43887	43951
44102	44137	44171	44184
44185	44226	44264	44333
44482	45576	45668	47623
73157	75002	75009	90069

Diesel locomotive:
D3993

29 locomotives on shed

Class '0F' 0-4-0 tank No 41535 was a Deeley Midland design of 1907, allocated to this depot.

BETWEEN GLOUCESTER AND LYDNEY

Steam locomotives:

4929	5218	6365	6909
7741	70016		

Gloucester (Horton Road) depot: A general view of the yard and depot from the turntable. The buildings consisted of a six-road and a four-road shed.

LYDNEY DEPOT

Steam locomotives:

1631	1632	1642	3721
6415	8701		

6 locomotives on shed

for a change, and as we had a little spare time, to purchase half pints of lager and lime. We both saw the appetising menu and could not resist having a crusty ploughman's lunch - such a meal, with no chips or doughnuts, was completely out of character for us! Having consumed this we were now fully revitalised and continued our Railrover journey by catching a train to Bristol, travelling via Severn Tunnel Junction, then

BETWEEN BRISTOL AND TAUNTON

Steam locomotives:
2232   46506   82001

Diesel locomotives:
D2133 D2140 D2141 D3507 D3998

from Temple Meads to Taunton via Highbridge and Bridgwater. It was approaching midnight as we made the few minutes walk from Taunton station to the depot entrance in Station Road.

FRIDAY 2 JUNE (Day 7)

Oddly enough, my previous visit to Taunton depot had also taken place in the early hours - 2.40 am - when on an SR Railrover in August 1960.

It now remained for us to visit the Penzance area and St Blazey before catching a train to London and then making our way home to Portsmouth. We still had a few miles to go at this stage, and 'Inky' had not rejoined us.

We had a considerable wait on Taunton station before boarding our train for Exeter, which departed at 3.10 am. We were diesel-hauled by 'Warship' Class No D835 *Pegasus*. On our arrival at Exeter (St David's) we rested in the same small waiting room that I had used on the SR Railrover in August 1960. Departure was at 5.17 am on the 1.10 am from London to Plymouth.

A total of 20 steam and 13 diesels were noted on the way to Plymouth; only one SR engine was noted, Class 'Z' 0-8-0 tank No 30950.

TAUNTON DEPOT

Steam locomotives:

3669	3733	3736	4117	4604	4644	4663	4915	4932	4991	4992	5198	5516
5542	5571	5780	5793	5798	5999	6140	6320	6375	6390	6812	6874	6914
6995	6999	7031	7305	7337	7436	7713	7916	8745	9608	9646	9647	9663
9757												

Diesel locomotives:
PWM652   D2142

42 locomotives on shed

LAIRA (PLYMOUTH) DEPOT

Steam locomotives:

1363	2841	2871	3787	3862	4591	4679	5511	5541	5560	5568	5572	6301
6400	6771	6804	6823	6824	6836	6860	6921	6944	6988	7328	7335	

Diesel locomotives:

D601	D604	D805	D813	D834	D841	D847	D867	D868	D2127	D6301	D6303	D6304
D6311	D6317	D6322	D6323	D6327	D6334							

44 locomotives on shed

We arrived at Plymouth (North Road) station at 7.40 am and made the 2-mile walk to Laira shed; any remains of tiredness were dispelled as we made the walk at a brisk pace.

After completing the 2-mile return walk to North Road station, we found 5 minutes for a welcome cup of tea before setting off to Penzance. Steam locomotives noted at Truro were Nos 3702, 4566, 6824, 6870 and 8486.

A Western National bus was waiting near Penzance station, which could have taken us to the depot entrance, but as it was a sunny day we decided to stretch our legs and make the brisk 20-minute walk. The depot was a brick-built, four-road dead-end shed with a single-road repair shop. Of note at the depot were no fewer than eight 'Grange' Class 4-6-0s (6800 to 6876 in the accompanying list).

PENZANCE DEPOT

Steam locomotives:

1003	1004	4563	5515
6800	6808	6814	6824
6854	6868	6873	6876
9433	9475		

Diesel locomotives:
D821   D839   D6318   D6320

18 locomotives on shed

Back at Penzance we found that we still had time to spare before our next train departed for St Blazey, so we both looked around the town and bought some food and drink to take on the train. We also purchased several souvenirs

and some rock to take home. We boarded the train and as we were looking for an empty compartment we were both surprised and relieved to once again be reunited with our travelling companion, 'Inky'. All three of us then continued together.

St Blazey depot was an open-style semi-roundhouse building, very uncommon on BR. Others of similar appearance that I had visited were located at Horsham and Guildford. I had the pleasure of 'cabbing' Class '1600' 0-6-0 pannier tank No 1624 (83E).

St Blazey was the final depot of this Railrover. We caught the mid-day train to Paddington, being diesel-hauled by No D6334. It was a crowded train but we managed to get a seat as we had done all the week. Our earlier differences of opinion had now been forgotten and the three of us settled down

ST BLAZEY DEPOT

Steam locomotives:

1468	1624	1626	3790
4565	5539	5570	6413
6875	7446	7715	8702
8719	9755		

Diesel locomotives:
D848 D4005 D6322 D6323

18 locomotives on shed

ST BLAZEY AND PLYMOUTH AREAS

Steam locomotives:

3787	3790	5532	5538
5562	6324	8737	

SWINDON, READING AND PADDINGTON AREAS

Steam locomotives:

L91	3758	3810	5906
5913	9413	9419	9420
9658	9706		

Diesel locomotives:
D2195 D3114 D3520 D3754
D3761 D5502 D5696

No L91, a Class '5700' 0-6-0 pannier tank, ex-BR No 5757, was at this date allocated to London Transport stock (Neasden area).

ready for the long journey to London, talking about our separate experiences since we had split up 36 hours earlier.

On arrival at Paddington at 4.40 pm we immediately transferred to a London Transport tube train bound for Waterloo, where we purchased single tickets to Portsmouth & Southsea, departing on the 5.50 pm electric unit train via Guildford. We travelled on one of the 4-COR electric corridor motor units for the final 70 miles to Portsmouth. These units were nicknamed 'Nelsons' because one front window, or 'eye', was 'closed' to accommodate the destination number, and the other was 'open', which was the driver's cab.

Their number series was 3101 to 3158.

Despite our differences regarding the purchase of food, all three of us thoroughly enjoyed this seven-day Western Region Railrover and no doubt it will always hold some vivid memories for us. We travelled almost to our limits, with very little sleep or decent food, in order to maintain our pre-planned timetable and to

get the maximum benefit from our tickets, which cost us £9 10s. As the end of the escapade was nearing its finale, we reflected on the past week's visits and it was agreed that we had enjoyed great value from our tickets. All 45 depots, three workshops and a scrapyard that had been planned to visit were successfully completed, and over 30 photographs were taken, the majority of these being in Wales. The timetable, which Eddie Rooke had set out, went as planned, and the use of *The British Locomotive Shed Directory* proved to be most helpful, especially in locating some of the lesser-known engine sheds.

From notes that I made, it appears that I took about £4 spending money, and it was recorded that, after three days, I had exactly £3 remaining; this meant that I could spend about 15 shillings a day, but of this total I would need to retain 18 shillings for tube fares and a single ticket at 15/6d in order to catch the electric train from Waterloo to Portsmouth.

My 'greatest adventure' had certainly lived up to its name, and all three of us returned home to portray excitedly our adventures to all our train-spotting friends who gathered on Fratton station footbridge.

TOUR OF SOUTH WEST ENGLAND

SATURDAY 22 AND SUNDAY 23 JULY

I travelled 'pillion passenger' on Eddie Rooke's Lambretta scooter,

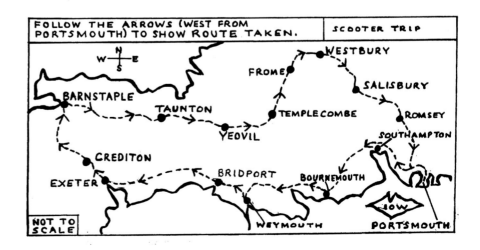

FOLLOW THE ARROWS (WEST FROM PORTSMOUTH) TO SHOW ROUTE TAKEN.   SCOOTER TRIP

WTP 977, for this two-day tour of South West England. We took a tent (jointly owned), together with other small items. The route for our visits was as follows: Southampton, Bournemouth, Weymouth, Bridport, Exeter, Crediton, Barnstaple, Taunton, Yeovil, Templecombe, Frome, Westbury, Salisbury, Romsey and Fareham.

The main reason for this trip, including the visit to Barnstaple, was the hope of noting Class 'M7' 0-4-4 tank No 30253 (allocated to Barnstaple Junction), as this was my *last* Southern Region steam locomotive; if noted it would 'clear' all SR locomotives for me. (My first was noted in 1955, so it had taken me six years to note all the approximately 1,250 SR steam locomotives.)

SATURDAY 22 JULY (Day 1)

Departure from Portsmouth was at 1.30 pm. It was agreed that I would pay half towards the cost of petrol (it was very cheap in those days!).

BOURNEMOUTH DEPOT (71B)

This, together with the Central and West stations, was visited and the steam locomotives noted at all three were Nos 3742, 30031, 30056, 30057, 30105, 30107, 30108, 30111, 30112, 30476, 30539, 30548, 30790, 30857, 30912, 31639, 31810, 33024, 34004, 34016, 34020, 34037, 34040, 34045, 34053, 35018, 35023, 35024, 75067, 76053, 76057 and 76069.

The vintage Class 'M7' 0-4-4 tanks could always be seen in and around the Bournemouth area, being used extensively on the Swanage and Lymington branch lines. Nos 30031/56/57/105/07/08/ 111 and 112 in the list shown were all 'M7' tanks.

After Weymouth we continued on the road to Bridport. On our

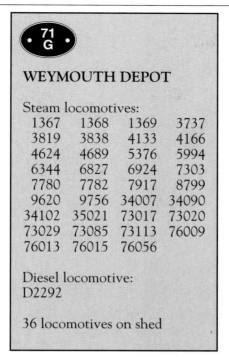

71 G

WEYMOUTH DEPOT

Steam locomotives:

1367	1368	1369	3737
3819	3838	4133	4166
4624	4689	5376	5994
6344	6827	6924	7303
7780	7782	7917	8799
9620	9756	34007	34090
34102	35021	73017	73020
73029	73085	73113	76009
76013	76015	76056	

Diesel locomotive:
D2292

36 locomotives on shed

arrival at the single-road, stone-built engine shed we found that it was empty, although the building was intact together with the water tower in the yard. There was a DMU at the station.

Leaving Bridport we travelled along the coast road to Exeter.

Weymouth depot: No 1368, one of the three Collett-designed Class '1366' 0-6-0s with outside cylinders that were 'on shed'. Note the bell above the running plate, used to warn road traffic when assisting boat trains between the station and the docks. The street railway was a main feature of Weymouth's rail system.

EXMOUTH JUNCTION DEPOT (72A)

This was next visited and we found to our delight that it was 'all steam', 52 being noted. The small SR tanks included 'M7' and 'O2' types, but the large side tanks, the Class 'Z' 0-8-0s used for 'banking', were also much in evidence, Nos 30950, 30952, 30953, 30955 and 30957. The usual Bulleid 'Pacifics' were noted (12 on this visit). At this date Class 'U1' 2-6-0s, LMS 2-6-2 tanks and Standard Class '2' 2-6-2 tanks had been re-shedded here from such areas as Neasden and Tonbridge to replace withdrawn locomotives.

We then travelled the short distance into Exeter, where we visited the WR depot.

EXETER DEPOT (83C)

This was a complete contrast to Exmouth Junction in that it only had 28 locomotives 'on shed', of which 26 were steam, 15 of them tank designs. The two diesels noted were 'Warships' Nos D842 *Royal Oak* and D846 *Steadfast*.

Moving on to the Central station we looked in briefly to note Nos 30951, 30956, 34033, 34098 and 84021.

It was about 9 pm as we set off on the Lambretta from Exeter; we were looking for a suitable piece of land to pitch our tent for the night. We

headed north towards Barnstaple, which was to be our first depot next morning. We chose a field near Crediton, but had much difficulty in erecting the tent; it took us about 30 minutes. We had no sleeping bags, and our only protection was plastic macs and caps.

SUNDAY 23 JULY (Day 2)

It was exactly midnight when something woke me. I stood up, forgetting that I was in a tent, and immediately brought the whole lot down! Eddie had a few choice words to say! We erected the tent again, much quicker than before, and settled down for a well-earned rest. The night was quite warm and there was little or no wind.

We were both rudely awoken at 5.30 am by the sound of cattle. When we peered out of the tent we realised that we were surrounded by a herd of cows! We made a very hurried departure, to say the least, the tent being pulled down in record time and put on to the scooter, and we were off just in time to avoid an approaching angry farmer! All sorts of things went through our minds - the thought of dogs being set upon us, or even a farmer wielding a shotgun - but luckily we got away from our illegal camp site unscathed!

It was a dull, misty morning as we made our way along the road towards Barnstaple, where we arrived at 7 am.

BARNSTAPLE JUNCTION DEPOT

Steam locomotives:
7304	7305	30023	30247
30251	30253	30254	31836
34065	34076	34081	41290
41294	41297	41298	41310
41312	41313	41314	

19 locomotives on shed

As hoped, with Class 'M7' 0-4-4 tank No 30253 - the one that I had set out to see - I had now 'cleared' the complete allocation of SR steam locomotives.

Leaving the depot we continued on the scooter to Taunton. We noted 'U' Class 2-6-0 No 31840 at Portsmouth Arms station. Our visit to Taunton depot (83B) was abruptly ended when we were confronted by the foreman who told us firmly, 'We do not issue permits for this depot'. But by this time we had already noted 34 engines, of

YEOVIL (PEN MILL) STATION

Steam locomotives:
5994   6822   9732

YEOVIL DEPOT

Steam locomotives:
3679	4656	5554	9764
30125	30129	30131	30823
30844	30845	31632	31637
31792	31802	31805	34005
34048	34110		

18 locomotives on shed

which 31 were steam - he then ordered us out!

Our next visit was to Yeovil depot, prior to which we briefly visited Yeovil (Pen Mill) station.

We then continued by road to our next depot, Templecombe.

TEMPLECOMBE DEPOT (82G)

This depot produced a mixture of GWR, LMS and 'Standard' locomotives, all but two of which were

Barnstaple Junction depot: This is the scene at 7 am as we entered the yard. Engines are Class 'M7' 0-4-4 tank No 30254, LMS Class '2' 2-6-2 tanks Nos 41298 and 41313 and Class 'M7' 0-4-4 tank No 30253. Note the wooden engine shed.

A view of Yeovil (72C) depot. The locomotives quietly resting in the yard are rebuilt 'West Country' 4-6-2 No 34048 *Crediton* with Class 'U' 2-6-0s Nos 31632 and 31802. On the far left is Class 'M7' 0-4-4 tank No 30129, awaiting departure from the Town station. Eddie Rooke is on the right, taking notes of the locomotives.

Templecombe depot: Two 'stored' locomotives in the yard are Class '2P' 4-4-0 No 40537 of 82E, Bristol (Barrow Road) and Class '2251' 0-6-0 No 2215 of 86A, Newport (Ebbw Junction).

Templecombe depot: Class '7F' 2-8-0 No 53810 of 82F, Bath (Green Park), used on the Somerset & Dorset Railway. Note the raised footplate above the cylinders.

in working order. A total of 18 steam were 'on shed', comprising Nos 2215, 2223, 3215, 3216, 3720, 4691, 40537, 40564, 40569, 40634, 43216, 43682, 44557, 44558, 47542, 53810, 75027 and 82001.

Of note was Class '3F' 0-6-0 No 43216 (82G) of 1896, built for the S&D and taken into LMS stock in 1930 - and still in working order on this visit.

I had noted Class '2P' 4-4-0 No 40537 of 1912, a Fowler rebuild of a Johnson locomotive with super-heater and piston valves, 'stored' at Templecombe on both of my previous visits (September 1959 and August 1960). Its former depot of allocation was Bristol (Barrow Road) (82E) I 'cabbed' the engine and noted that the fittings from the cab had been almost completely stripped; one brass handle was on the cab floor, and I retained it as a souvenir. At a later date it was transferred to a 1926

FROME DEPOT
Steam locomotives:
3629   7784   9615   9628
4 locomotives on shed

Aveling & Porter steam roller owned by a Mr D. Bird of Portsmouth.

On completing Templecombe shed we continued on the road to Frome. This was a sub-depot of Westbury, and all the engines were Class '5700' 0-6-0 pannier tanks and allocated to Westbury. It was a very small depot, having room to house about six tanks within its area. The single-road shed was built of timber.

We then continued to the final depot of our visit, Westbury, previously visited in August 1956.

Having completed our tour of South West England on the scoot-

82 D

WESTBURY DEPOT			
Steam locomotives:			
2200	2206	2268	3614
3675	3735	4607	4636
4941	4974	5092	5410
5526	5542	5689	5921
5940	5950	5962	5963
5980	6625	6809	6842
6951	6955	7302	7324
7917	8711	8790	9612
9668	9769	48459	
35 locomotives on shed			

er we made our way back to Portsmouth via Salisbury, Romsey and Fareham. We arrived home at 5.30 pm. The total miles travelled was 420 and I paid 10 shillings towards cost of the petrol. It had been an eventful trip.

ANDOVER, SWINDON, EASTLEIGH AND FRATTON

SUNDAY 30 JULY

I went on this trip again as a pillion passenger on Eddie Rooke's Lambretta scooter. Leaving Portsmouth at 7.45 am, our first visit was Andover Junction shed, this being a sub-shed of Eastleigh. This was my first visit to this depot.

Including our visit to Andover, the journey to Swindon took us

ANDOVER JUNCTION DEPOT
Steam locomotives:
6327   31626   31810   31818
4 locomotives on shed

⊙·82C·⊙ SWINDON DEPOT

Steam locomotives:

1015	1658	2291	2842	2852	3645	3684	3711	3763	3780	4088	4567	4656
4697	4972	5001	5015	5023	5064	5547	5934	5964	5997	6858	6873	6951
7031	7035	7413	8433	9467	9605	9754	9790	73027				

Diesel locomotives:
D2086 D2137 D2193 D2196 D2372 D3262

41 locomotives on shed

Swindon Works yard: Tanks on the turntable are Class '7200' 2-8-2 No 7222 (ex-works) and Class '5700' 0-6-0 pannier No 3670.

three hours. We first made a brief visit to the Junction station, where we noted steam locomotives Nos 3758, 7002, 7238, 7413, 7421, 7904 and 9720, and diesels Nos D817, D852, D2087, D2088 and D2143.

'Castle' Class 4-6-0s could always be noted when visiting Swindon - ten were noted on this visit. After the depot we visited Swindon Gas Works Yard.

Many of the locomotives seen in the scrapyard still had their shed-plates and number-plates intact; in fact the majority of these, which were all tank designs, appeared to be in fair external condition. Some of them had fallen victim to dieselisation

SWINDON GAS WORKS YARD

Steam locomotives:

5815	6309	6941	7748

SWINDON SCRAPYARD

Steam locomotives:

1361	1366	1433	1647
3657	3676	3724	4203
5103	5110	5176	5177
5195	5771	6426	7700
7745	7761	7798	8429
8705	8722	8726	8740
8777	8789	8796	9414
9735	9736	9762	9767
9771	9781		

SWINDON WORKS YARD

Steam locomotives:

1009	1454	1604	1634	1640	2516	2839	3667	3670	3805	3817	3852	4003
4099	4916	4928	5074	5080	5088	5158	5166	5208	5936	5949	6004	6021
6027	6901	6905	6959	6969	7222	7756	7775	7826	8721	8783	8798	9400
9749	9751	78001	78008	92234	92245							

Diesel locomotives:
D811 D850 D2188 D2195 D6311 D7003

Above Ex-Basingstoke (70D) Class 'G6' 0-6-0 tank No 30258 with Class 'T9' 4-4-0 No 30313 behind, ex-Exmouth Junction (72A), bide their time before being towed to Eastleigh Works scrapyard. Someone had chalked the words 'DON'T SCRAP THIS ENGINE' on the smokebox door of No 30258, but it was to no avail; it was eventually cut up.

Right Fratton depot: An unusual visitor was Type '2' No D5093 (14A) with an excursion from the North London area.

rather than being in a state of unrepair.

Swindon workshop produced 78 locomotives, of which 39 were diesels. The most notable difference between this and previous visits was the appearance of the diesel. Although there were 39 steam 'in works' and a further 45 in the works yard, there was no doubting that the 'diesel age' was rapidly beginning to emerge.

The D600s, D800s and D1000s (the latter being built) were all intended for main-line passenger use, and would eventually replace steam Classes such as the 'Kings', 'Castles' and 'Counties'.

It is also of note that only five tank-design steam were 'in works', Nos 4573, 5503, 7221, 7233 and 82031 - this suggests that the very common pannier tanks, together with the many side tanks, were being replaced by the standard 0-6-0 diesel shunter.

Having completed our visit to Swindon we travelled direct to Eastleigh. It was now late afternoon, and steam noted in the works yard were Nos 30837 and 31113, the latter a Class 'C' 0-6-0.

EASTLEIGH DEPOT (71A)

This was successfully 'bunked' and a grand total of 91 steam were recorded. Of note were two GWR pannier tanks, Nos 3742 and 3759, but on the 'dead line' we noted Nos 30258, 30313, 30317, 30349, 30582, 30669, 30691, 30709, 30717, 31061 and 31498.

Returning to Portsmouth, we were joined by David Copus for a visit to Fratton shed, where we found 18 steam, including two 'Hall' Class 4-6-0s, Nos 5936 *Oakley Hall* and 5944 *Ickenham Hall*.

EASTLEIGH 'OPEN DAY'

WEDNESDAY 9 AUGUST

I visited Eastleigh for the Annual Open Day with four local enthusiasts. Both the Works and the Carriage Works were open to visitors on payment of a small fee, which benefited local charities and railway orphanages.

No 32694, noted in the scrapyard, was the ex-Fratton Class 'E1' 0-6-0 tank best remembered for its many years of service on the daily Fratton sidings to Portsmouth Dockyard goods. It was hoped that a preservation society may have wanted to save her, but it was not to be and she was soon to be cut up.

Other steam awaiting the 'torch' were Class 'M7' 0-4-4 tanks Nos 30031, 30109 and 30248; 'King Arthur' Class 4-6-0 No 30453 *King Arthur*; Class 'T9' 4-4-0 No 30715;

Class 'S15' 4-6-0 No 30837; and 'Lord Nelson' Class 4-6-0 No 30865 *Sir John Hawkins*.

A brief visit was then made to the depot yard followed by a short stop on Campbell Road bridge, where steam locomotives Nos 6392, 30127, 30695, 92206 and 92239 were noted. We were quite surprised to note Class 'M7' 0-4-4 tank No 30127 (71B) hauling a *nine-carriage* passenger train in the direction of Southampton - it had obviously been called upon in an emergency!

EASTLEIGH WORKS

Steam locomotives:
 3620   3633   9653   30072
30494 30496 30497 30510
30514 30773 32339 32353
34019 34038 34051 34084
34091 35009 41272 41309
41315 73017 73082 75073
76067 80016 82016 84028
WD600

Diesel locomotives:
D3223 D3472 15213 D5008
D5009 D6530

Electric locomotive:
E5005

36 locomotives in works

No WD600 *Gordon* was a War
Department freight locomotive, at
this date allocated to the Longmoor
Military Railway, Liss, Hampshire.

EASTLEIGH SCRAPYARD

Steam locomotives:
30031 30109 30248 30453
30715 30837 30865 31113
32694

The Eastleigh 'Open Day' was an annual event looked forward to by many local train-spotters. Un-rebuilt 'West Country' Class 4-6-2 No 34006 *Bude*, in ex-works condition, is attracting quite a bit of attention. Note the steam crane on the right.

EASTLEIGH WORKS YARD

Steam locomotives:
 3754   30060 30306 30831
32341 33010 34006 34025
34030 35028 75065 76064
80013 80152

Diesel locomotives:
11222 D3272 D3667 15232

Electric locomotive:
E5008

EASTLEIGH CARRIAGE & WAGON WORKS

Steam locomotive:
30200

Diesel locomotive:
DS600

The Class 'O2' 0-4-4 tank and the
0-4-0 diesel were used in the extensive works yards for hauling and general shunting of both new and old
carriages and wagons.

ADDITIONAL HIGHLIGHTS OF 1961

**LONDON: SUNDAY
8 JANUARY** - We visited two
depots, NEASDEN (14D) - 40
steam and two diesels 'on shed' -
and CRICKLEWOOD (14A) - 53
steam and 12 diesels. Of note at
this depot was SR Class 'H16' 4-6-2
heavy freight tank No 30520
(70B), which had recently been
involved in a collision and was in
the roundhouse awaiting repair.
These tanks, of which there were
only five in the Class, were
designed to work interchange traffic between Feltham and Brent
sidings, Cricklewood, or
Willesden.

**LONDON: TUESDAY
8 AUGUST** - Four depots were
visited, WILLESDEN (1A) - 34
steam and 13 diesels; OLD OAK
COMMON (81A) - 48 steam
and six diesels; KING'S CROSS
(34A) - 63 steam and two
diesels; and HORNSEY (34B),
where we noted 11 steam, all
tanks and the majority 'stored'.

They were Nos 68073, 68894,
68896, 68931, 68950, 68971,
68991, 69498, 69512, 69543 and
69579. There were also 13 diesels
'on shed'.

**LONDON: SUNDAY
10 SEPTEMBER** - I travelled pillion passenger on Eddie Rooke's
scooter to visit Stratford depot.
We knew in advance of a party of
enthusiasts visiting on this date,
and the time (11 am), so we were
able to join them.

STRATFORD DEPOT

Steam locomotives:

32	33	35	44	61156	61226	61233	61253	61375	64667	64669	64677	64692
64697	65361	65445	65453	65460	65462	65464	65476	65507	65554	67701	67706	67708
67709	67726	67728	67735	67736	67737	68538	68542	68552	68556	68565	68566	68570
68600	68613	68621	68642	68646	68649	69618	69632	69640	69646	69653	69668	69670
69673	69678	69686	69693	69697	69698	69710	69713	69723	69724	69728	69730	69732
80131	90196	90528										

Diesel locomotives:

D200	11132	12103	12106	12110	12130	D2215	D2224	D2954	D2958	D3301	D3608	D3609
D3683	D5034	D5036	D5048	D5058	D5064	D5505	D5506	D5511	D5516	D5517	D5538	D5551
D5558	D5563	D5596	D5597	D5623	D5627	D5637	D5653	D5663	D5694	D5696	D6703	D6705
D6707	D6711	D6717	D8228	D8232	D8233	D8234	D8400	D8401	D8406	D8407	D8408	

119 locomotives on shed

Nos 32, 33, 35 and 44 were Departmental Stock, allocated to Stratford depot works.

Above Class 'J69' 0-6-0 tank No 68556, in company with many other tanks, in Stratford depot yard.

Above Birkenhead depot (6C): Class '2F' 0-6-0 tank No 47164. Partly visible on the right is Class '0F' 0-4-0 saddle tank No 47005.

Below Nottingham depot (16A): Class 'B1' 4-6-0 No 61083.

LMS RAILROVER

Two of my closest friends, David Copus and Frank Allen, undertook an LMS Railrover in 1961. David's ticket is reproduced here; it cost £9 10s. David took numerous photographs; above right and right are just two.

THE PORTSMOUTH AREA DURING 1961

An unusual visitor to Fratton shed, seen here undergoing minor repairs on the lifting crane, was Class 'A1' 0-6-0 tank Service locomotive No DS680, which at this date was allocated to Lancing Carriage Works, Sussex. This tank was introduced in 1872, a Stroudley 'Terrier' design. Perhaps it was sent to Fratton with a view to working the Hayling Island branch? May 1961. *Doug Willis*

FRATTON: MONDAY 17 JULY

- A rare visitor noted passing through Fratton station at 5.50 pm with a return excursion to the east London area was Class 'B1' 4-6-0 No 61200 (34A).

FOOTBALL AND TRAINS

Many of my railway colleagues were avid supporters of Portsmouth Football Club - 'Pompey'. We attended their home games regularly (railway trips permitting) and often travelled to away games, especially when British Railways laid on Football Specials - the London clubs always proved the most popular ones.

Many of my friends were at this date between the ages of 15 and 20, and the majority played for local soccer teams in Portsmouth at weekends, as long as railway trips had not been arranged - they always took priority. David Copus and Eddie Rooke together with several others played for a team called Ferndale. David originally came across this name when visiting engine sheds in the South Wales area; in fact, Ferndale was a sub-shed of Treherbert (88F). In the late 1950s when he visited this area, he suggested on returning to Portsmouth that their Sunday league football team should be called Ferndale, and his friends agreed. This was probably during the 1960-61 season, and the name still lives on today in the City of Portsmouth.

DINNER GONG STRIKES!

Our vocal support for 'Pompey' was, at this date, accompanied by a somewhat bizarre and unusual-sounding object, a large, heavy, brass dinner gong! It was taken into Fratton Park for most of Portsmouth's home games and, indeed, was also taken to numerous away matches, including many

London games. I believe the furthest it travelled was to St James's Park, Newcastle. We probably had the distinction of being the only football fans ever to use a dinner gong to encourage support at a football match.

Walking was one of our favourite pastimes - it was healthy and it kept us fit. Usually there would be three or four of us, and we would quite often cover 5 or 6 miles around Portsmouth. I'm sure it helped us whenever we undertook railway visits to engine sheds and stations, which always seemed to involve much walking.

It was while on one of our local walks that we chanced to notice this brass dinner gong in an antiques shop window in Queen Street, Portsmouth. I was urged to go in and find out its cost - my friends suggested that it could be taken to Fratton Park to

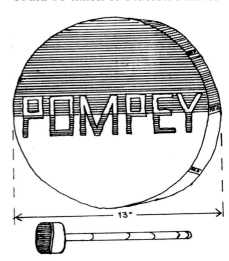

The 'Pompey' gong and its stick. The shaded area was blue, and the rest white, except for the red bands on the side.

promote encouragement for the team, rather than the then common wooden rattle. I did not take too much persuasion and I promptly purchased it for the sum of £1!

We would position ourselves at the rear of the covered Fratton end terrace and the gong would be heartily bashed whenever the home team scored a goal or made a good move - it had a most distinctive sound and I am sure some old supporters may well recall hearing it.

As mentioned, it was also taken to many away games and one such proved to be a bit out of the ordinary. A party of about 14 railway enthusiasts from the Portsmouth area, including David Copus, travelled by rail on a Special Excursion to Crystal Palace on Saturday 4 November to see the FA Cup First Round match at Selhurst Park - a crowd in excess of 30,000 saw our team put up a great performance and win 3-0, with Ron Saunders scoring two goals. However, at the final whistle thousands of Portsmouth supporters swarmed on to the pitch, including us to congratulate the players. David, carrying the gong, accidentally collided with the match referee who crumpled to the ground; we saw that he soon recovered, but did not stay around too long before mingling with the crowds of people! When we read the Sunday papers covering the 'Pompey' match we were quite amazed to read a line that said '. . . and at the end of the game Portsmouth supporters rushed on to the pitch and the referee was felled from behind by a heavy object'!

This particular season, 1961-62, saw my team in Division 3, but it proved to be only a 'one season' stay - they gained promotion with an impressive record of 27 wins and 11 draws out of 46 games and finished as champions. I wonder if the gong helped.

I also remember this season as I bought my first ever new bicycle for £25 from Allen's of Albert Road, Southsea; it was a three-speed Raleigh 'New Yorker'.

Western Region Class '4300' 2-6-0 No 7303 (71G) waits quietly in Fratton yard after bringing in an excursion from the West Country on Sunday 21 May.

COME TO SUNNY SOUTHSEA!

To conclude 1961 and the local scene, I have included a photograph of a steam locomotive in Fratton depot yard - it had just brought in an eight-carriage excursion train from the West Country. It had deposited its passengers at Portsmouth Harbour station to enjoy a four to five hour stay in 'Sunny Southsea', as the local guide-book of the time always seemed to say.

The guide-book always encour-

aged people to travel to Portsmouth & Southsea by rail, and information was always printed in the annual guide with the emphasis particularly focused on 'Southsea'. These Sunday excursion trains would always terminate at the Harbour station; the alighting passengers could then choose between catching the adjacent ferry to Ryde on the Isle of Wight, where they had the option of a coach tour, or

The Southsea Miniature Railway. This is the early 1960s scene as I remember it, and what happy days they were! Yet another full train-load of excited children, and often adults too, enjoy a summer-time ride behind a steam engine on this popular attraction. *By kind permission of Portsmouth City Council*

they could decide to stay in Southsea, with a visit to the beach and all its attractions.

Other attractions included a visit to the nearby historic Royal Naval Dockyard to view Nelson's flagship *HMS Victory* in its dry dock berth, or maybe, if you were a railway enthusiast and you had children to entertain, a visit to the Southsea Miniature Railway would be an ideal choice, as it was located virtually next to the beach.

A BRITISH RAILWAYS POSTER THAT NEVER WAS!

In the late 1950s the Southern Region of British Railways produced a large colour poster depicting a very scantily dressed female, which was intended to promote Portsmouth and Southsea as a sunny holiday resort.

I well remember much criticism, not only from local councillors, but also from the general public on the publication of this poster - in those days it was looked upon as far too revealing! As a result of this criticism the poster was subsequently withdrawn from the general public's eye!
The poster displayed the following information:

'FREQUENT ELECTRIC TRAINS FROM LONDON (WATERLOO). THROUGH TRAINS FROM THE WEST, MIDLANDS & SOUTH WALES. 'OBTAIN YOUR HOLIDAY GUIDE (9d P.O.) FROM ENQUIRY BUREAU, CASTLE BUILDINGS, SOUTHSEA, HANTS.'

This is the poster issued by the Southern Region of British Railways that was withdrawn from the public eye. *Reproduced by kind permission of Portsmouth City Council*

BRIGHTON

TUESDAY 9 JANUARY

Doug Willis, a train-spotting companion of myself and David Copus, was employed by British Railways, based at Eastleigh depot, and he made a working trip to Brighton via Fareham, Cosham and Chichester. The lists comprise two sections, 'on line' and 'on shed'.

Doug Willis, complete with coal shovel, is pictured in Eastleigh depot yard shortly before setting out on this trip as fireman. His driver was Mr Frank Collins (right), seen here in the cab of Class 'Q' 0-6-0 No 30540 at Eastleigh depot.

NOTED ON LINE

Steam locomotives:
30321	30540	30781	30936
31631	31791	31844	31905
31912	32351	33025	34016
34094	41261	41311	41329
73118	82014	82015	82016
92211	92239		

Diesel locomotives:
D3012	D3270	D3467	D3665
D3720	D5005	D6504	D6505

BRIGHTON DEPOT (75A)

Notings included six Class 'K' 2-6-0s, one of which, No 32337, was ex-Fratton. Another ex-Fratton engine was Class 'E4' 0-6-2 tank No 32479. If I recall rightly, there were several 'Schools' and 'West Country' Class main-line engines in the yard, awaiting their duties, one of which was No 30926 *Repton*.

SR electric units noted were Nos 2011, 2636, 2638, 2922, 3012, 3017, 3025, 3042 and 3052.

SR ELECTRIC UNITS

These were commonplace at Fratton station in the years that I and my friends were train-spotting, and very few records of their numbers existed after the end of steam. I do have a typical list noted at Fratton station dating from the early 1960s; they consist of the usual two-coach formations of 2-BIL and 2-HAL, and four-coach formations of 4-COR and 4-RES, together with a few four-coach suburban units. Nos noted were 2010, 2015, 2020, 2046, 2057, 2061, 2092, 2142, 2152, 2616, 2618, 2622, 2638, 2656, 2657, 2666, 2675, 3061, 3062, 3066, 3107, 3108, 3138, 3150, 4109, 4372 and 4668.

These green-liveried SR two-carriage electric units (2-BIL) were an everyday part of the Portsmouth scene at this date. Here we see a headcode '62' - an all-stations Brighton to Portsmouth Harbour train - departing from platform 3 at Fratton station; it is composed of three 2-BIL sets. *Doug Willis*

FROM TRAIN TO SCOOTER TO CAR

STEAM . . . NUMBERS DWINDLE

At the start of 1962 the rate of steam engines being withdrawn and scrapped had increased considerably. Not only were the pre-1900 classes being withdrawn, but also main-line types introduced in the 1920s and 1930s. With this and the thought of diesels taking over, the interest in steam among railway enthusiasts at Fratton had begun to wain and it was no surprise that fewer train-spotters now gathered on the station footbridge.

LOCAL VISITS

Eddie Rooke and I made numerous visits to both Fratton station and the engine shed between 1962 and 1967. We were often joined by David Copus, and the visits were mainly photographic.

Eddie Rooke, having first acquired a scooter, now had a car, and we continued our railway visits by road as well as rail. Local visits were made by road to such places as Havant, Hilsea Gas Works, Hayling Island, Gosport, Droxford, Bedhampton (scrapyard), and the old favourite, Eastleigh.

One such visit to a sub-depot of Eastleigh, Winchester, took place early in 1962. The tiny depot was built to house one small tank locomotive, and Adams-designed Class 'B4' 0-4-0 (outside-cylinder) tank No 30102 was 'on shed'. Situated in

the up yard of Winchester City station, it had often been passed by when travelling on trains to and from Portsmouth. A notice displayed near the depot read as follows: THE ONLY ENGINES PERMITTED TO PASS THIS BOARD ON Nos 1 AND 2 ROADS ARE THE B4 CLASS AND 204 H.P. DIESEL

THE SPORTING INTEREST CONTINUES

As already mentioned, my interest as a supporter of Portsmouth Football Club had taken me on rail excursions to many away games, and this combination continued well into the late 1960s. I recall my first ever visit to Fratton Park to see 'Pompey',

in the 1948/49 season; their opponents were Derby County in the FA Cup. 'Pompey' won 2-1, and the crowd was a record that will never be beaten, 51,385!

Cricket was also one of my sporting interests - many a time I would travel the short distance from Fratton to Portsmouth & Southsea or the Harbour station and make the 5-minute walk to Burnaby Road ground to see Hampshire. I would position myself to note the passing trains travelling between the Town and Harbour stations. I had my favourite players back in the 1960s, namely opener Roy Marshall and accurate bowler Derek Shackleton (how did he manage to bowl so many maiden overs?).

Above right An unusual angle of Urie-designed Class 'S15' 4-6-0 No 30514 (70B) in Fratton depot yard - its tender was under repair on the depot crane.

Right This photograph is just one of many that I took during 1962 at Fratton depot, and shows a very clean-looking Class 'U' 2-6-0 No 31633 (70C).

LONDON

SUNDAY 13 MAY

This was a visit with David Copus to London depots, and departure from Fratton was around 7.30 am. Permits were obtained for all depot visits.

Complete 'on shed' lists for this trip are not provided. The accompanying table highlights the steam/diesel ratio of the depots visited, and will give the reader an indication that 1962 saw the emergence of the diesel locomotive.

Steam noted at KING'S CROSS STATION: 60526, 60870, 61912 and 69523; diesels: D278, D5061, D5678 and D9021.

Diesels noted at ST PANCRAS: D12, D69, D313 and D5384.

Code	Location	Steam	Diesel	Total
1B	Camden	16	27	43
14B	Kentish Town	34	5	39
30A	Stratford	58	86	144
-	Stratford Works	-	10	10
81A	Old Oak Common	85	26	111
1A	Willesden	80	20	100
14D	Neasden	30	2	32
14A	Cricklewood	43	9	52
(A separate diesel depot contained 18 diesel and 10 DMUs.)				
34A	King's Cross	54	7	61
73C	Hither Green	-	42	42
Totals		400	244	644

Right Willesden depot: 'Britannia' Class 4-6-2 No 70018 *Flying Dutchman*. Class '9F' 2-10-0 No 92075 is behind.

Below Stratford depot: Class 'B12' 4-6-0 No 61572 (32A). It had been withdrawn from its home depot of Norwich Thorpe and sent to Stratford, but was lucky enough in later years to be preserved.

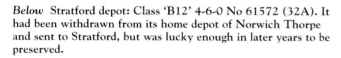

Below right Old Oak Common depot: 'Castle' Class 4-6-0 No 7037 *Swindon* was one of the locomotives in the depot yard on this visit.

Stratford depot: Class 'J15' 0-6-0 No 65445 of Parkeston depot (30F).

Old Oak Common depot: Class '5700' 0-6-0 pannier tank No 3646 waits in the yard.

BY SCOOTER TO LANCASHIRE VIA WALES

SATURDAY 9 TO TUESDAY 12 JUNE

SATURDAY 9 JUNE (Day 1)

This four-day trip to Wales and Lancashire was planned by Eddie Rooke, and I once again travelled as a pillion passenger on his Lambretta scooter. We took the camping gear with us; the tent was purchased jointly, each of us paying half towards the cost and any repairs needed. We made quite sure that everything needed for the three days ahead had been

packed; this included a very large bag of sandwiches, a bottle of orange squash, transistor radio, plastic mac and cap, and a camera. Our departure from outside Eddie Rooke's house at Fratton was at 6 am, and we travelled via Southampton to Salisbury. We then made a brief visit to Stonehenge on Salisbury Plain. Our route to Cardiff was via Chippenham and Gloucester, and several stops were made on the way for food and drink; our arrival

Camp at Porthkerry. Taking a night-cap in the form of a bottle of Brain's Brown Ale - and still in my sleeping bag! *E. C. Rooke*

at Cardiff was in the late afternoon. We then travelled several miles west of Cardiff to Porthkerry, where we located a camping site. Having set up the tent we travelled into Cardiff to purchase fish and chips and bags of crisps. We stopped at an off-licence and I purchased a quart bottle of Brain's Brown Ale, then returning to the tent we ate our food and had a drink. We finally dropped off to sleep after listening to Radio Luxembourg on Eddie's transistor.

SUNDAY 10 JUNE
(Day 2)

We were both awake just before 6.45 am - breakfast consisted of several sandwiches, a packet of crisps and the remains of the Brown Ale from the previous night. Having packed up the tent we departed from the camp site and headed for Woodham Brothers' scrapyard at Barry Island. Eddie and I had visited many of the locations on this trip as recently as 1961 (Western Region

Railrover), so complete engine shed lists have, in the main, been omitted here, but brief notings are shown for each location.

BARRY SCRAPYARD
This produced just 19 GWR tank engines, many of which still had

their rods and number-plates intact; Nos 5547 (88D) and 9499 (82B) both had their shed-plates intact.

BARRY DEPOT (88C)
Arriving at this nearby depot we were confronted by a shed official; at first we thought he would eject us as we had no permit for our visit, but on conversing with him we found that he was a friendly Welshman and we talked to him for several minutes - he informed us that there was a 'stored' pannier tank at the rear of the shed building. We then continued our visit, noting 26 locomotives 'on shed', of which 25 were tank designs, the sole passenger engine being 'Hall'

Below A general view of Barry locomotive depot. The 'Hall' Class referred to is just visible on the left.

Bottom An unexpected tank locomotive at the rear of Barry depot was pannier 0-6-0 Class '5400' No 5416 of Westbury. As can be seen, it has a tarpaulin over its chimney and is stored, pending further use.

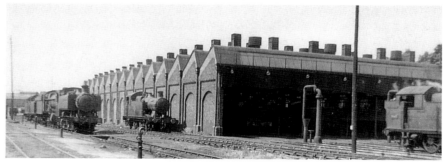

Class 4-6-0 No 4956 *Plowden Hall*. The 'stored' tank was located, and it proved to be quite a surprising find, a Westbury (82D)-allocated Class '5400' 0-6-0 pannier No 5416.

At Barry Island station we noted steam locomotives Nos 4177, 4619, 5627 and 5664, then travelled the short distance to Cardiff.

CARDIFF (CANTON) DEPOT (88A)

Here we noted 49 steam locomotives, all Western Region types, of which 32 were tanks. The following main-line locomotives had all been withdrawn from active service and were 'in store' pending disposal: 'King' Class 4-6-0s Nos 6003 and 6024, and 'Castle' Class 4-6-0s Nos 4090, 5041, 5048, 5062, 5080 and 7028.

Travelling the coast road to Newport, our next scheduled shed visit was Ebbw Junction.

NEWPORT (EBBW JUNCTION) DEPOT (86A)

We did not have a permit, but past experiences at this location told me that if we sped past the gateman's hut on the scooter we could enter the depot - this we achieved, and once again a very irate gateman was seen waving his arms, both as we entered and once again on our departure!

Once again this depot proved well worth a visit. We noted no fewer than 75 steam locomotives, of which over half were 'in steam'. Classes ranged from 0-6-0 pannier tanks to Class '4300' 2-6-0s, of which Nos 5330, 6325, 6366 and 7325 were noted. The tank locomotives were plentiful, in fact 61 were noted, 29 of them panniers. Only three were under repair in the large depot workshop.

We then travelled through Llantrisant and Monmouth and took the A466 via St Weonards to Hereford.

HEREFORD DEPOT (86C)

This was visited without a permit, and was 'all-steam', 25 being noted. All were Western Region engines. An impressive sight was 'County' Class 4-6-0 No 1024 *County of Pembroke* (82B), blowing off steam in the yard. The majority of engines were inside the shed and included six Class '2251' 0-6-0s, Nos 2241, 2242, 2249, 2256, 2295 and 3201.

Our route then took us via Kidderminster and Leominster to Craven Arms depot. This was a sub-depot of Shrewsbury. We stopped off on our journey at Leominster to view the shed (a sub-shed of Hereford), but this two-road through shed had officially closed two months previously and was consequently empty.

CRAVEN ARMS DEPOT

This was a brick-built, four-road dead-end shed, and contained four steam locomotives, Nos 4617, 42182, 48369 and 48761.

We then continued our journey via Church Stretton to Shrewsbury.

SHREWSBURY DEPOT (89A)

This had over 35 steam 'on shed', of which 24 were GWR engines, including two 'Hall' Class 4-6-0s with tarpaulins over their chimneys. Their numbers were not specifically noted, but they were in the following list: Nos 4951, 5942, 5971, 5976, 5991 and 7922. Other steam classes included LMS 'Black Five' 4-6-0s, '8F' 2-8-0s and Standard Class '5' 4-6-0s.

Leaving Shrewsbury, we made our way via the A5 in a north-westerly direction, eventually arriving at Oswestry, where we adjourned to a small cafe located near the railway station. We were both quite hungry and promptly consumed a meal of sausage, egg and chips followed by cups of tea. Refreshed, we then visited the depot.

OSWESTRY DEPOT (89D)

Here we saw just 15 steam 'on shed', including two Class '1400' 0-4-2 tanks, Nos 1434 and 1438 - the total was made up of eight 0-6-0 pannier tanks and five Class '2251' 0-6-0s, of which Nos 3200 and 3208 were Oswestry engines.

It was late evening as we located a field, only a short distance from the engine shed and adjacent to a railway track - it seemed to be an ideal spot to pitch our tent. After erecting the tent we settled down for some much-earned rest and to consume some fizzy drink as we listened to Radio Luxembourg on Eddie's transistor radio. Sleep eventually overcame us as it neared midnight.

MONDAY 11 JUNE (Day 3)

At 6 am we were both woken by the sound of a very loud voice. We peeped out of the tent to see in the distance an angry farmer waving his arms and shouting, 'Get out of my field, now!' We did not hang around to confront him; it was probably the quickest getaway we had ever experienced, although a similar incident had occurred the previous year in a field at Crediton, Devon!

We took the road to Wrexham, stopping off at a lay-by to consume our breakfast, some biscuits and the remains of a bottle of Tizer.

CROES NEWYDD DEPOT (89B)

We noted 23 steam 'on shed', including ten pannier tanks. The only tender locomotives of GWR design were Class '2800' 2-8-0 No 2859 and Class '4300' 2-6-0s Nos

Croes Newydd depot: Collett-designed Class '5600' 0-6-2 tank No 6694 complete with 89B shed-plate.

7302, 7313 and 7341. The most unlikely locomotive noted was Eastern Region 'B1' 4-6-0 No 61239 (9G, Gorton).

Leaving Wrexham we continued north to Liverpool, passing through the Mersey Tunnel. Bank Hall depot (code 27A) was passed; we did not make a visit, but noted two steam and one diesel shunter on passing. Our camping site for the third day was to be Blackpool, but we had planned to visit Preston on the way.

PRESTON DEPOT (24K)
This depot had been badly dam-aged by fire and only the brick walls and some of the charred supports to its roof remained intact. There were 13 steam 'on shed', of which 11 were 'Patriot' Class 4-6-0s: Nos 45505, 45507, 45510, 45513, 45518, 45524, 45533, 45546, 45547, 45549 and 45551. These, along with two 2-6-4 tanks, were virtually 'out of use' - many were destined for Derby Works for scrap.

We then travelled to Blackpool where we set up our tent at an official camp site on a farm only a few miles from the town. We purchased food and milk from the farm, then set off to enjoy ourselves amidst the bright lights of Blackpool. We did not visit any more depots that day.
It started to rain late in the evening as we returned to the farm camp site. We were looking forward to a good night's sleep.

TUESDAY 12 JUNE (Day 4)

Thunder and lightning and torrential rain during the night kept us awake; the tent had not been waterproofed and consequently the rain came through and soaked us and our sleeping bags! At first light we decided to fry a small breakfast of egg and sausage on my paraffin stove; this we did and it made us feel a little warmer. We had originally planned to visit some locomotive depots on the way home to Portsmouth, but because we and our equipment were soaked, we decided to make the journey home as quickly as possible. Our departure time from the camp site was 8 am - and it was still pouring with rain.

Travelling via the M6 motorway, we eventually found ourselves at a transport cafe on the outskirts of Stoke-on-Trent. We then had a breakfast of baked beans and chips, which was most welcome. A pintable in the cafe, on which we had several shillings to spend, proved lucky for us; we managed a high score that paid out to the winner a packet of 10 cigarettes - but neither of us smoked!

We eventually arrived safely home in Portsmouth during the early evening, having travelled nearly 600 miles on the scooter. Planned by Eddie, the trip unfortunately did not end as expected - it left two very weary, rain-soaked railway enthusiasts cursing the British weather!

ISLE OF WIGHT

MONDAY 20 AUGUST

This visit was made with my parents, although the engine sheds and works were visited on my own. This was, in the main, a photographic visit, capturing the Class 'O2' 0-4-4 tanks both 'on shed' and 'on line'.

Ryde Works, situated adjacent to Ryde (St John's) station, also undertook repairs to carriages and

---

70 H

RYDE (IOW) DEPOT

Steam locomotives:

14	17	18	20
22	24	29	30
31	36		

10 locomotives on shed

RYDE WORKS

Steam locomotives:
27   33

2 locomotives in works

---

wagons. No 27 *Merstone* was on shunting duties in the yard, while No 33 *Bembridge* was undergoing repairs inside the works. I also noted the boiler of an ex-Isle of Wight steam engine on a wagon in the works yard.

In later years I was to become a member of the then Wight Locomotive Society, and my passion for the island and its railways led me to help restore some passenger carriages in Newport sta-

Above Ryde depot: The signal box at St John's station forms the background to Nos 27 *Merstone* (left) and 17 *Seaview*.

Above right Ryde Pier Head station: No 22 *Brading* departs with a train for Ventnor. The 20 mph speed limit is displayed on the signals, with the water tower behind, while on the right is the signal box with the town of Ryde forming the background. The bell on the post, to the right of the engine, is shrouded in mystery - its most likely use was to inform engine crews that the steamer had just arrived at the pier. The sign on the post read: 'Engines must not pass this board unless the platform starting signal is off'. *I acknowledge the assistance of the Isle of Wight Steam Railway for this information.*

Right Ventnor station: No 16 *Ventnor* gets some attention from the driver while taking water. No 16 has just been uncoupled from its carriages, and after these duties it will run round its carriages and couple up ready for its return journey to Ryde Pier Head. Of interest is the number board '9' on the engine; this was a Duty Number and the figure was painted white on a black background. The SR introduced these numbers during the 1930s: Nos 1-11 relating to Ryde shed, and

13-24 Newport. When Newport closed, all numbers related to Ryde. They were of special significance on summer Saturdays.

tion - in the summer months a complete weekend would be taken in, and nights would be spent in one of the carriages.

The standard gauge tracks that ran at this date adjacent to the BR tracks between Ryde Pier Head and Esplanade stations, a distance of half a mile, conveyed two Drewry petrol railcars (introduced in 1927). These, especially in the summer months, would carry the bulk of the passengers and their luggage after disembarkation from the ferries and take them to the Esplanade. The single fare for this half-mile journey was 2d. Those passengers who were bound for Sandown, Ventnor and other stations would catch the BR train at Ryde Pier Head.

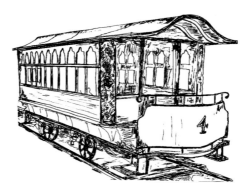

Ryde Pier tram (1871): This is Britain's oldest surviving tram-car, though it is not as old as had previously been thought (1867). Built under the supervision of the Clerk of the Ryde Pier works, Mr Harvey, using axles and wheels by Starbuck of Birkenhead, it ran as No 4. It was unique in having rounded corners with the monogram 'RPC' (Ryde Pier Company). Intricate carvings included bunches of grapes, and the car was consequently nicknamed 'The

Grapes'. From the opening in 1862 until steam locomotives were introduced in 1881, the Ryde tram-cars were pulled by horses. No 4 remained in service until 1935, when it was pushed through the buffer stops at Ryde Pier Head by a Drewry petrol car and wrecked! It was withdrawn from service and brought to the City of Kingston upon Hull Museum in 1936 by the late Dr H. C. Winstone, where it was restored, unfortunately incorrectly numbered 3.

ADDITIONAL HIGHLIGHTS OF 1962

SCOTLAND, HERE WE COME!

As already mentioned in Volume 1, this book sets out to describe primarily my own train-spotting escapades, but I feel it appropriate to include a much condensed version of an extraordinary trip undertaken by two of my closest friends, David Copus and Frank Allen. This trip took in the North East of England, Scotland and Carlisle, but unfortunately I could not join them as my holidays were planned for a later date.

A seven-day 'Freedom of Scotland' Silver ticket was purchased for £6 6s, and the trip began on Saturday 21 July and ended on Monday 30 July. All the photographs were taken by David Copus, who, as readers of Volume 1 will recollect, died shortly before the book was published.

Frank Allen will now unfold his story:

I worked in a Southsea guest house during my school holidays to fund my ticket, working an 80-hour week as a waiter for £3 10s, plus tips. David had persuaded his father to pay for his ticket.

SATURDAY 21 JULY

We departed from King's Cross at noon on the 'Queen of Scots' for Newcastle. No engine shed permits or sleeping arrangements had been made for this trip; accommodation for the first night was found in a communal room in a Newcastle guest house, which we shared with three complete strangers who proceeded to play cards noisily until just before dawn - this experience persuaded us to look for alternative forms of shelter for the remaining days!

Ex-NER 'J72' 0-6-0 tank No 68723 was the station pilot at Newcastle Central, and still retained its pre-nationalisation green livery.

SUNDAY 22 JULY

Engine sheds visited were HEATON (52B); PERCY MAIN (52E); GATESHEAD (52A) (apart from 50 steam on shed we noted 'in works' Nos 60052, 62002, 63365, 63466, 65788 and 65812); TYNE DOCK (52H); BLAYDON (52C); THORNABY (51L) and WEST HARTLEPOOL (51C). These depots produced a total of 350 steam.

MONDAY 23 JULY

We left Newcastle at 12.54 am on the 'Aberdonian' to Aberdeen. Early morning visits were made to both FERRYHILL and KITTY-BREWSTER sheds, but the latter only produced 13 diesels.

Our route to Inverness via Elgin saw just two steam, one being WR 0-6-0 pannier tank No 1649, and the other ex-Caledonian 4-4-0 No 54482 in the yard at Inverness depot. INVERNESS (60A) was visited, then we moved north to THURSO and WICK, both depots being visited. We slept on Wick station. Being ardent 'Pompey' FC fans, it was David who decided to take with us no fewer than 5,000 gummed stickers printed in royal blue and bearing the legend 'PLAY UP POMPEY'. These, needless to say, were plastered throughout the trip for the edification of the unwary! By the end of our travels they had been

displayed from Wick in the north, through the west coast including two ferries, and around Glasgow, Edinburgh and Aberdeen!

TUESDAY 24 JULY

We made our way south to Inverness from where we caught an evening train via the scenic route to Kyle of Lochalsh. We spent the night in a railway carriage in the station sidings, and this was where David's rather old-fashioned alarm clock came into its own - it had large bells on top of its face and a powerful gong action, and this we needed to wake us in time to catch the early ferry.

WEDNESDAY 25 JULY

We departed from Kyle of Lochalsh pier on the 5.10 am ferry to Mallaig; our ticket cost 8s 3d. We arrived in time to connect with the 7.54 am train to Fort William, where on arrival we were rewarded with the sight and sound of live steam. On shed at FORT WILLIAM (63B) were Nos 44225, 44975, 62011, 62012, 65300 and 65313. A hearty breakfast was consumed at a small cafe, topped with limitless supplies of tea, all for 2 shillings. We then caught the afternoon ferry to Oban, staying on deck to view some stunning scenery.

63 C

OBAN DEPOT

Steam locomotives:
44959   46460   78052

Diesel locomotives:
D5349 D5364 D5365 D5369

7 locomotives on shed

We next caught an early evening train to Glasgow, where we spent the night in Queen Street waiting room. This was not a good idea as frequent interruptions by both the law and local drunks ensured that we got very little sleep.

THURSDAY 26 JULY
It was exactly 5.30 am as we raised our weary heads to witness the sunrise over Glasgow. Engine sheds visited were DAWSHOLM (65D), where of note were four preserved steam, Nos 49, a GN 4-4-0, 103, a Highland 4-6-0, 123, a Caledonian 4-2-2, and 256, an NB 4-4-0; EASTFIELD (65A); ST ROLLOX (65B); POLMADIE (66A); PARKHEAD (65C); and KIPPS, where we saw two Class 'Y9' 0-4-0 saddle tanks, Nos 68104 and 68117. At this date there were only four working specimens of this Class, and we were lucky to note both Nos 68095 and 68101 within the next 24 hours. MOTHERWELL (66B) and CORKERHILL (67A) were visited; we had the distinction of being ejected from the latter by the foreman, but not before we had noted 90% of the engines.

We caught the 6.50 pm Glasgow (Central) to CARSTAIRS, where we visited the depot (66E) and found 42 steam 'on shed'. The night was spent on Princes Street station, Edinburgh, following a visit to a fish and chip shop. We inevitably ended our day with an identical menu to the previous day - large bags of greasy chips smothered in salt and vinegar and washed down with swigs of fizzy Tizer!

FRIDAY 27 JULY
Our schedule began at 7.15 am, and depots visited were HAYMARKET (64B), where steam noted were Nos 60099, 60160, 60162, 60838, 61219, 61221 and 65243; DALRY ROAD (64C); ST MARGARETS (64A); DUN-

St Margarets (Edinburgh) depot (64A): This was one of the four diminutive Class 'Y9' 0-4-0 saddle tanks, still in existence at this date, that David enthused over. As can be seen, No 68095 had had its smokebox door handle and its shed-plate removed, a sure sign that it had been taken out of active service. This Class were built to a Holmes NB design of 1882 and some of them must have had a somewhat unusual appearance in that they had a permanently attached wooden tender.

FERMLINE (62C); ALLOA; STIRLING (65J); and PERTH (63A). The latter had a strongly cosmopolitan atmosphere, with WR 0-6-0 pannier tank No 1646 rubbing shoulders with two 'Pacifics', Nos 60002 *Sir Murrough Wilson* and 60037 *Hyperion*, 'Princess Royal' No 46201 *Princess Elizabeth*, a selection of 17 'Black Five' 4-6-0s, and two Caledonian 4-4-0s, Nos 54466 and 54482.

DUNDEE DEPOT (62B) was visited, quickly followed by its subshed DUNDEE WEST. We then made the journey to THORNTON (62A), and another day concluded with a night spent on a station platform in Edinburgh accompanied by the usual menu of chips.

SATURDAY 28 JULY
The day dawned and we witnessed pouring rain; it seemed to be set to continue for most of the day, but it did not blunt our enthusiasm to carry on, as we were at this date the proud owners of the famous 'plastic macs' - these proved to be the forerunners of the modern-day anorak. I recall this particular

event because we discovered that David's mac had been sabotaged; when it was unfolded a sticky, stale cake revealed itself, smelling awful!

BATHGATE (64F) was visited by bus. Edinburgh (Waverley) was our departure point for POLMONT (65K), and next was GRANGEMOUTH (65F). Two scrapyards then came into our schedule, BO'NESS DOCKS and CARNBROE SOUTH.

Bo'ness Docks scrapyard: Although awaiting scrap, Class 'N15/1' 0-6-2 tank No 69183, ex-65A (Eastfield), looks to be in a fairly good external condition. It had seen 52 years of active service.

The non-stop rain must have left us looking a sorry and bedraggled sight, but we eventually dried out and by 5.30 pm had set off for KILMARNOCK WORKS, then HURLFORD (67B).

Leaving Hurlford, we made our way to Glasgow (St Enoch) station where we noted five 'Jubilee' 4-6-0s, Nos 45621, 45665, 45687, 45707 and 45711. We kipped the night on this station, and had a virtually trouble-free sleep.

SUNDAY 29 JULY
We left St Enoch at 9.20 am for DUMFRIES (68B); it was 'all steam'. We were then steam-hauled to Carlisle by 'Jubilee' 4-6-0 No 45677 *Beatty*, arriving at 12.28 pm. A taxi was used to visit both KINGMOOR and UPPERBY depots; the former (12A) had 85 steam 'on shed', the latter (12B) 71. We then caught the 4.48 pm

train to Edinburgh to connect with the 8.05 pm overnight train to London, for which we purchased reserved seats at 2 shillings each. It would be bliss to get home and return to normal living hours, real food, a soaking in the bath and a proper bed - all this after having to confront what must have been two sets of anxious parents awaiting our safe return!

A GEORDIE ESCAPADE

NEWCASTLE: AUGUST 24-26

Portsmouth FC were playing a League Division 2 match at Newcastle on Saturday 25th and Eddie Rooke and I decided to travel to Newcastle by road. We departed from Portsmouth mid-afternoon on the Friday; I travelled pillion passenger on Eddie's scooter as far as Reading, where we parked it in the car park at the General station. Here, as arranged, we met up with one of our train-spotting friends, Trevor Robson - originally from Southsea, he had later moved to Bath, and had motored up to Reading, meeting us in the early evening.

We then travelled north via the A1 in Trevor's grey Ford Popular (JAP 591), but nearing Ripon in Yorkshire the car became 'ill' - there was much spluttering and it eventually ground to a halt! Trevor called out the AA to assist, and they towed us about 10 miles into a garage forecourt in Ripon. Being late Friday evening there were no mechanics to attend to the car, so we slept in it overnight, and very early on Saturday morning the garage staff replaced a gasket that had blown - all this only took a few hours. After thanking everyone concerned, we continued our journey north.

Prior to the match, we visited Trevor's family friends' house at Fence Houses, near Houghton le Spring, about 10 miles south of Newcastle; on our arrival they greeted us with food and drinks.

On many previous football excursions I had taken with me the Pompey 'gong', and this trip was no exception; I remember Trevor's family friends marvelling over the use of a dinner gong painted in Pompey colours, and they were amazed to learn that we were taking it to the match! Theirs was only a small terraced house in Pinewood Street, but the incessant bashing of the gong in their back yard must have aroused many a neighbour on that Saturday morning! I recall watching the TV, and when the local football preview was shown we were quite surprised to see that a group of so-called 'Pompey' supporters had gained entrance to St James's Park overnight and painted the goal-posts blue!

Although no rail excursion was laid on, thousands of 'Pompey' supporters made the long trek north, some by ordinary rail services and others by coaches, cars and even hitch-hiking. Our close train-spotting friend, David Copus from Southsea, had decided to travel up by rail and to include several engine shed visits prior to attending the football.

We eventually left for Newcastle, and visits were made to the station before and after the match - steam locomotives were: Nos 60072, 60088, 60913, 61019, 67645, 67647, 67653, 68723, 68736 and 69025; diesel locomotives Nos D274, D277, D2045, D2322, D3321, D5099, D5102 and D9008.

We didn't meet up with David, but for information purposes his engine shed lists were as follows:

SUNDERLAND DEPOT (52G)
Steam locomotives noted were Nos 62064, 63342, 63345, 63418, 63456, 64701, 64703, 64704, 64843, 64846, 64847, 64851, 64853, 64854, 64858, 65817, 65830, 65832, 65833, 65835, 65841, 65853, 65854, 65865, 65869, 65870, 65871, 65872, 65873, 65874, 65883, 65885, 65887 and 65892; diesel locomotives Nos D2044, D2249, D3241 and D3679. 38 locomotives on shed.

CONSETT DEPOT (52K)
Steam locomotives: Nos 62002, 62023, 62027, 62050, 62060, 63346, 63359, 63368, 63406, 63427, 63439 and 63455. 12 locomotives on shed.

As regards the football, the match ended 1-1 with Tony Barton scoring for Portsmouth.

Details of our return journey are rather vague, but we motored back to Reading, having first stopped off at Trevor's family friends' house to say farewell. Several stops were made for refreshments during the long journey through Saturday evening and the early hours of Sunday. On our eventual arrival at Reading we said goodbye to Trevor, who then motored on to Bath; Eddie and I then rode the scooter from General station on the final stage to Portsmouth with the gong safely held in my grasp. The roads were virtually traffic-free and the weather was quite warm as we arrived back in Portsmouth at about 7 am on the Sunday morning - it had certainly been quite an eventful weekend!

THE PORTSMOUTH AREA DURING 1962

BEDHAMPTON

This private scrapyard (known as Sullivan's) was located in a chalk pit in Portsdown Hill Road, Bedhampton, Portsmouth. I travelled the 5 miles from Fratton as a passenger on Eddie Rooke's scooter for this unofficial visit.

As well as the locomotives illustrated, the scrapyard also included a Hunslet 0-4-0 diesel, works No 2147, built at Leeds in 1940.

Sullivan's scrapyard: Ex-Portsmouth Royal Navy Dockyard steam locomotives await their fate on Saturday 30 June 1962. Three saddle-tanks can be seen; left to right they are No 15, Avonside, works No 1659, built 1915; No 10, Andrew Barclay, works No 2039, built 1937; and No 18, Bagnall, works No 2602, built 1938. Also there but not in the picture was No 14, Avonside, works No 1658, built 1915. At about this date Portsmouth Dockyard had several 0-4-0 saddle-tank steam locomotives still in use, including No 17, an Andrew Barclay outside-cylinder type, and No 21, a Hudswell Clarke, also with outside cylinders.

THE HAYLING ISLAND BRANCH: SUMMER OF 1962

The Hayling Island branch opened in 1865 for 1 mile between Havant and Langstone, then in 1867 the full 4½ miles of single track to Hayling Island terminus was opened. There were two stations, one at Langstone

Halt (1 mile), the other at North Hayling, which was situated across the water from the mainland. The water was crossed by an impressive trestle bridge with an iron rail on each side. The terminus had one platform with brick station buildings and a covered roof. There were several sidings used for carriages and others for goods; the latter included a goods shed.

The steam locomotives used in 1962 were Class 'A1X' 0-6-0 tanks, previously allocated to Fratton but now transferred to Eastleigh (71A), although some could still be noted at Fratton shed.

The journey from Havant to Hayling Island terminus took 13 minutes. The route followed the west coast of the island, with the shore of Langstone Harbour lapping at one side of the track, and the other side giving passengers some pleasant views of farmland and scattered dwellings.

THE HAYLING BILLY ENGINES

These engines were designed by William Stroudley in 1872 and originally classed as 'A1', later 'A1X'. They were the only type of engine allowed to cross Langstone Swing Bridge; this restriction took effect from their introduction date and continued right up to the closure of the line in 1963.

Local train-spotters at Fratton shed would always be able to note at least one of these 'A1X' Class tanks whenever they made a visit, and they were probably the most loved and most photographed type at this location.

It is of particular note that of the 50 'Terriers' built, a grand total of ten still survive today in preservation; as they were all constructed between the years 1872 and 1880, this really is a magnifi-

cent achievement, and all credit must go to their designer in providing an engine that would virtually last for ever. One would doubt very much whether any of today's diesel and electric locomotives would have a life-span anywhere near that of an 'A1X' 0-6-0 tank engine.

We would often travel the Hayling branch in the summer months to visit the beach - it was a welcome change from our local Southsea beach - observe the many shipping movements in Spithead and, of course, enjoy the views of the Isle of Wight. Bearing in mind that by now we were all teenage boys, our thoughts often turned to the fairer sex, and we can all recall some fond memories of time spent on the beach and visits to the funfair! We could easily reach West Hayling by the short ferry crossing from the Eastney district of Portsmouth, but being rail enthusiasts we more often than not chose the rail route.

With its holiday camps and beaches, Hayling Island was a magnet for summer holidaymakers, not only from the local counties and London but also from the Midlands and the North. But Beeching arrived in 1962: 'Lack of passengers in winter months and the viaduct needs replacing'. Despite much local outcry, the last train ran in November 1963.

'Terrier' No 32636 approaches North Hayling during the summer of 1962.

1963

A 'CASTLE' 'IMPOUNDED'

MARCH: FOUR FOOTBALL SPECIALS IN FOUR WEEKS!

The year began with the 'big freeze' - an exceptionally heavy fall of snow - and it was most unusual to see Langstone Harbour frozen over! We continued our railway trips, albeit on a smaller scale, and our visits to Fratton Park were still frequent; from notes that I made, admission to the ground was just 3/6d!

As mentioned on previous pages, the cinema was a favourite leisure-time attraction for us, and in 1963 we had no fewer than 14 cinemas to choose from in our area. The Gaumont at Bradford Junction, Southsea, was visited frequently; some films that I recall were *Shane*, *Conflict of Wings* and *Robin Hood*, the latter being viewed at least three times!

I travelled in the company of David Copus and numerous other friends on no fewer than four football 'specials' during March! The famed 'Pompey' gong was taken on several of these rail trips. All departures were from Fratton.

SOUTHAMPTON: SATURDAY 2 MARCH - On this first occasion local rivals the 'Saints' caused some degree of embarrassment for us 'Pompey' supporters, as we lost 4-2. It was hard to take, especially when I returned to work on the Monday to be confronted by several jubilant workmates who were 'Saints' fans! The only conso-lation was that a Southampton player scored an 'own goal'!

COVENTRY CITY: SATURDAY 16 MARCH - Portsmouth were away to City in the fourth round replay of the FA Cup. The result was a 2-2 draw.

PORTSMOUTH TO LONDON

Steam locomotives:
30072   31407   31870   33035
33038   82018   82022

EUSTON STATION

Steam locomotives:
42234   42350   42566   42604
44910   45669   46129   48531

Diesel locomotives:
D317   D5003   D5018   D8037

EUSTON TO COVENTRY

Steam locomotives:
31913   42577   42958   43018
44938   45198   45299   45331
45448   46431   47241   47500
47501   48600   48624   61059
73039   84004   92021   92078

Diesel locomotives:
D228   D318   D321   D324
D328   D371   D2909   D2910
D3016   D3051   D3834   D3847
D3850   D5001   D5002   D5016
D5035   D5075   D5146   D8012

TOTTENHAM: TUESDAY 19 MARCH - The replay against Coventry City was played at White Hart Lane, Tottenham Hotspur's ground. We finally bowed out of the FA Cup by losing 2-1.

LIVERPOOL STREET

Diesel locomotives:
D209   D5695   D6727   D6737
D8229

CHARLTON: SATURDAY 30 MARCH - This was a League Division 2 game, and once more my team ended on the losing side, going down 2-0.

GUILDFORD AND WATERLOO AREAS

Steam locomotives:
31868   31872   80072   80087
82012   82019

Diesel locomotives:
D3272   D6516   D6527   D6537
D6563   D6576   D6582

Electric locomotive:
E5011

LONDON: A PHOTOGRAPHIC FAREWELL

SUNDAY 28 APRIL

This day trip was chosen as a 'Photographic Farewell' rather than as a train-spotting trip. Visits to five engine sheds were planned, all of which had over a period of six years been visited on numerous occasions - at this date they were gradually being 'run down' to eventually make way for the diesel. I travelled with David Copus and Frank Allen.

WILLESDEN DEPOT (1A)

There were 99 locomotives 'on shed', of which 70 were steam. These included nine 'Black Five' 4-6-0s, an assortment of 'Patriot', 'Jubilee' and 'Princess Coronation' Classes, together with no fewer than ten 'Britannia' 4-6-2s, Nos 70000, 70004, 70010, 70018, 70024, 70031, 70032, 70034, 70043 and 70048. Main-line diesel No 10001 was also 'on shed'.

Willesden: Class '7P' ('Patriot') 4-6-0 No 45530 *Sir Frank Ree* in very smart condition.

OLD OAK COMMON DEPOT (81A)

There were 112 locomotives 'on shed', of which 77 were steam. 'Castles' were prominent - those noted were Nos 4074, 4087, 4098, 5001, 5014, 5041, 5060, 5076, 5091, 7009, 7017, 7018, 7020, 7025, 7026, 7027, 7029, 7034, 7035 and 7037. 'Warship' Class diesels: D806, D809, D822, D827, D843, D850, D857 and D865.

Old Oak Common: 'King' Class 4-6-0 No 6010 *King Charles I* has sadly been side-lined for scrap. Part of its front bogie, chimney capping, numbers and name-plates have already been removed.

CRICKLEWOOD DEPOT (14A)

There were 45 locomotives 'on shed', of which 41 were steam. 'Standards' were plentiful and included Nos 73157, 73158, 76035, 76037, 76038, 76039, 76040, 76041, 76043, 76048, 76085, 76086, 76089 and 92009.

Cricklewood: 'Royal Scot' 4-6-0 No 46163 *Civil Service Rifleman*.

CAMDEN DEPOT (1B)

There were 36 locomotives 'on shed', of which only seven were steam, Nos 46225, 46228, 46239, 46240, 46245, 46251 and 46252. All seven were 'Princess Coronation' Class 4-6-2 main-line passenger types, introduced in 1937. These Stanier-designed locomotives were enlargements of the 'Princess Royal' Class originally introduced in 1933. Their main duties were hauling expresses between Euston and Glasgow, but at this date they were being gradually replaced with diesel

locomotives. The depot building was in a run-down state and we were informed on this visit that it was due for closure in September 1963.

Camden: 'Princess Coronation' Class 4-6-2 No 46251 *City of Nottingham*.

KING'S CROSS DEPOT

Steam locomotives:
60007	60010	60026	60029
60061	60136	60150	60157
60880	60897	60924	61075
61179	61200	61393	61912
90154	90246	90514	92180
92181			

Diesel locomotives:
D278	D1501	D1509	D1516
12131	D3331	D3693	D3715
D5659	D5680	D9016	

32 locomotives on shed

King's Cross depot was due for closure in June 1963, and like the others that we had visited on this trip, was in a run-down state, although some of the steam engines were kept very clean externally.

King's Cross: 'A4' streamlined 'Pacific' No 60007 *Sir Nigel Gresley* simmers amidst other main-line locomotives in the depot yard.

King's Cross: Class 'A1' 4-6-2 No 60150 *Willbrook* waits in the yard in the company of Class 'A4' No 60010 *Dominion of Canada.*

FRATTON AND HAYLING ISLAND

SUNDAY 9 JUNE

Both Fratton depot and the Hayling Island branch line were visited, and just a few of the photographs that I captured on that day are shown here.

Bound for the seaside at Hayling Island, a very happy bunch of children are aware of my presence as Class 'A1X' 0-6-0 tank No 32678 (fitted with spark arrestor) departs after a brief halt at North Hayling.

Above Contrasting designs, side by side, at Fratton: on the left is Class 'Q1' 0-6-0 freight locomotive No 33020 and on the right Class 'N' 2-6-0 'Mogul' No 31412.

Below Hayling Island terminus station: In the distance Class 'A1X' 0-6-0 tank No 32646 waits in the bay platform with the train for Havant. The taxi driver is engrossed in a newspaper while he waits for the next train to arrive from Havant. Note the gas lamp on the right still in use.

No 5050 'IMPOUNDED' AT FRATTON DEPOT

TUESDAY 25 JUNE

Nearest the camera is 'Castle' Class 4-6-0 No 5050 *Earl of St Germans*, 'impounded' at Fratton. In front of No 5050 are two Class 'Q1' 0-6-0s and a 'Standard' Class '5' 4-6-0, while in the left background can be seen one of the Class 'A1X' 0-6-0 tanks that were used on the Havant to Hayling Island branch. *Bruce R. Oliver*

Local railway enthusiasts were very surprised to find that a 'Castle' Class locomotive had arrived in Portsmouth. News of its arrival soon got around, but being a Tuesday, not too many 'spotters' were around to see it. This main-line 4-6-0 Western Region passenger locomotive, No 5050 *Earl of St Germans*, appeared with a schoolchildren's special train from Bristol.

According to British Railways officials, 'Castle' Class locomotives, total weight 126 tons 11 cwt, were too large for the Southern Region loading gauge and their outside cylinders would have made slight contact with the platform edge at Fareham station, where a very tight curve (now eliminated) existed. When British Railways officials found out that the 'Castle' had hauled the special train through to Portsmouth Harbour, via Fareham, No 5050 was immediately 'impounded' on a siding in Fratton depot yard, 'NOT TO BE MOVED' signs were displayed on it and several other locomotives were placed in front of it to prevent it from being moved. *Earl of St Germans* remained there for well over three weeks until a decision was made as to what action to take and how to return this locomotive to its home depot of Bristol (St Philip's Marsh). Rumours spread that the 'Castle' had stayed at Fratton because it had broken down.

No 5050 eventually departed, under its own steam, on Sunday 21 July - but with a speed restriction of 10 mph between Fratton and Salisbury. ('Castles' often worked between Bristol and Salisbury, run-ning via Bath Spa and Westbury, and on their arrival at Salisbury a Southern Region locomotive or a Standard would take over for the Portsmouth train.) On its arrival at Bristol No 5050 was put into its home depot roundhouse and from that day was subsequently put 'in store' and never used again - eventually it was scrapped. A Standard Class '5' 4-6-0 locomotive was used to haul the return schoolchildren's special between Portsmouth Harbour and Salisbury.

On a visit to Bristol on Tuesday 3 September 1963 I noted No 5050, still intact, in St Philip's Marsh roundhouse. Although no damage appeared to have arisen from its route through Fareham station, no other details were made known. This was the *last ever visit* of a 'Castle' to Portsmouth.

Going back to the 1930s, local enthusiast Mr B. Batten recollected that a 'Castle', No 5019 *Treago Castle*, ran 'light engine' on a wheel test to Portsmouth Harbour. Another 'Castle' recorded by Mr Batten was No 4082 *Windsor Castle*, on an excursion from Worcester to Portsmouth Harbour; the year is unknown, but it was a Sunday. Also from Worcester, *circa* 1936, No 4086 *Builth Castle* appeared in Portsmouth with an excursion.

Coming back to 1963, prior to the 'impounding' an excursion from Kidderminster to Portsmouth Harbour arrived behind 'Castle' No 5063 *Earl Baldwin* (84A). One wonders therefore what all the fuss was about; having learned that 'Castles' had visited Portsmouth (via Fareham) frequently in the past - perhaps the re-alignment of platforms at Fareham station was the reason?

JUNE AND JULY: A TRAIN-SPOTTER'S DIARY

Between 1 June and the end of July 1963 I made various visits to local railway stations. I have listed the locomotives noted, together with the locations and any other information. Also included are other items of interest of which I had made notes. Listening to and attending pop music dances was also very popular about this date.

SATURDAY 1 JUNE -
Purchased a new suit at Jackson's,

Commercial Road, Portsmouth, for £10.00. Cricket: Hampshire 349 for 5 v Kent; H. Horton 139.

SUNDAY 2 JUNE - Whit Sunday. I travelled on the Hayling Island branch line. Class 'A1X' 0-6-0 tanks working were Nos 32646, 32650 and 32678. Western Region 'Hall' 4-6-0 No 6951 *Impney Hall* brought an excursion into Portsmouth.

FRIDAY 7 JUNE - Purchased 45 rpm record 'String Along' by Ricky Nelson; also ordered two LPs by the same artist. At this date I had in my collection seven LPs, 13 singles and two EPs, all by this artist! He was my pop idol of the 'sixties.

SATURDAY 8 JUNE - Attended the first day of the three-day County Cricket match at Burnaby Road, Portsmouth. Hampshire v Lancashire. Class '9F' 2-10-0 freight locomotive No 92212 was noted at Fratton. Nos 92211 and 92239 were also noted at about this date. They were also used on goods trains between Salisbury and Chichester at various dates in 1963.

SATURDAY 29 JUNE - During the final months of trolleybus workings in Portsmouth I noted Nos 301, 305, 306, 307 and 313. Steam locomotives noted at Fratton station were Class 'Q1' 0-6-0 No 33018, and Class 'Q' 0-6-0 No 30531 employed on a Bertram Mills Circus train. Passenger train information: Standard Class '4' 2-6-0 No 76017 brought a Nottingham train into Portsmouth, while another of the same class, No 76009, took out the 12.15 pm to Plymouth from Portsmouth & Southsea (Low Level), platform 1.

SUNDAY 30 JUNE - Saw the 'Teenbeats' pop group at the Savoy, Southsea.

END OF JUNE - Twelve steam-hauled passenger trains were departing from Portsmouth on Summer Saturdays; these included through services to both Nottingham and Sheffield.

SATURDAY 6 JULY - Midland Region Class '2' 2-6-2 tank No 41325 was noted on a pw train at Littlehampton, Sussex.

TUESDAY 16 JULY - Purchased Johnny Burnette LP from Weston Hart record shop, Portsmouth; cost 35 shillings.

SATURDAY 20 JULY - I went on a coach outing to London with the Grosvenor Press Sports and Social Club. I had just completed a six-year apprenticeship as a hot metal compositor with this company.

SUNDAY 21 JULY - It was rumoured that two Beattie well-tanks were to be 'stored' at Fratton; 'West Country' Class 4-6-2 No 34014 *Budleigh Salterton* was noted on a Brighton to Cardiff train; 'A1X' No 32662 was working the Hayling Island branch; and Standard Class '4' 2-6-0 No 76064 was noted at Bognor.

MONDAY 22 JULY - Two saddle-tanks were noted at Hilsea Gas Works; also one (in red livery) in the one-road shed at the southern end of the gas works. Also noted at this location was 0-6-0 diesel *Fleet No 1139*. Class 'Q1' No 33031 was shunting at Littlehampton. Class 'A1X' No 32670 was working the Hayling Island branch. Noted at Fratton were Standard Class '4' 2-6-0s Nos 76006 and 76058.

TUESDAY 23 JULY - Class 'A1X' 0-6-0 tank No 32650 was working the Hayling Island branch. Class 'Q1' 0-6-0 No 33021 was shunting at Chichester; also noted at this location was Class 'CC' electric locomotive No

20003 (introduced in 1948). 'A1X' No 32640 was on shunting duties at Littlehampton yard; also seen there was Midland 2-6-2 tank No 41325. Class 'Q' 0-6-0 No 30543 was on shunting duties at Barnham station.

FRIDAY 26 JULY - Standard Class '5' 4-6-0 No 73018 was noted at Fratton. Had my first ride on the new City of Portsmouth Leyland passenger transport buses, on No 211 on the Arundel Street to Commercial Road route.

MORE 1960s MUSICAL MEMORIES FROM MY DIARY - ROCK 'N' ROLL AND RHYTHM 'N' BLUES - My own favourite rock 'n' roll artist was without a doubt Ricky Nelson, followed closely by such artists as Buddy Holly, The Crickets, Chuck Berry, Eddie Cochran, Del Shannon and The Everly Brothers. Although

Eddie Rooke's first car! Eddie (top) and Trevor Robson pose for a photograph, complete with genuine 'Charlotte Street' caps (Portsmouth's street market). Eddie purchased the 1937 Austin Seven from a milkman employed at Walkers Dairy, Guildford Road, Fratton, for the sum of £5. I helped to hand-paint it brightly in yellow, blue and black, and it ran regularly for nearly 12 months. I remember it reaching a speed of 90 mph on a local bypass, but after this it broke down - Eddie then sold it to a sailor for £17!

neither I nor my close friends ever did get into playing 'live' music, we did get together at Eddie Rooke's house and attempt to record some very silly songs, the tune being recognisable, but the words changed! I had a six-string guitar (purchased new for £5 from Musical Homes, Fratton Road), whilst Eddie Rooke and David Copus would play such instruments as a jews harp, kazoo, biscuit tin and tea cups! We recorded on to tape, and some of these still remain to this day.

Local 'live' music venues were many, but two particular artists remain in my thoughts to this day, these being American blues singer John Lee Hooker 'live' on stage at 'Kimbells', Osborne Road, Southsea, and at the same venue a 12-string guitar blues artist from the USA, Jimmy Reed.

Some of the 'local' rock 'n' roll groups that I saw in 1963 were Johnny Devlin and the Detours (Bognor), Terry Franks and the Avalons, Mike Anger and the Wild Ones, and Chris Ryder and the Southern Sounds.

SOUTHAMPTON

SATURDAY 27 JULY

I travelled first to Eastleigh on the 7.33 am from Fratton (Reading train), being steam-hauled by Standard Class '4' 2-6-0 No 76058. I had planned also to visit Winchester, but my main objective was to visit Southampton Central station and take some photographs.

I was delighted to be steam-hauled between Winchester and Southampton by an immaculately turned out 'West Country' Class 4-6-2 No 34001 *Exeter*.

SOUTHAMPTON AREA			
Steam locomotives:			
34053	34061	34071	34085
34103	34105	73119	76017

Plenty of activity at Southampton as 'West Country' Class 4-6-2 No 34105 *Swanage* eagerly awaits its departure from platform 1 with the Bournemouth to Birkenhead train. On the left is Standard Class '4' 2-6-0 No 76017 with a Cardiff General to Portsmouth train. This view shows the old station building at platforms 1 and 2 before it was demolished and replaced with modern office-type buildings. Note the impressive clock tower, just visible behind the plumes of steam; sadly, this was also demolished. On a summer Saturday this location was a spotters' paradise, as can be seen by the boys here whose attention has been caught by *Swanage* 'blowing off'. By coincidence both of these locomotives have been preserved on the 'Watercress Line' in Hampshire. This is one of my favourite photographs, so much so that I produced a painting 'in oils' capturing this scene.

BRISTOL

TUESDAY 3 SEPTEMBER

I travelled with railway enthusiast John Jones. Nos 2229, 3606, 3632 and 8725, noted at Barrow Road, were waiting their turn to be towed to the breaker's yard. Only Western

BETWEEN FRATTON AND BRISTOL			
Steam locomotives:			
3203	3739	4626	4630
4636	4699	5904	6977
7250			

Region steam locomotives were recorded on this visit, except No

92225, a Class '9F' 2-10-0, 'on shed' at St Philip's Marsh.

Nos 1365, 4102, 4700, 4947, 4960, 4999, 5040, 5050, 5940, 6312, 7338, 9601 and 9729 were all withdrawn from service and awaiting to be towed to scrapyards. Of note was No 1365, a Class '1361' 0-6-0 saddle-tank, previously allocated to Swindon.

We then travelled by DMU from Temple Meads to

BRISTOL (BARROW ROAD) DEPOT

Steam locomotives:

2229	3606	3632	3643
3675	3677	4131	4619
4684	6148	8725	9623

12 locomotives noted

BRISTOL (ST PHILIP'S MARSH) DEPOT

Steam locomotives:

1011	1021	1028	1365
3696	3742	3752	3815
3838	3844	3856	4090
4102	4700	4947	4960
4999	5040	5050	5091
5929	5937	5939	5940
5975	5978	6312	6408
6769	6810	6821	6831
6840	6846	6857	6878
6950	6952	6954	6987
6990	6997	7338	7901
7924	9601	9729	92225

48 locomotives noted.

No 5050 *Earl of St Germans* was the 'Castle' Class engine 'impounded' at Fratton depot during June and July.

Avonmouth Docks, noting en route steam locomotives Nos 2277, 6320, 8102 and 9660.

Although not known at this date, this was to be my final visit to engine sheds in Bristol. My first had taken place on 16 June 1957 and during my many visits, accompanied by my fellow enthusiasts, Bristol had become a firm favourite as an interesting railway centre - the noting of steam engines both ancient and modern was always possible.

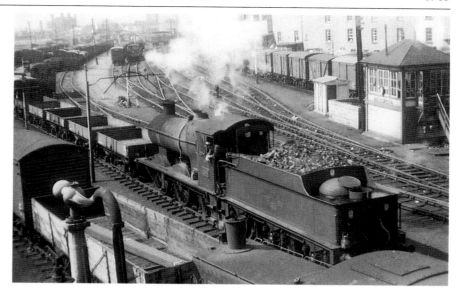

Barrow Lane Sidings: Class '2251' 0-6-0 No 2217 is busy at work on shunting duty. In the foreground is diesel shunter No D2134 and another diesel shunter can be seen in the yard. Note the clock on the front of the signal box.

CARDIFF FOOTBALL EXCURSION

SATURDAY 7 SEPTEMBER

Our departure on this 2nd Class Day Special Football Excursion from Portsmouth Harbour station was at 8 am. Both David Copus and Roy Davidson accompanied me and we paid a return fare of 27/6d. Standard Class '5' 4-6-0 No 73119 hauled our train via Eastleigh and Romsey to Salisbury, where GWR 'Hall' Class 4-6-0 No 6953 *Leighton Hall* took over for the journey to Cardiff General via Westbury and Bath Spa.

'On line' we noted 35 steam and 30 diesels. Named steam were 'County' Class 4-6-0 No 1021 *County of Montgomery*, 'Castle' Class 4-6-0 No 5071 *Spitfire*, and 'Hall' Class 4-6-0 No 5978 *Bodinnick Hall*.

On arrival we changed platforms and quickly boarded the

13.16 pm train to Radyr; we had no time to purchase tickets as the train was waiting to depart. The ticket collector at Radyr issued us with excess fare tickets when we arrived; the fare was 1s 5d.

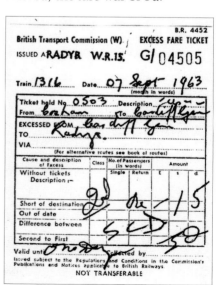

We then made our way via the cinder path running parallel to the main line, and a 10-minute walk brought us to the depot.

RADYR DEPOT (88B)

My previous visit here had taken

BETWEEN CARDIFF AND RADYR

Steam locomotives:
  6116   6624   6626   6635
  8469   9473

Diesel locomotives:
D3258 D3427 15104 D6832
D6859 D7037 D7086

place in 1961. This was a 'tank' shed with its allocation mostly serving the Welsh valleys, employed on coal and freight workings. In all, 30 steam tank engines were 'on shed', together with four diesels, of which three were of the newly constructed Type '3' English Electric main-line type, Nos D6820, D6832 and D6838. The steam locomotives were Nos 3400/1/2/3/5/6/9; 3672/81; 4166/77; 4289; 5608/13/72/97; 6606/7/14/38/59/60/99;

7205/50; 8466/97; and 9456/72/80. Nos 3406, 4289, 5608 and 6607 were awaiting scrapping.

As described in previous pages, the 'Pompey' gong was taken to many of Portsmouth Football Club's away games and this trip was no exception. I recall that as we ended our visit to Radyr depot (successfully 'bunked' without a permit!) David, who had been lumbered with carrying the gong, removed it from its plastic bag and crept up behind an elderly railwayman and produced four hearty strikes. The startled railwayman was heard to exclaim 'What's going on?'. Even nearby offices were aroused - faces peered out of windows and doors were opened in quick succession, but the offending instrument was quickly put back in the bag and we made a somewhat hasty retreat!

Returning to Cardiff we caught a local DMU to Ninian Park station, from where we walked to

the football ground. It was a League Division 2 match and we positioned ourselves with the gong behind some local supporters, taking turns in making ourselves heard whenever 'Pompey' scored or made a good move. The Cardiff supporters did not seem to mind - in fact, several commented that it was a novel method of making our support heard. Portsmouth won the match 2-1 with Summersby and Blackburn scoring.

We then walked back to Cardiff General station and were steam-hauled on the return excursion to Portsmouth by the same two locomotives that were used on the forward journey, Nos 6953 and 73119. Steam locomotives noted on way home were Nos 1028, 2818, 3813, 5091, 5235, 6810, 6935, 6985 and 92242, and diesels Nos D1046, D3806, D3807, D6841, D7000, D7007, D7032, D7058, D7064 and D7066.

ADDITIONAL HIGHLIGHTS OF 1963

EASTLEIGH - A PHOTOGRAPHIC SESSION: FRIDAY 2 AUGUST - As conditions were ideal for photography, I

decided to visit this location in the early evening. No 'on shed' list was recorded, but here are a selection of photographs.

Below left Rebuilt 'West Country' Class 4-6-2 No 34022 *Exmoor*. The fireman is busy cleaning ash from the smokebox as a young spotter looks on.

Below Class 'B4' 0-4-0 tank No 30089 (ex-Guildford) awaits its fate. This outside-cylinder tank, with driving wheels of only 3 ft 9¾ in diameter, was an Adams LSWR design basically for dock shunting duties. Note that the connecting rods have been removed.

Withdrawn Class '0298' 2-4-0 well-tank No 30586 (ex-Wadebridge). Note that the connecting rods have also been removed from this locomotive.

Bulleid-designed 'Battle of Britain' 4-6-2 No 34084 *253 Squadron* (of Exmouth Junction) in ex-works condition, its gleaming paintwork exaggerated by the sunlight.

LEEDS, THE NORTH WEST AND NORTH WALES: SATURDAY 27 JULY TO SUNDAY 4 AUGUST - A HECTIC TIMETABLE!

As highlighted in previous years, some railway trips in which I unfortunately did not participate proved to be quite interesting. This particular trip, undertaken by my two close friends David Copus and Frank Allen, was one such adventure.

I have included just *three* days of this nine-day trip purely to show the hectic timetables that young train-spotters of those days set themselves in order to visit, photograph and make notes of as many locomotives and to visit as many depots as possible within 24 hours.

The twilight of BR steam was now fast approaching and my two friends decided to purchase a seven-day Freedom of Wales Railrover ticket, giving unlimited travel on BR anywhere in Wales on the LMR and Western Regions. It was a 2nd Class ticket costing £5 5s, and they paid additional fares to travel to other areas on Saturday 27 and Sunday 28 July. The photographs are by David Copus.

All but one of the actual lists of engine numbers have been omitted, but the total numbers of locomotives 'on shed' are shown for each depot visited.

This, then, was the hectic timetable for just three of the nine days:

SATURDAY 27 JULY

The day started off at Fratton station at 7 am by catching an electric unit train to London (Waterloo), where a tube train was taken to King's Cross. Departure from King's Cross was at 9.20 am on the 'White Rose', arriving at Wakefield Westgate at 12.35 pm. 35 steam and 50 diesels were noted 'on line'.

WAKEFIELD DEPOT (56A) - 'On shed' were 75 steam and two diesels. Depart Wakefield Kirkgate 1.53 pm, arrive Normanton 2.00 pm.

NORMANTON DEPOT (55E) - 'On shed' were 19 steam and one diesel. Depart Normanton 2.44 pm, arrive Mirfield 3.04 pm. 'On line': six steam and eight diesels.

MIRFIELD DEPOT (56D) - 'On shed' were 18 steam and two diesels. Depart Mirfield 3.41 pm, arrive Huddersfield 3.49 pm.

HUDDERSFIELD DEPOT (55G) - 'On shed' were 23 steam and three diesels. Depart Huddersfield 5.18 pm, arrive Sowerby Bridge 5.56 pm.

SOWERBY BRIDGE DEPOT (56E) - 'On shed' were 13 steam and one diesel. Depart Sowerby Bridge 6.29 pm, arrive Halifax 6.35 pm. Bus to Low Moor.

LOW MOOR DEPOT (56F) - 'On shed' were 27 steam and no diesels. Depart Low Moor 7.56 pm, arrive Bradford Exchange 8.03 pm. Bus to Bradford.

BRADFORD (MANNINGHAM) DEPOT (55F) - 'On shed' were 14 steam and two diesels. Bus to Bradford (Hammerton Street).

BRADFORD (HAMMERTON STREET) DEPOT (56G) - 'On shed' were five diesels and no steam. Depart Bradford Forster Square 9.40 pm, arrive Shipley 9.45 pm, depart Shipley 9.47 pm, arrive Leeds City 10.10 pm. Sleep on station platform and in waiting room.

SUNDAY 28 JULY

A combination of buses and taxis were used to visit six locomotive depots in and around Leeds. An 8 am start was made.

LEEDS (HOLBECK) DEPOT (55A) - 'On shed' were 29 steam and 21 diesels.

COPLEY HILL DEPOT (56C) - 'On shed' were 12 steam and no diesels.

FARNLEY DEPOT (55C) - 'On shed' were 39 steam and three diesels.

STOURTON DEPOT (55E) - 'On shed' were 24 steam and six diesels.

No 3442 *The Great Marquess* (BR No 61994) at Neville Hill was the preserved Class 'K1' 2-6-0 of Gresley design, introduced in 1937

Farnley depot: 'Jubilee' Class 4-6-0 No 45695 *Minotaur* at its home depot in excellent condition.

Leeds (Neville Hill) depot: Eastern Region Class 'A3' 4-6-2 No 60084 *Trigo* simmers in the depot yard. Of note is the ornate water tower with clocks on two sides - as can be seen, this photograph was taken at 11.53 am.

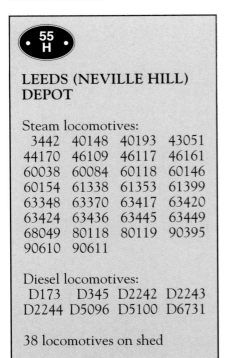

55 H

LEEDS (NEVILLE HILL) DEPOT

Steam locomotives:
3442	40148	40193	43051
44170	46109	46117	46161
60038	60084	60118	60146
60154	61338	61353	61399
63348	63370	63417	63420
63424	63436	63445	63449
68049	80118	80119	90395
90610	90611		

Diesel locomotives:
D173	D345	D2242	D2243
D2244	D5096	D5100	D6731

38 locomotives on shed

especially for use on the West Highland line in Scotland. It was in LNER livery and was undergoing some minor repairs.

ARDSLEY DEPOT (56B) - 'On shed' were 59 steam and three diesels.

Returning to Leeds City station they caught the 4.50 pm train to Manchester Exchange, travelling via Huddersfield. 'On line' were 20 steam, eight diesels and two electrics. Arrive Manchester Exchange 7.21 pm, then by taxi to:

HEATON MERSEY DEPOT (9F) - 'On shed' were 32 steam and two diesels.

STOCKPORT (EDGELEY) DEPOT (9B) - 'On shed' were 26 steam and two diesels. Depart Stockport 10.45 pm, arrive Crewe 11.25 pm. 10-minute rest in waiting room.

MONDAY 29 JULY
CREWE SOUTH DEPOT (5B) was visited shortly after midnight! 'On shed' were 97 steam and five diesels.

Visits to both Crewe North (5A) and Gresty Lane (sub-depot of Crewe South) were originally planned, but time did not allow it. Depart Crewe 2.29 am, arrive Holyhead 6.10 am. 'On line': ten steam and two diesels.

HOLYHEAD DEPOT (6J) - 'On shed' were 20 steam and one diesel. Depart Holyhead 7.05 am, arrive Bangor 7.59 am.

BANGOR DEPOT (6H) - 'On shed' were 25 steam and no diesels. Depart Bangor 9.25 am, arrive Llandudno Junction 9.59 am.

LLANDUDNO JUNCTION DEPOT (6G) - 'On shed' were 27 steam and no diesels. Depart Llandudno Junction 11.30 am, arrive Chester General 1.06 pm. 'On line': 18 steam and three diesels. Taxi for 19-mile round journey to:

MOLD JUNCTION DEPOT (6B) - 'On shed' were 21 steam and one diesel. Also planned, but time did not permit, was a visit to Chester (Midland) depot (6A). Depart Chester General 3.25 pm, arrive Wrexham General 3.46 pm. 'On line': 11 steam and three diesels.

CROES NEWYDD DEPOT (89B) - 'On shed' were 17 steam and no diesels. Depart Wrexham General 5.32 pm, arrive Gobowen 5.58 pm and change. Depart 6.05 pm, arrive Oswestry 6.13 pm. 'On line': 11 steam and no diesels. Only 52 minutes had been allowed to visit both the depot and the Works, the latter being separate from the depot. Entry in engine number notebook: 'DO THESE TWO WITH GROSS SPEED'!

OSWESTRY DEPOT (89D) - 'On shed' were 22 steam and no diesels.

OSWESTRY WORKS - 'In works' were two steam only. Depart Oswestry 7.05 pm, arrive Gobowen 7.13 pm and change. Depart 7.19 pm, arrive Shrewsbury 7.45 pm. SHREWSBURY DEPOT (89A) - 'On shed' were 56 steam and four diesels. Night was spent on Shrewsbury station.

When one reflects back on such a hectic timetable, it seems impossible, compared to today's travelling experiences on BR, that these kinds of timings could be kept. In fact, in the early 1960s we very rarely encountered late or cancelled trains, and on the odd occasion that we did, a taxi or a bus was always at hand.

THE PORTSMOUTH AREA DURING 1963

'MERCHANT NAVY' 4-6-2s IN PORTSMOUTH - Rare visiting steam locomotives to Portsmouth during the summer months were two Bulleid 'Pacifics', rebuilt 'Merchant Navy' Nos 35011 *General Steam Navigation* and 35022 *Holland-America Line*, both being employed on excursions originating from the Midlands via London. Another of the same class, No 35026 *Lamport & Holt Line*, appeared in Portsmouth with a van train.

BASIL BATTEN'S NOTINGS -

Living in close proximity to the triangle of tracks north of Portsmouth, Mr Batten, a local railway enthusiast of long-standing reliability, had over a period of years noted some unusual steam locomotive classes at this location. His personal favourite Class was the Stanier 'Black Five' 4-6-0, and the following were some of his notings of this class:
No 44768 - Sunday excursion
No 44770 - Air Force troop train
No 44909 - Sunday excursion
No 45046 - SO Leeds-Portsmouth Harbour
No 45246 - Early morning newspaper train
Other steam locomotives of note recorded were 'Britannia' Class 4-6-2 No 70017 *Arrow* and Class '9F' 2-10-0s Nos 92004 and 92206. Class '8F' 2-8-0s also appeared from time to time.

FIVE SHILLINGS TO SEE THE BEATLES!

An up and coming Liverpool pop group was seen at the Savoy Ballroom on Sunday 7 April, namely The Beatles. This Sunday Club could be joined for the fee of 1 shilling, and we enjoyed many rock 'n' roll dances in the company of such groups as The Nashville Teens and Nero and the Gladiators. Admission, if I remember rightly, was 5 shillings. Our chance to see The Beatles was just prior to them becoming famous and hitting the big time. The man responsible for that and other 'big name' bookings at the Savoy Ballroom at that time was the manager, Mr George Turner.

LAST DAY FOR TROLLEY-BUSES

Some of my fondest memories of Portsmouth City Transport derive from travelling on their pollution-free trolleybuses. We often used them to get to Portsmouth Town or Harbour stations from Fratton Bridge at the start of a railway trip. Sadly, Saturday 27 July 1963 was the last day of trolleybus operation in the city, after a reign of nearly 30 years.

AN ENGINEMAN'S 'TURN'

Some of my train-spotting friends, including Frank Allen, Doug Willis and Dave Pallett, had at one time worked for British Railways and were actively involved in footplate work on both steam and diesel locomotives and depot duties at this date. The following 'turns' in which Doug Willis was involved, based at Eastleigh depot (71A), are taken from his records of 1963 and they show some typical workings and duties:

Passenger to Canute Road Box (Southampton Terminus) and relieve Nine Elms goods. Work into Docks and leave train. 'Light' to locomotive depot and dispose. SR Class 'U', SR Class 'LN', BR Standard Class '5'.

Prepare engine and shunting in new loco works. Relieved in loco works. SR Class '700', BR 0-6-0 diesel shunter.

Passenger to Romsey and relieve. Work goods train to Southampton Old Docks and leave train. Work parcel van train to Eastleigh yard. 'Light' to depot and dispose. SR Class 'U' 31809, BR Standard Class '5' 73043.

Passenger to Northam Yard and relieve. Work petrol wagon train to Fawley. Shunt passenger to Eastleigh. Type '3' Bo-Bo diesel.

Passenger to Bournemouth Central. Walk to depot. Requirements on engine. 'Light' to Eastleigh depot and dispose. BR Standard Class '5' 73002. (Speed at one point about 96 to 100 mph!)

Prepare engine. Work parcel van train to Southampton Terminus. 'Light' to Eastleigh yard. Work goods train to Basingstoke. Relieved in station. Work parcels van train to Eastleigh yard. 'Light' to depot and dispose. SR Class 'S15' 30515 (to Basingstoke) and 34104 *Bere Alston* (return).

Engine prepared. Work ballast train to Alresford and back to Eastleigh yard when job finished. 'Light' engine to depot and dispose. BR Standard Class '4' 76XXX.

Prepare engine. Work parcels van train to Southampton Terminus. Work stopping passenger train to Bournemouth Central. Leave train. 'Light' engine round Branksome triangle and turn. Take water in Branksome depot. 'Light' to Bournemouth West. Work stopping passenger over Bournemouth old road (via Poole, Ringwood and Wimborne) to Brockenhurst. 'Light' to depot and relieved. BR Standard Class '4' 76029.

Work cement train to Poole after relieving men in up yard (dump). 'Light' engine from Poole to Bournemouth depot. Turn engine. 'Light' to Eastleigh depot and dispose. SR Class 'WC' 34105 *Swanage*.

Doug Willis recalls:

It's the unexpected that turns a routine day's events into something to be remembered, even for the strangest reasons - and so it was with one particular late 'turn' one chilly winter afternoon in 1963.

I was rostered on a rather unexciting shunting duty into Southampton Docks; the steam locomotive was LMS Class '2' 2-6-2 tank No 41319. The cab was enclosed, so it wouldn't be draughty travelling bunker-first. We left Eastleigh shed in the gathering dusk, southbound, for calls at both Bevios Park and Northam (two marshalling yards on the approaches to Southampton); this was followed by a run into the Terminus yard, then across Canute Road into the Old Docks.

It was here, during a welcome break for a cup of tea and a sandwich, that a figure appeared in the orange pool of light below the footplate thrown from the open firebox door.

'D'yer want any bananas, mates?' My driver and I both said we would. 'Run forward to the other shunter' came the order from beneath a peaked cap and deep within a muffler. The engine came to a standstill alongside a tarpaulin-covered wagon; the cover was thrown back to reveal not just hands, but fists and arms of bananas!

'They're gonna be dumped 'cause they're too ripe,' said the muffler. 'Take some for the lads back at the depot.'

Across they came, bunch after bunch after bunch, great big stalks full of tropical yellow fruits, all over the footplate, under the seats,

in the lamp lockers and finally into the bunker!

The run back to Eastleigh shed was quite incredible - we needed to be constantly ducking and climbing to avoid the mountain of fruit! On our arrival back at Eastleigh shed, many willing hands soon moved the bunches of bananas to car boots, cycle pannier bags and carrier bags.

I had to return home to Portsmouth as a passenger on a train with a bag of about a dozen bananas; this, with my other items, was as much as I could carry without looking too much like a greengrocer! Needless to say, my 'afters' and sandwiches for the next several days consisted of bananas!

HAYLING ISLAND 'FINALE': SATURDAY 2 AND SUNDAY 3 NOVEMBER

The final day of public operation between Havant and Hayling Island was Saturday 2 November, when Class 'A1X' 0-6-0 tanks Nos 32650, 32662 and 32670 all worked the line.

On Sunday the Locomotive Club of Great Britain ran a special train, 'The Hayling Farewell Railtour'. It started off from Waterloo steam-hauled by Class 'S15' 4-6-0 No 30512 and travelled via the 'Watercress Line' and Fareham to Fratton. There it was taken over by Class 'U' 2-6-0 No 31791, which, after a visit to the Portsmouth Dockyard branch, was coupled to 'Battle of Britain' 4-6-2 No 34088 *213 Squadron*; they then hauled the special train to Havant. Changing trains here on to the five-coach special, the passengers made their final trip into Hayling headed by No 32636 with No 32670 at the rear.

The train then returned to Havant and, disembarking their passengers there, the two 'Terrier' tanks

Class 'A1X' 0-6-0 tank No 32636, with LCGB headboard, is seen crossing Langstone Bridge viaduct, the five coach train being assisted at the rear by another 'A1X', No 32670. *A. D. Davies*

forming presumably the very last Class 'A1X'-hauled train to perform a run along a current main line. Meanwhile, the LCGB passengers headed back to London (Victoria) steam-hauled by two Maunsell-designed Class 'Q' 0-6-0s, Nos 30531 and 30543. Thus ended a much-loved local branch line.

In later years attempts had been made to run an ex-Blackpool tram-car (No 11), purchased by the Hayling Light Railway Society, but unfortunately it stood in the up siding of Havant station yard until the late 1960s when it was removed - all the suggestions and ideas that had been put forward came to nothing.

One of the main factors for the closure was said to be the replacement of the ageing wooden viaduct that linked Hayling Island with the mainland. The estimated cost of its replacement or extensive repair stood at £400,000, and this amount was obviously not forthcoming. A proposed bypass and lack of passengers in the winter months also contributed to its closure.

Ticket 54418 was one of those issued on the final day of public operation, Saturday 2 November 1963.

1964

STOKE FOOTBALL EXCURSION

SATURDAY 4 JANUARY

I was accompanied on this Football Excursion by David Copus and Frank Allen; the latter resided at this date at Jessie Road, Southsea. A Refreshment Car was included, and the return fare was 37/6d. It was an 8 am departure from Portsmouth Harbour station, and we were steam-hauled to Basingstoke by 'West Country' Class 4-6-2 No 34037 *Clovelly*. At Basingstoke 'Modified Hall' 4-6-0 No 7920 *Coney Hall* took over the train. We noted 24 steam between Reading West and Banbury; of note was 'Britannia' 4-6-2 No 70030 *William Wordsworth*, an ex-March (31B) engine, near Leamington Spa. *Coney Hall* was taken off at

BETWEEN LEAMINGTON SPA AND STOKE

Steam locomotives:
41231 41272 45001 45089
45181 45257 45599 45627
46430 47478 47485 48054
48101 48154 48264 70044
70049 75014 75030 75056
76044 92249

Diesel locomotives:
D221 D236 D373 D2508
D3054 D3107 D3108 D3109
D3112 D4144

Leamington Spa and replaced by 'Black Five' 4-6-0 No 45392 (1H), which took us through to Stoke.

The excursion arrived at Stoke at 1.20 pm. Stoke-on-Trent, to give it its full name, is the centre of the pottery industry in England. At the date of this visit the industry had declined somewhat, but in its hey-day the smoke drifting from its many kilns made Stoke a very dirty city.

It was a very foggy afternoon, and David and I set off for the depot not realising that Frank was still at the station. We expected him to catch us up at the depot or the football ground, but we did not see him until after the game! He told us later that he stopped for some food and then went to the engine shed and the football match.

STOKE DEPOT (5D)

The depot was set in an industrial area at the junction of the Stafford and Uttoxeter lines, some distance south of Stoke railway station. It was very grimy and run-down, consisting of two separate buildings, one of which was, due to the ravages of time, an 'open top' roundhouse! We did not have a permit for our visit, but David Copus did look out a previous Stoke permit, which we took with us, duly amended to be dated 4 January 1964! Fortunately, we completed the shed visit without being questioned.

We noted 50 steam 'on shed'. Steam classes were varied and included no fewer than 11 'Black Five' 4-6-0s, and three Ivatt Class '4' 2-6-0s, Nos 43003, 43019 and 43113, these having been introduced as late as 1947. An eerie sight was the movement of 'Jinty' tanks Nos 47628 and 47664, slowly

making their way through the yard amidst the fog; we certainly had to be 'on our toes' to ensure a safe visit. Others of the same class were Nos 47587, 47596 and 47609.

A sprinkling of 'Standards' included Nos 75018, 75056, 76022, 76023, 76051, 78017 and 78056. From my notes at least eight engines were 'stored' with tarpaulins over their chimneys; these included Nos 44354 and 44499 (both Class '4F' 0-6-0s) and 'Black Five' 4-6-0 No 45446.

Leaving the depot, we caught a bus to the Victoria Ground to see the Stoke City v Portsmouth FA Cup Third Round match, arriving just prior to the kick-off. The Portsmouth team was Armstrong; Gunter, Lunniss; Campbell R., Dickinson, Lewis; McClelland, Gordon, Saunders, Harris, H., and Lill.

Portsmouth lost 4-1. It was noted from the programme, which cost 6d, that a packet of 20 Park Drive cigarettes at this date would cost you just 3/5d.

The return football excursion departed from Stoke at 5.30 pm - despite the result, the 'Pompey' supporters were still in good voice. We arrived home at Fratton at 10.50 pm, the excursion having been very well patronised.

BETWEEN STOKE AND READING

Steam locomotives:
5971 7340 7920 44068
48623 75063 92245

Diesel locomotives:
D3958 D7048 D7059

SWINDON AND EASTLEIGH

SUNDAY 26 JANUARY

This was a trip by car in the company of Eddie Rooke, David Copus and Trevor Robson. At Swindon station, in the depot and 'on line', notable sightings were Nos 1006, 1664, 2291, 3808, 4507, 4996, 5017, 5815, 6106, 7826, 48650 and 73023; diesels noted included Nos D1018, D2194, D3003, 15100 and D7069.

We next travelled south to Eastleigh (71A) where we noted 33 steam and four diesels before being ejected by the shed foreman! One tank of particular note was Wainwright-designed Class 'H' 0-4-4 No 31543, ex-Tunbridge Wells West (75F), which had found its way to Eastleigh for scrapping.

SWINDON WORKS, WORKS YARD AND SCRAPYARD

Steam locomotives:

1440	2818	3653	3665	3668	3733	4111	4644	4690	4987	5202	5261	5645
5691	5570	5573	5787	5922	6000	6010	6025	6151	6163	6350	6674	6816
6848	6849	6850	6854	6859	6976	8106	8425	8464	8738	9422	9425	9429
9600	9645	9677	9791	42954	42983	43002	43044	44411	73053	73093	76037	76041
76075	76076	76081	92220	92232	92250							

Diesel locomotives:

D809	D811	D812	D817	D821	D823	D827	D843	D845	D1000	D1013	D1014	D1027
D1028	D1029	D1036	D1040	D1056	D1069						

FRATTON DEPOT - A LOCOMOTIVE STORE

SUNDAY 8 MARCH

Fratton's former code of 70F had now been deleted, and it was officially a 'closed depot'. I was accompanied on this visit by David Copus and Frank Allen.

Never before had there been noted so many unusual classes of steam locomotives at Fratton depot! It had become a 'storage location' for redundant locomotives, both in the yard and inside the depot building. The Class '0298' 2-4-0 well-tanks usually ventured as far east as Eastleigh, but only when visiting the works. The 'Z' Class, like the '0298', was probably also making its first ever visit to Fratton. The majority, if

FRATTON DEPOT

Steam locomotives:

30120	30245	30538	30587
30777	30850	30925	30926
30952	31618	31625	31638
31806	31819	33022	33034
34076	73114	75067	75074
76011	76069		

Diesel locomotives:
D3010 D3046

24 locomotives on shed

Nos 30120 to 33034 were all 'stored'. Some were awaiting preservation, while others were less fortunate and awaited being towed to the breaker's yard.

not all, of this Class of eight were allocated to Exmouth Junction, where their main duty was 'banking' between Exeter St David's and Central stations up the very steep incline, which also passed through a tunnel.

BRIEF NOTES ON THE 'STORED' LOCOMOTIVES -
30120: Class 'T9' 4-4-0. Introduced 1899. Drummond LSWR design. Allocation: Eastleigh. **30245:** Class 'M7' 0-4-4 tank. Introduced 1897. Drummond LSWR design. Allocation: Nine Elms. **30538:** Class 'Q' 0-6-0. Introduced 1938. Maunsell design. Allocation: Norwood Junction. **30587:** Class '0298' 2-4-0 well-tank. Introduced 1874. Beattie LSWR design. Allocation: Wadebridge. **30777:** Class 'N15' ('King Arthur') 4-6-0. Introduced 1925. Urie LSWR design. Named *Sir Lamiel*. Allocation: Basingstoke. **30850:** 'Lord Nelson' Class 4-6-0. Introduced 1926. Maunsell design. Named *Lord Nelson*. Allocation: Eastleigh. **30925** and **30926:** Class 'V' ('Schools') 4-4-0s. Introduced 1930. Maunsell design. Named *Cheltenham* and *Repton* respectively. Allocation: Bricklayers Arms (both). **30952:** Class 'Z' 0-8-0 heavy tank.

Introduced 1929. Maunsell design. Allocation: Exmouth Junction. **31618, 31625, 31638** and **31806**: Class 'U' 2-6-0s. Introduced 1928. No 31806 rebuild of Maunsell Class 'K' ('River') 2-6-4 tank, introduced 1917. Nos 31618, 31625 and 31638 had detail differences from 31806. Allocations: Eastleigh, Guildford, Basingstoke and Fratton. **31819:** Class 'N' 2-6-0. Introduced 1917. Maunsell SECR design. Allocation: Dover. **33022** and **33034**: Class 'Q1' 0-6-0s. Introduced 1942. Bulleid design. Allocations: Guildford and Tonbridge. All the name-plates on the 'King Arthur', 'Lord Nelson' and 'Schools' loco-motives had been removed, obviously for 'safe keeping'.

EASTLEIGH

SUNDAY 18 OCTOBER

BULLEIDS GALORE!

EASTLEIGH DEPOT

34001	34019	34021	34022
34023	34028	34033	34034
34038	34047	34050	34053
34061	34065	34067	34072
34073	34077	34082	34090
34093	34095	34098	34102
34105	35006	35010	35016
35022			

Total 29 Bulleid 'Pacifics'

'Dead' Class 'Z' 0-8-0 heavy tank No 30952, awaiting its final few weeks before being cut up. It had previously been 'in store' at Fratton shed. Behind it is 'West Country' Class 4-6-2 No 34105 *Swanage*.

I travelled in the company of Eddie Rooke and David Copus to visit the depot (71A). In the works yard we noted steam locomotives Nos 34086, 92045 and 92150.

Although we recorded 83 steam 'on shed' on this visit, together with numerous diesels, the accompanying list of numbers highlights solely the Bulleid-designed 'Pacifics' of the 'West Country', 'Battle of Britain' and 'Merchant Navy' Classes.

EAST ANGLIAN DRUBBING!

SATURDAY 7 NOVEMBER

I travelled on this excursion train to Ipswich with David Copus, Roger Emptage, Pete Walsh and Jim Davidson. Our departure from Portsmouth Harbour station was at 9.20 am, and the fare was 27/6d.

Football result: Ipswich Town 7 Portsmouth 0!

It is of note that during our many

LIVERPOOL STREET AND AREA

Diesel locomotives:
D2550 D2551 D2552 D2905
D3298 D5044 D5524 D5566
D5591 D5800 D6703 D6704
D6705 D6714 D6717 D6724
D8212 D8234

Electric unit numbers noted on the Liverpool Street to Shenfield route were: 15, 18, 35, 55, 59, 62, 70, 73 and 86.

IPSWICH AREA

Diesel locomotives:
D202 D2049 D2556 D3680
D5040 D5049 D5520 D5623
D8214 D8226 D8241

travels to see 'Pompey', which nearly always incorporated visits to railway installations, our team did not seem to fare too well, as you can see from this score-line. If you think that this was a 'one-off', you're wrong! I recall a particular away match, Portsmouth's last of the 1962/63 season, when David Copus and I decided at the last minute to travel by rail (not an excursion) to Chelsea for an evening kick-off. We encountered a late arrival at Waterloo, a hold-up on the underground train which was packed tight with football fans, and long queues to get into Stamford Bridge. When we eventually got to the terraces about 15 minutes into the game, we asked some Chelsea fans the score. They smiled and said 'We're 2-0 up'. It went from bad to worse, and 'Pompey' went down again by 7-0! If I remember rightly, the crowd on that night was in excess of 50,000!

We then had to endure the company of jubilant Chelsea fans on the tube train, and we were glad to reach the comparative quietness of Waterloo station and board the electric unit train for Portsmouth. It certainly was a match to forget!

ADDITIONAL HIGHLIGHTS OF 1964

'ON THE ROAD' - A CAR JOURNEY OF NOTE

By 1964 rail fares had begun to increase and many local train-spotters turned to the road as an alternative method of visiting railway depots. One such trip in Eddie Rooke's pale blue Ford Popular car with Tony Ingram and Timothy Julnes covered no fewer than 1,469 miles! The itinerary was as follows:

Day 1
Portsmouth to Westbury
WESTBURY DEPOT - 31 steam, three diesels.
BATH (GREEN PARK) DEPOT - 22 steam.
LYDNEY DEPOT - empty.
NEWPORT (PILL) DEPOT - 14 diesels.
BARRY DOCKS - 35 steam.

Day 2
BARRY DEPOT - 11 steam, six diesels.
BARRY WORKS AND YARD - 38 steam.
DUFFRYN YARD DEPOT - empty.
NEATH DEPOT - 56 steam, three diesels.

ABERYSTWYTH (V of R) DEPOT - three steam.
ABERYSTWYTH DEPOT (WR) - eight steam.
MACHYNLLETH DEPOT - 12 steam.
OSWESTRY DEPOT - 20 steam.

Day 3
BIRKENHEAD DEPOT - 35 steam, five diesels.
BLACKPOOL DEPOT - 25 steam.
FLEETWOOD DEPOT - 20 steam, one diesel.
LOWER DARWEN DEPOT - 20 steam.
ROSE GROVE DEPOT - 27 steam.

Day 4
SKIPTON DEPOT - 14 steam, one diesel.
SUNDERLAND DEPOT - 23 steam, one diesel.
Stop at Fence Houses (friends).

Day 5
TEBAY DEPOT - nine steam, one diesel.
CARNFORTH DEPOT - 36 steam, two diesels.
LANCASTER DEPOT - 13 steam
LOSTOCK HALL DEPOT - 31 steam, one diesel

UTTOXETER STATION - one diesel.
UTTOXETER DEPOT - four steam.
BURTON DEPOT - 35 steam, five diesels.
COALVILLE DEPOT - 20 steam.
COALVILLE STATION - one steam.

Day 6
NORWICH THORPE DEPOT - three steam (departmental), 14 diesels.
YARMOUTH (VAUXHALL) STATION - three diesels.
SLOUGH DEPOT - two diesels, six DMUs.

An interesting table of mileages and petrol used on this trip is as follows:

Day	Petrol 'in'	Mileage
1	7 gallons	243
2	7 gallons	226
3	6 gallons	176
4	7 gallons	213
5	8 gallons	252
6	8 gallons	359
	Total mileage	1,469

THE PORTSMOUTH AREA DURING 1964

COSHAM STATION - Opened in 1848, it was enlarged in 1890; the direct Cosham-Havant service began in 1860. The station has two platforms connected by a footbridge bearing a plaque stating

'JOSEPH WESTWOOD & Co ENGINEERS LONDON 1890'. It is 5½ miles to Portsmouth Harbour and 20 to Southampton.

The cottages became uninhabited about 1985 and were finally demolished to make way for an office block in the early 1990s. The coal office was also demolished. The station was transformed in 1990 to coincide with the introduction of third-rail electric trains.

MARCH & APRIL: FINAL 'SPOTTINGS' OF SR 2-6-0s AT COSHAM

During these two months diesel locomotives were seen towing redundant steam engines to the breakers yards. D6528 was noted towing Class 'U' 2-6-0 No 31807 and Class 'N' 2-6-0 No 31829; D6532 towing Class 'U' 2-6-0s Nos 31626 and 31629; and D6545 towing Class 'N' 2-6-0s Nos 31830 and 31832.

FRATTON

Steam-hauled trains still operated between Portsmouth and Plymouth and Cardiff, these being the main daily cross-country workings. The engines did not use the turntable in the former depot, but ran round the Fratton triangle. 18 OCTOBER - A Sunday visit to the depot was made in the company of Eddie Rooke and David Copus. We met up there with Mr Ernie Middleton's Railway Enthusiast's Club from the North London area. We had a short conversation with him, giving him information on steam engines that were allocated to Fratton, and he seemed very interested, making some brief notes in his book. I recalled to Ernie that I and several friends from Portsmouth had travelled on a coach trip from London to Doncaster in the summer of 1958; he remembered me and asked if any of us were still interested in any trips to depots or works. All of his trips were by coach. It was a pleasant surprise to meet him so unexpectedly at my 'local' after not seeing him for six years.

Class 'M7' 0-4-4 tank No 30133

FRATTON DEPOT

Steam locomotives:
30133 30838 30926 33004
34004 34018 34037 35007
80010 80082

10 locomotives on shed

Sunday 18 October: A 'Merchant Navy' at Fratton. Eddie Rooke and I had visited Eastleigh depot earlier in the day and returned to Fratton for a depot visit. I was quite surprised to note rebuilt 4-6-2 No 35007 *Aberdeen Commonwealth* in the yard. It was in ex-works condition and being 'run in' prior to returning to its main-line duties. At this date its depot of allocation was Weymouth (70G).

was the only SR tank locomotive 'on shed'; it had previously been stored at Eastleigh depot yard, awaiting disposal, but it found its way to Fratton. It was rumoured at this date that its boiler may be used on Highland 4-4-0 *Ben Alder*, of the 'Small Ben' Class, No 2 which became ex-BR No 54398.

A (T)RAIN JOURNEY TO FORGET!

'Jim' Jackson, secretary of the South Hants group of the Ian Allan Locospotters Club, of which I was a member, organised numerous successful visits to locomotive depots all over Great Britain in the 1950s and '60s. However, he recalls that 'not all visits went as planned' - one such trip in 1964 falls into this category. Jim explains the details:

I had arranged for a party of about 20 teenagers from the Portsmouth and Southampton areas to visit engine sheds in Cardiff. It was a Sunday excursion and all train times, child fares and shed permits had been arranged beforehand and it promised to be just another trip.

The train started off in pouring rain and picked up its party via Fareham and Southampton Central, where I joined the train. Needless to say, everyone started off the day with a drenching! The excursion, which was steam-hauled, encountered severe flooding near Kimbridge Junction and near Dean station between Romsey and Salisbury, which obviously held up our progress. We learned that the track was liable to subsidence in these areas and speed was reduced to walking pace for a considerable number of miles. When eventually we were clear of the flooded areas, the train continued on its way, but it had cost us about 2 hours extra journey time.

The pouring rain followed us all the way to Cardiff and it never looked like clearing up. There were several more minor hold-ups before we arrived at Cardiff General station, and it was realised that we would not have time to visit the three or four depots intended; only Canton, the nearest to the station, would be possible if we were to return to the waiting excursion in the time allotted.

The dashing party of 20 trainspotters then got their second drenching of the day as they made their way to the depot. It was visited at great speed and there was no time for formalities such as handing the permit to the shed foreman or even informing anyone that our party had arrived! Anyway, we completed our visit without being questioned and once again made the dash through the rain back to the station to find our 'Hall' Class 4-6-0 locomotive waiting departure for Portsmouth.

According to the excursion leaflet we now had about 10 minutes' wait before the train departed, so we spent this removing our soaking wet plastic macs, shoes, socks and whatever we could to enable them to dry out.

We thought that we had experi-

Derailment at Fratton West: the actual date of this mishap is unknown, but it was during 1964. This is the scene looking towards Fratton station. Note the destination nameboard on the carriage: 'PORTSMOUTH SOUTHAMPTON BRISTOL NEWPORT CARDIFF'. The derailment happened as a set of maroon-liveried carriages were being reversed towards Fratton sidings. A Standard Class '4' 2-6-0 can just be seen above the carriage, while in the background a green-liveried 4-COR electric unit or 'Nelson' passes through platform 1 on a Portsmouth Harbour to Waterloo train. Also of note is the complete station footbridge, this being the gathering point of many local train-spotters. Note also the tall signal located at the southern end of platform 2. *David Copus*

enced some bad luck on the forward journey with the hold-ups caused by flooding, but we now had a further annoying wait of nearly 50 minutes in Cardiff General station - we were told that our locomotive had 'failed' and that the problem was being attended to! This just about capped it all, and by now I and the travelling party were all cursing the bad luck that had dogged us right from the start of their journey.

When the train eventually did get started it was a trouble-free run to Salisbury, where a Standard Class '4' took over from the 'Hall' on the run to Portsmouth. The pouring rain had now stopped and the flooding had receded, so arrival back in Portsmouth was only about 15 minutes late.

This was a one-off experience, and the chances of it being repeated were highly unlikely. However, it was, for those who travelled on that day, a (t)rain journey to forget!

STEAM LOCOMOTIVES OF NOTE IN THE PORTSMOUTH AREA - Of
particular note during the summer months was the appearance of BR's very last steam locomotive, No 92220 *Evening Star*, built at Swindon Works. It worked 'light' from Eastleigh to Three Bridges, passing through Fareham, Cosham and Havant via the north side of the Portsmouth triangle. Although not mentioned in earlier pages, the green-liveried *Evening Star* actually worked into Portsmouth in July 1961 with a passenger train from Cardiff General.

A most unusual visiting steam engine was Stanier Class '8F' 2-8-0 No 48408 of Bletchley shed, which had found its way into Portsmouth with a parcels train from Waterloo, travelling via Woking, Basingstoke and Eastleigh. It terminated at platform 1 of Portsmouth & Southsea Low Level.

On 6 December 'Britannia' Class 4-6-2 No 70004 *William Shakespeare* visited Portsmouth with a 'special'.

TRIALS ON THE DOCKYARD BRANCH - A Sunday was selected
for steam locomotive trials on the single-track Portsmouth Royal Naval Dockyard branch line. Retired Portsmouth railwayman John Scutt tells me that two steam locomotives were involved, a 'West Country' Class 4-6-2 and a 'Battle of Britain' 4-6-2 - both main-line types - and they were double-heading two Pullman carriages, possibly originating from Southampton Docks, into Portsmouth Dockyard.

Their route was as the usual daily freight trains from Fratton - via the up line of Portsmouth & Southsea (High Level) station, then crossing both Edinburgh and Alfred Road crossings and into the Dockyard marshalling yard. The guard on this train was Fratton-based Jimmy Stallard.

These workings were most likely 'weight' trials, as normally the only types of engines allowed on this line were small side tanks, sometimes a Class 'U' or 'N' 2-6-0, and occasionally an 0-6-0 diesel shunter.

The two locomotives made at least two return trips with the carriages from the marshalling yards along the branch and other trips with one locomotive at the front and the other at the rear of the carriages.

There were no official reports in any railway journal on this most unusual working, and the question of whether the outcome had any significance in later years must remain unanswered, as many of the men involved in these trials are now no longer with us.

A FEW MUSICAL MEMORIES FROM '64

As already described, I and many of my close railway enthusiast friends in Portsmouth frequented the local 'music scene' and I recall some great sounds of artists and groups playing the music of the day, rock 'n' roll. However, by this date an infectious sound known as

R & B (Rhythm and Blues) was sweeping the local clubs.

One of my best memories of rock 'n' roll came with a visit to the Thorngate Halls, Gosport, to 'bop the night away' in the company of Cliff Bennett and the Rebel Rousers.

Another popular venue was Kimbell's at Southsea, which during 1964 hosted Georgie Fame and The Blue Flames for a resident spot on Sunday evenings, all for a modest entrance fee of 4 shillings.

Cinemas and theatres were also patronised, and I remember a very young-looking Hughie Green performing in the pantomime *Cinderella* at the Kings Theatre, Southsea; if I recall correctly, we purchased the cheapest seats, way up in the 'gods', for 3 shillings.

We not only supported the music scene locally, but also often travelled out of the area, and I recall seeing Chuck Berry at the Gaumont, Southampton, on Whit Monday. His supporting acts included The Animals and the popular Liverpool group The Swinging Blue Jeans. Another visit to Southampton on Friday 16 October saw Billy J. Kramer and the Dakotas top the bill. Also 'on stage' that night were The Kinks, The Yardbirds, Cliff Bennett and the Rebel Rousers and The Ronettes - some show!

One of my favourite haunts was the Railway Hotel, located just behind the blocks of railway flats overlooking Fratton station. I especially remember Thursday evenings as it was R & B and the resident group was no other than Manfred Mann, with Portsmouth's own Paul Jones as their lead singer. These live performances took place in quite a small room, and as their popularity increased, so the premises proved to be inadequate.

MEMORIES ARE MADE OF THIS . . .

To round off 1964 I have included two rather silly photographs, which serve to reflect the kind of humour shared by us local train-spotters at this date. Trains, combined with travelling, pop music, football and the local scene generally, made this an era that was 'special' - but at no time did we relent from our interest in steam engines, even when countless scrappings were taking place.

We did not capture too many pictures of steam in its twilight years, because I'm sure that we found it far too depressing.

The ultimate in road travel was this Ford Popular owned by Eddie Rooke. Photographed here are Eddie leaning on bonnet with Tony Ingram (left) and David Copus (top), at a stop on the B4265 Bridgend to Barry road during one of our many visits to Wales in the mid-1960s. When stopped by the police, asking what the 'DANGER' sign was for, Eddie replied, 'It's us that are dangerous'. They asked for it to be removed! The camping gear is packed on the roof-rack.

'PC WONDERFUL' - In the 1960s there was a very popular policeman standing on a wooden platform controlling the traffic at Fratton Bridge. He was affectionately known as 'PC Wonderful', and his non-stop arm-waving and calling to drivers to 'stop' or 'proceed' was well known all over Portsmouth - he certainly kept the traffic flowing at this very busy junction. Drivers showed their appreciation for his efforts during the festive period by pausing and putting a 'Christmas Box' at his feet! Local train-spotters would also often gaze at his antics while at the same time keeping a look-out for trains below.

'DOING A SPONICAL' - My close train-spotting friend Frank Allen admits that he invented this unusual activity. It involved pinching the nose with the left hand, tilting back the head and moving the right hand on and off the throat while saying the word 'sponical' at a very high-pitched volume! He first performed it while at a 'Pompey' home game in the late 1950s, when a section of the crowd on the terraces became restless during a particularly goal-less and inept display by the home team - this eventually resulted in a barrage of high-pitched squeaking noises included Frank 'doing a sponical' to break the boredom! Apparently it did seem to make that section of the crowd a bit happier, but unfortunately did nothing for our football team! Whenever Frank accompanied us on any railway trips a 'sponical' was always to be heard, and it did not take too long before many of my train-spotting friends began to demonstrate their own versions!

The author 'doing a sponical' at Fratton depot, demonstrating the unusual pose involved. I am standing in front of redundant Class 'U' 2-6-0 No 31638 (waiting to be towed to Barry). The rods have been removed and the words 'BOILER OUT' were chalked on its tender. *David Copus*

1965 FAREWELL TO STANDARD GAUGE STEAM IN WALES

SHAWFORD

SATURDAY 10 JULY

Shawford station, situated on the main line between Waterloo and Southampton, is roughly half-way between Winchester and Eastleigh in Hampshire. I travelled on my own and spent almost 2½ hours train-spotting from the station platforms and other points nearby. This country location on a summer's day provided an ideal escape and a pleasant change from the hubbub of nearby Eastleigh.

The main feature of Shawford station at this date was its curved roofs and wooden platforms. The main building was painted cream, while all doors, seats and signs were in SR green. Sadly, this unique station building was demolished in the early 1980s, to become just another 'ordinary' station.

I recollect that my haversack contained endless goodies, including egg sandwiches, chocolate biscuits, apples and a bottle of Tizer, and it goes without saying that I thoroughly enjoyed my lunch that day in the presence of passing steam locomotives!

In between keeping an eye open for speeding expresses, my time was spent swatting wasps and exchanging brief conversations with passengers both entering and alighting from the occasional stopping train, commenting mostly on the sunny weather, although one old lady did ask me, 'When is the next train to Micheldever?'!

I took colour photographs of Bulleid 'Pacifics' Nos 34064, 34085, 34093, 34097, 34102, 34103 and 35004, but unfortunately they were not of a quality to include here.

Other steam locomotives noted there were Nos 6937, 34017, 34076, 34082, 35027, 35028, 73113, 75019, 76005, 76031, 80015 and 80065.

TOUR OF WALES AND BLACKPOOL

SATURDAY 24 TO WEDNESDAY 28 JULY

I travelled on this trip in Eddie Rooke's car, a Ford Anglia, SOE 99. We took the jointly owned tent and sleeping bags with us, together with all equipment needed for cooking meals. This trip could be described as a 'Farewell to standard gauge steam in Wales'.

SATURDAY 24 JULY (Day 1)

Departure was at 8.45 am and the weather was dry and sunny. Barry scrapyard would be our first visit, a previous visit to this location having been made in 1962, also with the camping gear but on that occasion on Eddie's scooter. A rough timetable for our journey to Barry was Salisbury, 10.00 am; Chippenham, 11.30 am; Gloucester, 1.15 pm; and Barry at 4.00 pm (there was no Severn Bridge in those days!).

Barry Island was possibly the 'mecca' of the South Wales holiday resorts at that time, boasting a sandy beach, Butlin's Holiday Camp, an impressive fun-fair and amusement arcades. A typical summer Saturday would see 100,000 visitors, the majority arriving by rail; the locomotive depot was well spread-out to cater for additional engines. Two other features of Barry Island were the extensive dockland, once the world's greatest coal-exporting port, and Woodham Brothers' scrapyard, our first destination.

The general view was quite depressing. Many locomotives still had coal in their tenders and bunkers, and their coupling rods were intact; some even looked in very good external condition, having been polished up prior to being sent to their doom!

On leaving the scrapyard we travelled the few miles into Cardiff where we 'looked in' at Canton depot. It had been dieselised, so we decided not to make a visit. We then returned in the direction of Barry, where we located the camp site. We then motored to Barry Island where we visited the large funfair to indulge in pastimes such as pin-tables and fruit machines, then purchased bags of chips and bottles of lemonade to take back to the camp site. We then experienced an enormous downpour of rain coupled with thunder and lightning, and on returning to the camp site we found that it was waterlogged! We had no option but to sleep the night in the car.

SUNDAY 25 JULY (Day 2)

We were both awake quite early; in fact, it was 5.50 am by my

BARRY SCRAPYARD

Steam locomotives:

2807	2857	2859	2861	2873	2874	2885	3612	3814	3822	3840	3845	4076
4141	4248	4270	4277	4561	4566	4588	4930	4936	4942	4953	4979	4983
5029	5043	5051	5080	5164	5193	5199	5227	5239	5253	5504	5521	5526
5532	5538	5539	5541	5552	5553	5557	5572	5619	5637	5794	5900	5952
5967	5972	6023	6024	6619	6692	6695	6960	6989	7027	7200	7202	7220
7722	7903	9468	9629	30499	30506	30541	30825	30828	30830	30841	30847	31618
31625	31638	31806	31874	34016	34027	34028	34058	34067	34070	34072	34073	34081
34092	34095	34108	35006	35009	35018	35025	45690	45699	48431	53808	53809	92207
92245												

105 locomotives noted.

Class 'U' 2-6-0 No 31638 was an ex-Fratton allocation. Nos 53808 and 53809 were both Class '7F' 2-8-0s used on the S&D. Three unidentified locomotives were also present.

Right The depressing scene at Barry scrapyard. The town is in the right background, and the works, at this date closed, is on the left.

Below right Radyr depot: Two lines of 'stored' tanks in the yard. These included Class '5700' 0-6-0 panniers Nos 9615, 9622 and 9667. Note also the breakdown crane, probably in working order.

watch as we managed some biscuits and lemonade for our breakfasts. We wasted no time in making our way from the adjacent flooded camp site, although by now the rain had stopped. Our first depot visit was Radyr, an ex-sub-shed of Cardiff (Cathays).

Leaving the Cardiff area, we travelled west looking in at some depots on our planned route.

ABERCYNON - No steam. Ten diesels 'on shed'.
MERTHYR - No steam. Six diesels 'on shed'.
BRECON - We had difficulty in locating the depot, but after asking an elderly gentleman we found out why - the railway had closed and the shed had been demolished! We took a brief look at the site where it once stood.
ABERAYRON - The depot had closed.
ABERYSTWYTH - We did not enter the depot, as we could see from the station that it was empty.

On arrival at Aberystwyth we had a welcome hot meal and drink,

RADYR DEPOT

Steam locomotives:

1612	1655	3784	4650
5691	5692	6654	6672
9615	9622	9667	9780

12 locomotives noted

We noted eight 'dead' tanks in the yard; the others were inside the shed, only three of them in use. There were diesels 'on shed' but we did not record their numbers.

Aberystwyth: The Vale of Rheidol, BR's only steam-operated narrow gauge railway. No 8 *Llewellyn* is in the yard, while No 9 *Prince of Wales* is inside the building on the right.

followed by a visit to the Vale of Rheidol narrow gauge depot. All three of the line's engines, Nos 7, 8 and 9, were present. We then purchased return tickets for the journey to Devil's Bridge, these costing 6 shillings. This was my first visit to this line, which at this date started from its own platforms situated near the British Railways station (the trains later used the BR station). The line runs for 12 miles through some quite breath-taking scenery up the Rheidol Valley to Devil's Bridge; starting at sea level, it rises to 680 feet in a journey time of 1 hour. The maximum gradient is 1 in 50. This was British Railways' only narrow gauge steam railway.

We then continued along the coast road to Machynlleth.

MACHYNLLETH DEPOT

Steam locomotives:
7812 7819 46521 75013 80104 80105

6 locomotives on shed

Following this visit we decided to look for an official camp site; continuing along the west coast we eventually came across one at Towyn, where we parked the car and set up the tent. We fried some chips and had a drink. It did not take us long to get settled down in our sleeping bags, and for a change the weather was quite warm. We listened to the transistor radio for almost an hour before sleep overcame us. In the 1960s the 'in' radio station was to be found at '208' on the dial (Radio Luxembourg), where we could listen to all the latest sounds of rock 'n' roll.

MONDAY 26 JULY (Day 3)

We awoke at 7.30 am, cooked a small breakfast, then packed up our tent, leaving the site at 9.30 am.

I travelled on the Talyllyn narrow gauge railway from Towyn Wharf to Abergynolwyn on the first train of the day, the 10.25 am. This line, 2 ft 3 in gauge, covers some very picturesque scenery. One stop was made on the way, at Dolgoch Falls. On arrival at Abergynolwyn (11.10 am) I walked down the disused line, where I collected some ferns and viewed a waterfall. I returned to Towyn on the 11.55 am train. The return fare was 5 shillings.

It was 12.45 pm as we continued in the car. Our route was via Dolgellau, then along the A487 to Portmadoc, then the A493 coast road via Llwyngwril to Penmaenpool.

PENMAENPOOL - We found out that this depot had been long closed. It was a wooden-built, two-road dead-end shed.

We continued north through Merioneth until we came to Trawsfyndd Lake, near where we spotted a double-decker bus stored in a private yard. On closer inspection it was found to be an ex-Southdown vehicle; the words 'SOUTHDOWN' could still be seen and it retained its original green paintwork. It would be interesting if any bus enthusiast could throw any further light on the fate of this vehicle.

TRAWSFYNYDD - We were unable to trace any signs of an engine shed or railway, although we were to learn later that this one-road shed, built on the side of a goods shed, was subsequently used for agricultural purposes.

PORTMADOC - This depot, a sub-depot of Machynlleth, had been demolished.

We continued west on the A497 via Criccieth (castle viewed), then along the Lleyn Peninsula to PWLLHELI. It was late afternoon as we entered the depot, a brick-built, two-road dead-end sub-shed of Machynlleth. Three steam were 'on shed', Nos 7819 *Hinton Manor*, 75055 and 80097.

We then travelled on the A499 to Caernarvon, and in the Bangor area saw steam locomotives Nos 45184 and 75009. A brief visit was made to Bangor station, but the engine shed had closed in early 1965.

Llandudno Junction depot con-

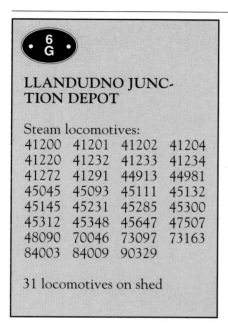

LLANDUDNO JUNCTION DEPOT

Steam locomotives:

41200	41201	41202	41204
41220	41232	41233	41234
41272	41291	44913	44981
45045	45093	45111	45132
45145	45231	45285	45300
45312	45348	45647	47507
48090	70046	73097	73163
84003	84009	90329	

31 locomotives on shed

sisted of four through roads; it was a brick-built shed and there was a turntable.

On leaving the depot we travelled along the North Wales coast on the A546 road to Colwyn Bay, then continued eastwards to an official camping site at Pen-sarn, just 4 miles west of Rhyl and very near the town of Abergele. We had a 'wash and brush up', then located a fish and chip shop, purchasing large amounts for supper. We erected the tent as darkness was falling, and it did not take us long to fall asleep.

Below Although I did not acquire this unusual platform ticket on this visit, I think it appropriate to include it as we were touring this area. In fact, this ticket was purchased on 7 August 1964 during a previous visit with Eddie Rooke. The station with the 'longest name' still survives today, albeit its name abbreviated to LLANFAIRPWLL.

TUESDAY 27 JULY
(Day 4)

We left the camp site at 7.30 am, and travelled via Rhyl, Prestatyn and Flint to Mold via the A548 and A5119. Some difficulty was experienced in locating Mold Junction locomotive depot, but after several enquiries we were told to look out for Saltney Ferry Road. It was a brick-built, eight-road, dead-end straight shed. Of the ten steam, six were Class '8F' 2-8-0 freight types; about five were 'in steam'.

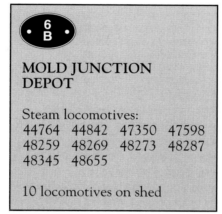

MOLD JUNCTION DEPOT

Steam locomotives:

44764	44842	47350	47598
48259	48269	48273	48287
48345	48655		

10 locomotives on shed

Above Mold Junction depot: I asked the driver of Class '8F' 2-8-0 No 48345 to stop the engine briefly for a photograph; he is seen leaning out of the cab window.

From the depot yard we could see across the main lines to Mold Marshalling Yard, which covered an enormous area; much activity was noted. Several 'Jinty' tanks, a pannier tank and 0-6-0 diesel shunter No 12020 were observed.

On leaving Mold Junction we took the Birkenhead road, travelling via Chester and Ellesmere Port. Birkenhead was a 16-road, dead-end straight shed, which we only partially visited, due to the fact that we had no permit and there were many railway staff in the vicinity. A notice at the depot entrance stated that 'GUARD DOGS PATROL THIS AREA'. It was most probably an 'all-steam' depot.

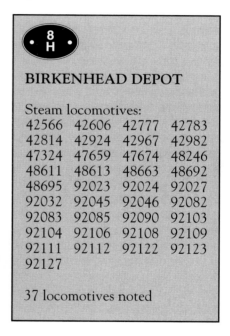

BIRKENHEAD DEPOT

Steam locomotives:

42566	42606	42777	42783
42814	42924	42967	42982
47324	47659	47674	48246
48611	48613	48663	48692
48695	92023	92024	92027
92032	92045	92046	92082
92083	92085	92090	92103
92104	92106	92108	92109
92111	92112	92122	92123
92127			

37 locomotives noted

Making a hasty departure, we then travelled via the Mersey Tunnel to Liverpool; this was the second time I had travelled through the tunnel. We continued to Blackpool, where it was pouring with rain. Luckily we located a very large camping site at a farm about 5 miles from the seaside and decided to set up camp for the night. We purchased milk and eggs at the farm together with some bread. We had already purchased

BRITISH RAILWAYS BOARD (M) BR 4405

LLANFAIRPWLLGWYNGYLLGOGERYCHWYRNDROBWLLLLANTYSILIOGOGOGOCH

B 50421

PLATFORM TICKET 3d.

AVAILABLE ONE HOUR ON DAY OF ISSUE ONLY
NOT VALID IN TRAINS, NOT TRANSFERABLE.

FOR CONDITIONS SEE OVER

B 50421

| 1 | 2 | 3 | 4 | 5 | 6 | 7 | 8 | 9 | 10 | 11 | 12 |

bacon and potatoes prior to our arrival, so we now settled down and cooked quite a substantial meal on the paraffin stove, despite the rain.

WEDNESDAY 28 JULY (Day 5)

We awoke at 7 am to find that the tent had flooded! The roof had been leaking, the sleeping bags were wet and we were very cold and damp. It was decided that we should pack all the camping gear and put it in the car boot, which we did very quickly. We didn't cook food on the stove because of the rain, which was still falling very heavily. Our breakfasts consisted of a tin of fruit and a packet of cream biscuits, which we ate sitting in the car before our departure on the long homeward journey to Portsmouth - in fact, this was an identical rain-soaked departure from the same site that we had experienced in 1962!

Leaving at 8 am we travelled via the M6 motorway, the M1 motorway, Coventry and Northampton, where we stopped for beans on toast and cups of tea. Bypassing London, we picked up the A3 road to Portsmouth.

ADDITIONAL HIGHLIGHTS OF 1965

CLAPHAM MUSEUM

MONDAY 21 MARCH

I travelled with my parents from Fratton to Waterloo via Petersfield and Guildford. The main attraction was a visit to the British Transport Museum, then at Clapham.

Steam locomotives noted between Portsmouth and Waterloo were Nos 34038, 34098, 35023, 41287, 73026, 76064, 80015, 80016, 80133 and 82019.

The reverse reads: 'We hope you have enjoyed your visit to CLAPHAM. Have you been to the other Transport Museums at YORK and SWINDON?'.

No	Name	Class or type/ wheel arrangement	Built	Previous owner
3	Coppernob	-/0-4-0	1846	Furness Railway
23	-	'A'/4-4-0	1866	Metropolitan Railway
82	Boxhill	'A'/0-6-0	1880	LBSCR
87	-	'S56'/0-6-0	1904	GER
490	-	'T26'/2-4-0	1895	GER
506	Butler-Henderson	'D11'/4-4-0	1920	GCR
563	-	'T3'/4-4-0	1893	LSWR
737	-	'D'/4-4-0	1901	SECR
790	Hardwicke	'Precedent'/2-4-0	1892	LNWR
1000	-	'4'/4-4-0	1902	MR
3020	Cornwall	-/2-2-2	1847	LNWR
4468	Mallard	'A4'/4-6-2	1938	LNER
-	Pet	18 in gauge/0-4-0	1865	LNWR
807	-	Tram loco/0-4-0	1872	Metropolitan Railway
-	Wren	18 in gauge/0-4-0ST	1887	LYR

PRESERVED STEAM LOCOMOTIVES AT THE BRITISH TRANSPORT MUSEUM - CLAPHAM

THE PORTSMOUTH AREA DURING 1965

EARLY MORNING STEAM

At this date there were only two regular steam workings on the Portsmouth 'direct' line. One was the 5.10 am Guildford to Portsmouth parcel van train, the other the Waterloo to Portsmouth newspaper train, which departed in the early hours, I believe about 2.30 am, and persisted until the end of steam. The latter was often used by naval personnel and the like of us young train-spotters who, after attending a show or maybe a pop concert in London, inevitably missed the last regular train home to Portsmouth.

The absence of any ticket collectors at Waterloo station, on the train or on arrival at Fratton made it an ideal train to use. I remember on quite a few journeys the guard walking through the train and checking whether anyone had fell asleep and missed their station, but we had no problems as we always held a ticket, even though it bore the previous day's date. This train took over 2½ hours, as it stopped at many stations for long periods to pick up and off-load newspapers. At this date the usual motive power would be a Standard Class '5' 4-6-0 or Class '4' 2-6-0.

THE PORTSMOUTH SCENE

By this date the Western Region had assumed control of the lines west of Salisbury, and steam-hauled trains ceased from Saturday 12 June 1965; on Monday 14th WR four-carriage DMUs took over the duties on the Cardiff/Bristol to Portsmouth Harbour trains.

Class '33' diesels had appeared from time to time on the Brighton to Salisbury workings, these being noted at Cosham station at regular intervals, but they were found to be unsatisfactory in the winter months due to the removal elsewhere of the coaching stock with compatible train heating equipment. Consequently in October steam made a return to this route, and I would often note a 'light' Bulleid 'West Country' or 'Battle of Britain' 4-6-2, or sometimes a Class '5' Standard 4-6-0 employed on these trains. This steam-hauled reprieve actually carried on until the end of April 1966, when the final train was hauled by 'West Country' No 34098 *Templecombe*.

SUNDAY 3 OCTOBER - 'West Country' Class 4-6-2 No 34002 *Salisbury* hauled a railtour from London (Victoria) to Portsmouth Harbour. It had a special diversion *en route*: its carriages were hauled up the Midhurst branch to Lavant by a couple of Class 'Q1' 0-6-0s.

LAST STEAM ON THE SALISBURY LINE

One of my last steam notings on the Portsmouth to Cardiff service was the working of Bulleid 'Pacific' No 34102 *Lapford* on the 9.30 am from Portsmouth as far as Salisbury on Saturday 12 June. Even though steam had officially ended on this route, it was still possible to note the occasional Bulleid 'Pacific' deputising for a 'failed' diesel, and one such was noted on Saturday 3 July when a 'West Country' worked through to Cardiff on the 10.29 am from Portsmouth, and returned 'light' to Eastleigh later in the day.

'FIRST' AND 'LAST' GWR 4-6-0s INTO PORTSMOUTH

To complete 1965's railway reminiscences are some notes on 'days gone by' and the *first* GWR 4-6-0s to visit Portsmouth, in the early and mid 1930s. These will be of interest compared to my notings of similar locomotives in Portsmouth over 30 years later, when I noted and photographed some of the *last* 'Hall' Class 4-6-0s to visit Portsmouth.

Long-standing Portsmouth railway enthusiast Mr B. Batten tells me that long before the 'Hall' and 'Grange' Class 4-6-0s visited Portsmouth, the city was graced with Great Western trains hauled by 'Star' and 'Saint' Classes in the early and mid 1930s.

The first ever GWR four-cylinder 'Star' 4-6-0 to visit Fratton running shed was No 4027 *Norwegian Monarch*, having brought an excursion into Portsmouth Harbour. Other 'Stars' noted in Portsmouth were Nos 4001 *Dog Star*, 4034 *Queen Adelaide*, 4058 *Princess Augusta* and 4068 *Llanthony Abbey*; the latter, when withdrawn in 1938, had parts utilised in 'Castle' Class No 5088, which was also named *Llanthony Abbey*.

The 'Saint' Class, the fore-runners of the 'Hall' and 'Grange' 4-6-0s, also visited Portsmouth, having, like the 'Stars', brought in excursions. 'Saint' 4-6-0s noted at Fratton running shed were Nos 2909 *Lady of Provence*, 2918 *Saint Catherine*, 2926 *Saint Nicholas*, 2930 *Saint Vincent*, 2978 *Kirkland* and 2980 *Coeur de Lion*.

The first ever 'Hall' 4-6-0s to appear in Portsmouth arrived with Saturday FA Cup football excursions from Birmingham, these being Nos 4947 *Nanhoran Hall* and 4948 *Northwick Hall*.

Saturday 29 May: One of the last GWR 4-6-0s into Portsmouth. Western Region 'Modified Hall' Class 4-6-0 No 6959 *Peatling Hall* reverses its carriages past Fratton station and the carriage washing unit after bringing an excursion into Portsmouth Harbour. Although in reasonably good external condition, it had, by this date, lost its name-plates, a sure sign that it was nearing withdrawal from service, as well as being a precaution against removal by railway 'buffs' who would be able to sell them for a considerable amount of money.

The elegant lines of the 'Saint' Class 4-6-0. These passenger engines were the forerunners of the 'Hall' and 'Grange' 4-6-0s and appeared in Portsmouth in the 1930s and 1940s.

The last 'Hall' that I noted in Portsmouth was No 6937 *Conyngham Hall* on Saturday 10 July 1965. My last photographed 'Halls' at Fratton were on the 29 May 1965; they were Nos 6959 *Peatling Hall* and 7929 *Wyke Hall*. Also noted at Fratton on the same date, but not photographed, was 'Hall' No 7922 *Salford Hall*. All three were 'Modified Halls'.

The appearance of a 'Grange' Class 4-6-0, No 6848 *Toddington Grange*, on an excursion to Portsmouth Harbour as late as Saturday 7 August 1965 was almost certainly one of the last, if not *the* last Western Region 4-6-0 ever to visit Portsmouth on a scheduled BR working.

. . . AND THE MUSIC CONTINUED

Although our interest in travelling to visit locomotive depots was dwindling with the emergence of the diesel, the train-spotters of Fratton station footbridge would still meet, but on a less frequent basis. We would often share our leisure-time at the local dance hall or seeing a live pop group at the Guildhall, Portsmouth. One visit to the Thorngate Ballroom at Gosport is remembered: we travelled the short distance by ferry across Portsmouth Harbour in a party of about eight to dance to pop group The Hollies, supported by local group Karl and the Rapiers. Admission was 7/6d.

An Eastney-based live music venue, The Birdcage, was officially opened in October of 1965, and it proved to be an opening night to remember for a long time! I and many friends were present and the groups playing on that night were The Action, The Vagabonds and the hit parade top group The Walker Brothers; the host for the evening was none other than a certain Mr Jimmy Savile. What a line-up, and all this entertainment for just 6 shillings!

Needless to say, we returned again and again and enjoyed many a good R & B group. Some of the other bands I recall seeing at this venue were The Moody Blues, with Bo Diddley. Resident groups, if I remember rightly, were The Action, Julie Driscoll with Long John Baldry and various others. American rock and R & B artists were quite frequent visitors, and I recall seeing one of my favourites of the day, Arthur Alexander.

'GENTLEMAN JIM'

It could only be Jimmy Dickinson - 764 appearances for 'Pompey' and no bookings, a one-team man devoted to Portsmouth FC. I remember attending his well-earned testimonial match at

The Portsmouth FC programme front cover for the 1965-66 season; as can be seen, the cost was 6d.

Fratton Park v West Ham United in 1965. As a curtain-raiser to this game the skills of Stanley Matthews, Tom Finney and Nat Lofthouse were pitched against an ex-'Pompey' team. Match programmes were on sale at 6d.

The 1965-66 season saw Jimmy Dickinson take over as the 'Pompey' PRO, and our continued support saw a bright start to the season. I recollect no fewer than four 4-1 home wins prior to the end of October, but unfortunately their mid-season form was poor and included an 8-2 thrashing at Wolves and a 5-2 drubbing at home to local 'rivals' the Saints! However, our Division 2 position improved dramatically, and I recall with some satisfaction our revenge on Wolverhampton Wanderers, beating them 2-0 at Fratton Park.

GOSPORT STEAM SPECIALS

SUNDAYS 20 FEBRUARY AND 20 MARCH

On 20 February I and several local railway enthusiasts, which included David Copus and Mike Yerbury, travelled the short distance from Fratton station to Portsmouth Harbour, where we took the ferry across to Gosport. We were to witness the first of two steam-hauled railtours that would traverse the Fareham-Gosport branch line.

The last public passenger train had left Gosport station and trav-elled the 5 miles to Fareham in 1953. The Southern Counties Touring Society had organised this railtour starting from London (Victoria) and travelling via Lewes and Brighton to Fareham, via the north side of the Cosham triangle.

The steam locomotive was Class 'West Country' 4-6-2 No 34013 *Okehampton*, and on its arrival at Fareham Class 'N' 2-6-0 No 31411 took the train to Gosport and back and thence to Portsmouth Harbour station. From there the 'West Country' took over for the return trip to London.

On 20 March the RCTS (Railway Correspondence and Travel Society) railtour ran from London (Waterloo) to Salisbury, Southampton and Fareham and, as on the previous tour, found its way to Gosport station. This section of the tour was steam-hauled by Class 'U' 2-6-0 No 31639. Having arrived tender-first at Fareham, it coupled up to Standard Class '4' 4-6-0 No 75070, which had brought the special from Southampton Terminus, and the pair double-headed the train through Portchester, Cosham and Havant, then up the Portsmouth 'direct' line via Haslemere and Guildford to Waterloo.

The Gosport branch continued to handle goods traffic until 1969, when it was cut back to Bedenham sidings, allowing trains to continue to serve the Naval Armament Depot. In these and later years the line was frequented by a number of railtours, but they were all diesel-hauled.

SOUTHAMPTON

SATURDAY 9 APRIL

I often visited the Southampton area for train-spotting and the taking of photographs; in the mid-1960s I even made some inroads into tape-recording steam in this area.

One of my railway enthusiast friends, whom I was to meet in later years via the Mid Hants Railway Preservation Society (Portsmouth Group Meetings), was Tony Holley. Like myself, he frequented the Southampton area with his notebooks and camera, and two of his photographs are reproduced here.

One of my former train-spotting companions of the 1960s, Mike Yerbury, with whom I had lost contact after the demise of BR steam, was also reunited with me in later years via the MHRPS monthly meetings.

Southampton station: A Waterloo to Bournemouth express departs hauled by rebuilt 'Merchant Navy' Class 4-6-2 No 35008 *Orient Line*. *Tony Holley*

St Denys station: Eastleigh-allocated rebuilt 'West Country' Class 4-6-2 No 34098 *Templecombe* hurries through the station with a 'Springbok' boat train from London (Waterloo) to Southampton Docks. At this date it carried a 70D shed-plate - Eastleigh had now been downgraded from its familiar 71A code. *Tony Holley*

ISLE OF WIGHT

SUNDAYS 1 AND 29 MAY

On 1 May Class 'O2' 0-4-4 tanks noted between Ryde and Ventnor were Nos 18, 22, 24, 27, 29, 31 and 33. Of these, I was hauled by Nos 22 *Brading*, 27 *Merstone* (with 70G, Newport, shed-plate) and 31 *Chale*. No 18 *Ningwood* was withdrawn from service and No 26 *Whitwell* was awaiting scrapping. Nos 29 *Alverstone* and 33 *Bembridge* were at Ryde (70H) depot.

A 2nd Class single ticket from Ventnor to Wroxall cost 6d.

Shanklin, 29 May: Class 'O2' 0-4-4 tank No 24 *Calbourne* (now preserved at Haven Street, Isle of Wight) stands at the station with an early evening train for Ryde Pier Head. My mother is in the photograph, and note also the driver on the extreme right attending to the locomotive, which on this date was in a clean condition.

No 4472 *FLYING SCOTSMAN* STEAMS SOUTH

SATURDAY 17 SEPTEMBER

I went on this local rail trip with Mike Yerbury of Southsea, and the main attraction of our Eastleigh visit was the appearance of the world-famous Gresley 'Pacific', No

4472 *Flying Scotsman*. It had travelled down with its train from London to Brighton, then departed west along the coast route via Chichester, Havant and Cosham to Eastleigh. It returned later that day along the same route.

It is of note that no major visits to locomotive depots had taken

Class 'A3' 4-6-2 No 4472 *Flying Scotsman*, preserved and in excellent condition, rests in Eastleigh depot yard after stopping off during a railtour of the south of England. This class, introduced in 1927, was designed by Gresley and its former BR number was 60103. This was just one of many railway enthusiasts' tours that this locomotive hauled in the mid-1960s.

place during 1966. It was decided on this trip to take some photographs and to make tape recordings of many of the steam locomotives. Our route from Fratton to Eastleigh was via Botley, and the return was via St Denys and Netley.

Steam seen at Eastleigh station and depot other than No 4472 were Nos 34001, 34009, 35008, 41299, 73022, 80016 and 80152.

Mike and I then walked to Campbell Road bridge where we chanced to see a party of railway enthusiasts about to enter the works; we wasted no time and included ourselves in their party!

In the accompanying list No 2818 was a GW Class '2800' 2-8-0, undergoing restoration for preser-

---

EASTLEIGH WORKS

Steam locomotives:
2818 30053 30926 34019
34089 35007

6 locomotives noted

There were also diesel and electric locomotives 'on works' but we only recorded the steam.

---

vation. No 30053 was a Class 'M7' 0-4-4 tank of Drummond design,

introduced in 1925, also undergoing restoration for preservation prior to it being sent to America for 'static' display. No 30926 *Repton* was a 'Schools' Class 4-4-0, again undergoing restoration for preservation. This engine, along with No 30925 *Cheltenham*, were both 'stored' at Fratton depot in 1964. The remaining three steam 'in works' - Nos 34019 *Bideford*, 34089 602 *Squadron* and 35007 *Aberdeen Commonwealth* - were all Bulleid 'Pacifics' undergoing repairs prior to their return to BR main-line workings.

THE PORTSMOUTH AREA DURING 1966

MONDAY 2 MAY - This date saw the re-introduction of the Class '33' diesel engines on passenger trains running across the north side of the Cosham triangle. The carriage heating problems from the previous year had now been resolved.

WEDNESDAY 11 MAY - A most unusual and very interesting working via the Portsmouth 'direct' line took place when 'Britannia' Class 4-6-2 No 70002 *Geoffrey Chaucer* worked into Portsmouth Harbour station. No 70002, a Crewe North engine, had taken over the troop train that had originally started off from the far-reaching outpost of Elgin, near the east coast of Scotland!

Later that day No 70002 returned the 11 coaches to the LMR at Willesden via Clapham Junction, but Willesden depot was unable to coal and water the locomotive, as by this date the services had been curtailed. No 70002 was therefore returned 'light' engine to Nine Elms shed, who used it on various workings until it was returned to its home depot some eight days after its foray south.

SATURDAY 11 JUNE - 'West Country' Class 4-6-2 No 34012 *Launceston* hauled an excursion train through Cosham *en route* from Blandford Forum to Brighton, returning later that day; it was most likely to have been one of the last

Southern steam locomotives to traverse this line in both directions.

'BRITANNIAS' - As mentioned above, Portsmouth was graced with a few 'Britannia' Class 4-6-2s, including Nos 70000 *Britannia*, 70004 *William Shakespeare* and 70047 (un-named), the latter on 28 June 1964. The mid-1960s also saw further examples of this Class arrive in Portsmouth, all with 'specials': Nos 70017 *Arrow*, 70019 *Lightning* and 70037 *Hereward the Wake*.

STEAM INTO PORTSMOUTH IN 1966

Only a very limited number of steam workings were to be seen. One of

Fratton depot: Friday 22 July. In the roundhouse entrance leading to the main yard is Class '4' Standard 2-6-0 No 76067 (71A). The notice to the left of the entrance read: 'WARNING This roof covering is fragile. For your safety use permanent walking ways, duck or roof ladders, knee or crawling boards' - rather ironic at this date!

these, an old favourite with Fratton train-spotters, was the weekdays 6.10 pm arrival at platform 2 from Eastleigh. This train was known as the 'workmen's' as it conveyed many men employed at Eastleigh Works. Its 5.20 pm departure from Eastleigh (platform 4) was ideal for the workers returning home to Botley, Fareham, Portchester, Cosham, Hilsea, Fratton and Portsmouth & Southsea (Low Level), where it terminated.

This interesting working survived until the end of steam on the Southern Region. Having worked into Portsmouth, the engine returned to Eastleigh with the 11.30 pm parcel van train, and the carriages of the 'workmen's' formed the 7.30 am out from Portsmouth

Two Standard Class '4' 4-6-0s, Nos 75075 (left) and 75069, 'in steam' and awaiting their respective duties. No 75075 carried the BR emblem on its tender while No 75069's tender was plain. Note the water hoses still in use.

on the following morning, doubtless conveying much the same clientèle, to arrive at Eastleigh in time for another day's work.

The 7.30 am was normally worked to Eastleigh by the engine that had earlier worked in the 2.30 am newspaper train from Waterloo. At this date BR Standard Class '4s' and '5s' were normally to be noted, but as mentioned in previous pages this train did produce, among other types, a Stanier 'Black Five' 4-6-0, No 45246.

OIL TRAINS FROM FAWLEY

Trains from Fawley Oil Refinery, near Southampton, were despatched to many areas of Britain and were probably at their peak during the mid and late 1960s. The frequency of running varied from season to season, according to the demand for a particular product and in some cases depending on climatic conditions.

The main destination for these trains was Bromford Bridge (Birmingham), together with Northampton, and they were classed as 'regulars', usually running for five or six days a week throughout the year. The 'regular' trains carried spirit products, being delivered to such locations as Angel Road, Colchester, Colwick (Nottingham), Derby, Hitchin (Cadwell), Leicester, Oxford, Poole, Portsmouth (Hilsea), Reading, Tiverton Junction, Wolverhampton and also Eastleigh - miscellaneous. Bitumen was also carried by 'regular' trains to Cardiff, Diss, Hertford East, Plymouth (Cattewater), Preston, Purfleet and Scunthorpe (Santon). Propane/butane was delivered to Coleshill, Longport, Tipton and Washwood Heath (all West Midlands/Stoke areas). The 'occasional' train of spirit products would also run to Reading (Sonning), Waddon Marsh and Burton (Drakelow).

The very longest journeys were the 'occasional' propane/butane deliveries to Glasgow (Provan) and Thornton (Westfield). The 'irregular' spirit product trains ran to Cambridge, Denham, Hethersett, Purton and Salfords (for Gatwick Airport); these trains would probably only run two or three times a year, or sometimes only once a year.

During the mid-1960s trains from Fawley had often been noted passing through Eastleigh. One such oil train regularly worked into the sidings at Hilsea Gas Works, Portsmouth.

THE 'ONE MAN' BUS ARRIVES

As mentioned in previous pages, Portsmouth's buses were a popular mode of transport for us, and were used frequently. The mid-1960s saw the introduction of the 'one man'-operated single-deck buses in the city for the first time. The Leyland 'Tiger Cub' buses, like the one illustrated, were in fact delivered in 1959, but sat in Eastney bus depot for over a year before union officials allowed them to go into service; even then they proved unpopular, especially when they replaced the much-loved trolleybuses on the 15/16 services in 1963. The loss of the bus conductor proved unpopular with many passengers, and as a result much revenue was lost.

I photographed No 23 (TTP 997) at Clive Road stop (Fratton Road) in 1966 as it was working the No 7 service from Copnor to Clarence Pier via Fratton Bridge.

1967

RUNNING OUT
OF STEAM

WATERLOO STATION AND IPSWICH FOOTBALL EXCURSION

SATURDAY 25 MARCH

Departure was on the 9.20 am electric unit train from Portsmouth & Southsea (High Level) to Waterloo, arriving at 10.50 am. I was accompanied by David Copus, and the return fare was 30 shillings, excluding tube train fares across London. With the exception of two diesels, only steam numbers were noted on this trip.

On passing Guildford depot (70C) we noted Nos 30072 and 77014. No 30072 was the 'shed pilot', a Class 'USA' 0-6-0 tank. No 77014 was a Standard Class '3' 2-6-0, which, due to dieselisation in the North East, had been sent to the SR. Some of its many previous allocations included Blaydon, Blyth, Thornaby, Stourton and Northwich!

WATERLOO STATION

Steam locomotives:
34036 34037 34047 35007
35013 80140 80154

We spent almost an hour at Waterloo. Nos 34036, 34037 and 34047 in the accompanying list were rebuilt 'West Country' 4-6-2s. No 34036 *Westward Ho!* was

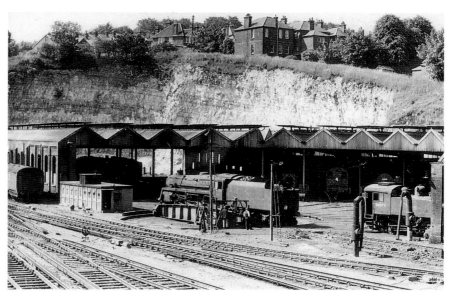

Guildford depot, seen from the road bridge in March 1967. This was one of only a few semi-roundhouse engine sheds on the BR system. Standard Class '5' 4-6-0 No 73155 (70D) is on the turntable, with 'USA' Class 0-6-0 tank No 30072, the shed pilot, on the right. This location had been passed on numerous occasions when travelling by rail between Portsmouth and Waterloo, but it is fitting to include this view on this trip as it proved to be my final glimpse of Guildford depot prior to its closure in July 1967 and eventual demolition.
Norman Hamshere

minus its front number and nameplates and covered in grime, while Nos 34037 *Clovelly* and 34047 *Callington* both had their numbers and name-plates intact and appeared to be in good external condition.

Nos 35007 and 35013 were rebuilt 'Merchant Navy' 4-6-2s. No 35007 *Aberdeen Commonwealth* was minus its front number and name-plates and in a grimy condition, while No 35013 *Blue Funnel* was in exceptionally good condition, its number and name-plates

intact and its casing cleaned.

Nos 80140 and 80154 were Standard 2-6-4 tanks. No 80140 was leaking steam and, like No 80154, was covered in grime. Both were allocated to Nine Elms depot and were employed on empty carriage duties between Waterloo and Clapham Junction.

We then travelled by tube train to Liverpool Street. We were diesel-hauled between Liverpool Street and Ipswich by Stratford-allocated (30A) Type '4' No D1772. Departure was at 12.30 pm and arrival at 1.50 pm.

On the return journey to Liverpool Street we were once again diesel-hauled by another Type '4', No D1768 (30A).

The Pompey supporters and their famous 'chimes' were somewhat 'muted' on the return journey as our team had lost 4-2 - Ray Pointer and Harry Harris were the scorers. Although we lost, it was nevertheless an improvement on my previous visit to the Portman Road ground (7 November 1964), when my team had been thrashed 7-0!

As mentioned earlier, David Copus and his travelling companions had 'PLAY UP POMPEY' stickers printed and they were put on walls, fences, public transport, cafes, station waiting rooms, to name just a few locations! Originally David had 5,000 printed and the majority of these were despatched all over Scotland, even as far north as Wick! By the mid-1960s further stickers were printed and distributed, and these were still in evidence on this trip. When we left a very crowded Ipswich station buffet, the staff must have cursed us as we had left stickers on the tables, chairs, plates and cups!

EASTLEIGH

SATURDAYS 1 AND 29 APRIL, 13 MAY AND 10 JUNE

With steam now extremely scarce in the Portsmouth area, I was forced to concentrate all my efforts towards Eastleigh. These four dates were chosen to visit Eastleigh to witness some of the last steam engines on the SR. Numbers noted on the first three dates have been included in one complete list, and those on my final visit as a separate list.

The forthcoming third rail electrification of the Waterloo to Bournemouth line in July would render Eastleigh depot redundant for the steam locomotive.

On Saturday 10 June I travelled on my own for my *final visit* to Eastleigh depot, being steam-hauled by Standard Class '4' 4-6-0 No 75076 (70D) on the 7.30 am departure from Portsmouth &

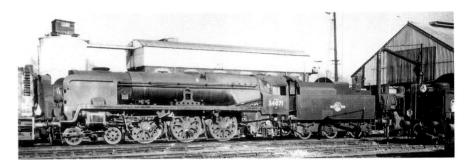

Above 'Dead': Rebuilt 'Battle of Britain' 4-6-2 No 34071 *601 Squadron*. Of note above the tender, fixed to the right-hand end of the water tank, is a small signal; this was used for testing the eyesight of train drivers.

Below 'Alive': Standard Class '4' 2-6-0 No 76009. On the right is Standard Class '5' 4-6-0 No 73115, its rods removed, waiting to be towed to the scrapyard.

EASTLEIGH DEPOT, STATION AND WORKS YARD

Steam locomotives:

DS233 30064 30069 30071 30073 34001 34005 34008 34025 34026 34036 34057 34060
34071 34077 34087 34093 34095 34102 34104 35008 35028 35030 41319 73018 73029
73037 73065 73085 73088 73089 73092 73113 73115 73117 73169 75069 75075 76016
76018 76033 76057 76063 76064 76066 80016 80019 80134 80139 80151

Diesel locomotives:

D824 D1693 D1923 D1924 D2040 D2179 D2251 D2255 D2292 D2293 D2998 D3014 D3097
D3223 15230 15231 15232 15234 D6512 D6531 D6553 D6554 D6583 D7058 D7078

75 locomotives noted over three visits

Steam and diesel side by side in the depot yard at Eastleigh. On the left is Standard Class '5' 4-6-0 No 73029 in green livery; it had recently been cleaned and also displays two white discs, denoting that it had been, or was about to be, used on the Waterloo to Bournemouth line. A green-liveried 'Crompton' diesel, its number not recorded, waits silently - these were soon to take over some of the steam duties on the Waterloo to Weymouth route.

Southsea (Low Level). I 'logged' the journey as follows:

Station	Arr	Dep	Miles
Fratton	7.33	7.34	-
Cosham	7.40	7.42	3¼
Portchester	7.45	7.48	6¼
Fareham	7.53	7.55	9¾
Botley	8.03	8.04	15¼
Eastleigh	8.15		20¾

The train took 3 minutes to pass Hilsea Halt, then slowed for signals on approaching Cosham Junction signal box. There was a 10 mph speed restriction south of the disused Knowle Halt station. Only one dead stop was made; this lasted for 30 seconds, as the train approached the main London to Southampton line at Eastleigh.

This last visit to Eastleigh depot produced a virtually identical list of locomotives to those noted on my three previous trips; the following steam were, however, not noted previously: Nos 30067, 34018, 34040, 34044, 34090, 75077 and 76007.

Since my inaugural visit to Eastleigh depot (71A) in 1955, I had made many official recorded visits, this final visit on Saturday 10 June 1967 being my 30th! I had made numerous other un-recorded visits, some being purely photographic and others where I and my friends had been ejected by the shed foreman for having no permit. Luckily, the latter did not happen too often!

BLUEBELL RAILWAY - STEAM LIVES ON

SUNDAY 25 JUNE

This was my first visit to this East Sussex preserved railway, which has the distinction of being the first standard gauge passenger line to be taken over by enthusiasts; the flowers that grow in abundance along the route provided its name and it is an entirely steam-operated line.

This 5-mile line once formed part of the Lewes to East Grinstead line. Closed by BR in 1958, it re-opened under the Preservation Society in 1960. At the date of this visit the line ran from Sheffield Park to Horsted Keynes; until 1962 trains had terminated at a halt platform just outside the latter.

I travelled by car from Portsmouth in the company of Eddie Rooke, Mike Yerbury and David Copus, and a selection of photographs were taken, of which a few are reproduced here.

Class '0415' 4-4-2 tank No 488. Built in 1885, it worked for many years on the East Kent Light Railway and spent 15 years on the Lyme Regis branch.

Plenty of steam in this shot of Class 'P' 0-6-0 tank No 27, built in 1910. *E. C. Rooke*

Former North London Class '2F' 0-6-0 tank No 2650. Built at Bow Works in 1880, it was formerly shedded at Devons Road (Bow) and carried BR No 58850.

SOUTHERN STEAM - A FAREWELL TOUR

SUNDAY 2 TO SATURDAY 8 JULY

With the third rail electrification of the Waterloo to Bournemouth main line due to begin on Monday 10 July, this week saw the last of the steam-hauled passenger trains. I purchased a 'Runabout' ticket valid for seven days' travel.

The loan of a friend's camera for this farewell tour proved to be a bad decision, as I failed to master it and consequently the batch of photographs that I took were not worthy of inclusion here. It seems that my use of cameras over the years had brought some very mixed results - and this week was no exception!

I vividly recall purchasing a fairly good second-hand camera in the mid-1960s. Its first outing was to Eastleigh Works, but it was dropped on the stone floor inside the works and attempts to repair it failed!

I had also planned to make tape recordings of some steam locomotives.

SUNDAY 2 JULY
(Day 1)

Departure from Fratton was on the 9.55 am train to Eastleigh. I

FAREWELL TRIPS BY TRAINS

Southern Region of British Railways says farewell to steam on July 10 when the Waterloo-Bournemouth line switches over to electric trains.

The end of a 137-year-old tradition will be marked on Sunday, July 9, when two "farewell" trains are to run from Waterloo.

The first will leave at 9.55 a.m. for Weymouth returning at 6.10 p.m. The second, which goes to Bournemouth, leaves at 12.20 p.m. and returns at 6.35 p.m.

This item of news appeared in the Portsmouth Evening News *on the evening of Friday 30 June.* Reproduced by kind permission of The News, *formerly* Evening News

---

changed there and travelled to Winchester, where I saw 'Merchant Navy' Class 4-6-2 No 35008 *Orient Line* on the first of two 'Specials' to mark the 'Farewell to Steam' on the Waterloo to Bournemouth line, which had departed from Waterloo at 9.55 am.

I then travelled to Salisbury, changing at both Eastleigh and Romsey. I walked to the depot for my first visit; how ironic that after 20 years of train-spotting I should finally succeed in eluding the foreman and gain entrance to the depot virtually at the 'death of steam'!

Salisbury depot, formerly 72B, was a ten-road dead-end shed with a turntable. There were 15 locomotives on shed: steam Nos 34006,

---

34052, 34056, 34060, 34090, 34098, 34108 and 76007, and diesels Nos D809, D867, D3011, D3101, D6503, D6508 and D6534

MONDAY 3 - FRIDAY 7 JULY
(Days 2-6)

Maximum travelling time was used during my seven days; engine sheds visited included BOURNE-MOUTH (at this date it had taken the code of 70F, the former Fratton code), BASINGSTOKE (at this date it was a sub-shed of Eastleigh), and EASTLEIGH, now 70D.

Highlights of the week included some nostalgic steam-hauled workings. I travelled behind the following: Winchester to Eastleigh by 'Battle of Britain' Class 4-6-2 No 34060 *25 Squadron*; rebuilt 'West Country' 4-6-2 No 34004 *Yeovil* on

---

REDBRIDGE RAILWAY SLEEPER WORKS (SOUTHAMPTON)

At this date the one-road depot had been demolished; it had been accidentally demolished at an earlier date by a large brake-van, and another small depot had been built, adjoining the works, to house one diesel-mechanical shunter. Ex-BR Standard Class '4' 4-6-0 No 75067 had been used as a stationary boiler at this location during 1965.

the 7.40 pm Bournemouth to Waterloo as far as Southampton; and Standard Class '4' 4-6-0 No 75074 on the 6.40 pm stopping train from Salisbury to Waterloo as far as Basingstoke.

SATURDAY 8 JULY (Day 7)

I paid the additional fare of 9/6d return from Southampton to Bournemouth and one of my many memories of steam on this day was seeing Standard Class '5' 4-6-0 No

73092 arrive at Bournemouth station with a Weymouth to Waterloo express. Hundreds of rail enthusiasts and local press photographers had converged at the London end of the platform - possibly for many this could be their last chance of seeing a BR steam-hauled train.

No 73092 had no front number-plate but someone had chalked its number in large numerals just above the buffer-beam. The words 'THE CUNARDER' were also chalked on the smokebox door,

which showed signs of rusting. Cameras were clicking and tape recorders were in use as the locomotive departed with its ten-carriage train.

Standard Class '3' 2-6-0 No 77014 was noted letting off steam in Bournemouth shed yard.

I was then diesel-hauled to Eastleigh by Class '42' ('Warship') No D801 *Vanguard* on the Weymouth to Swansea train, reaching its destination via Basingstoke, Reading West and the main line to South Wales.

NORTH WALES

SATURDAY 22 TO FRIDAY 28 JULY

I had one week's holiday in North Wales, based at Portmadoc. I travelled by train from Portsmouth via Waterloo, Euston, Wolverhampton, Shrewsbury and the North Wales coast to Portmadoc. I had pre-booked B&B at a terraced house in Portmadoc, and planned to travel by Crosville bus each day, taking in visits to various railways and visiting such places as Caernarvon and Betws-y-Coed.

I made the long journey south from Portmadoc to Aberystwyth to travel on the 1 ft 11½ in narrow gauge Vale of Rheidol Railway, which runs for nearly 12 miles to its terminus at Devil's Bridge, providing spectacular views *en route*. I was hauled in both directions by 2-6-2 tank No 8 *Llewelyn*.

I travelled the A470 road via Betws-y-Coed to Llandudno to visit the Great Orme Tramway. This cable-hauled tramway to the summit of the Great Orme is the only tramway of this type in Britain. It runs for 1 mile at 3 ft 6 in gauge and was opened in 1903.

Above Portmadoc: The Ffestiniog Railway, a former 1 ft 11½ in gauge slate quarry line, gives passengers some wonderful views as the line climbs above Portmadoc. *Linda*, in excellent condition, awaits its departure from the Wharf station.

Below Great Orme Tramway, Llandudno: This is one of the 1903-built electric tram-cars, on its way to the 650-foot summit, from which there are excellent views of Llandudno and Conway Bay. On a clear day the Isle of Man, Snowdonia, Anglesey and the Wicklow Hills of Ireland can be picked out.

Butlin's Holiday Camp, Pwllheli, was the location of preserved 'Princess Royal' Class 4-6-2 No 6203 *Princess Margaret Rose*. In later years she was to return to main-line duties, working enthusiasts specials.

SALISBURY - THE FINAL GATHERING

MONDAY 4 SEPTEMBER

I went on this photographic trip to Salisbury on my own. It was known that many steam, both tank and main-line designs, had been 'stored' at the depot after being sent from their respective depots, made redundant by the introduction of electrification and modernisation on the Waterloo-Weymouth line.

The end of steam on the Southern Region, in fact on most Regions, was now fast approaching, and as can be seen from the accompanying list, the 'final gathering' comprised no fewer than 60 steam locomotives. The majority were subsequently towed by diesels to various scrapyards in South Wales.

Salisbury depot (former code 72B) had officially closed on 8 July and its men had been made redundant, but due to the influx of withdrawn locomotives sent there the men were re-employed to prepare the locomotives for their final journey to the scrapyard.

A general view of Salisbury locomotive depot and yard from the station end. There were many weeds growing between the tracks and the depot building was in a deteriorating condition - demolition was not too far away.

SALISBURY DEPOT

Steam locomotives:

30064	30067	30069	30071	30072	34001	34008	34013	34018	34021	34024	34025	34037
34040	34047	34060	34087	34089	34090	34098	34100	34102	34104	34108	35007	35013
35030	41312	41319	73029	73037	73043	73065	73085	73093	73118	73155	75074	75075
75077	76005	76006	76007	76011	76031	76064	76066	76067	80015	80016	80085	80133
80139	80140	80143	80145	80146	80152	82019	82029					

60 locomotives on shed

THE PORTSMOUTH AREA DURING 1967

FRATTON: APRIL AND MAY

- There were a minimum of steam workings in Portsmouth at this date. The 2.30 am parcels from Waterloo, which arrived at Fratton at 5.20 am, was usually hauled by a Standard Class '4' 2-6-0. Two Eastleigh-allocated 0-6-0 diesel shunters were nearly always to be seen, one of which would inevitably be working in the goods yard adjacent to the depot.

COSHAM: SUNDAYS 11 AND 18 JUNE

- From time to time, due to engineering works and other reasons, steam-hauled trains on the Waterloo to Bournemouth line (and vice versa) would be diverted via the Portsmouth 'direct' line and travel through Cosham, then via the Netley line to join up with the main line at St Denys.

By this date only a few of my train-spotting companions still retained an interest in the local steam railway scene, but those that did found some satisfaction in noting the remaining Southern and Standard steam even though many of them were in a filthy external condition and devoid of their name and shed-plates; they were often seen to be leaking steam and were obviously being run down before being replaced by other motive power.

I would often travel by rail or bus to Cosham, especially if I knew that trains had been re-routed; this usually happened at weekends when engineering works were in progress, as mentioned above. One such diversion took place on Sunday 11 June when 'West Country' Class 4-6-2 No 34011 *Tavistock* was noted at Cosham. On one of my previous visits, another engine of the same Class, No 34008 *Padstow*, was noted on a Bournemouth express.

On Sunday 18 June a railtour from London (Waterloo) travelled via Woking, Petersfield, Havant and Cosham to Fareham - it was seen at Cosham double-headed by 'West Country' Class 4-6-2 No 34033 *Chard* and Standard Class '5' 4-6-0 No 73029. On its arrival at Fareham, the special was hauled by 'Battle of Britain' Class 4-6-2 No 34089 *602 Squadron* via the Netley line to Southampton.

FRIDAY 7 JULY - Standard Class '5' 4-6-0 No 73113 was noted with a breakdown train and crane at Somers Road Bridge, between Fratton and Portsmouth & Southsea; rail workers were repairing the signal gantry. From reports received, this engine was turned at Fratton shed and travelled to Eastleigh, the driver blowing his whistle most of the way - this procedure happened quite a few times around this date, as it was thought that the drivers were most likely to be on their final steam run!

THE LAST BR STEAM WORKING OUT OF PORTSMOUTH: SUNDAY 9 JULY

This was the day that the last steam train departed from Portsmouth. It consisted of empty carriages and departed from Fratton sidings mid-morning heading for Clapham Junction. The locomotive was Standard Class '5' 4-6-0 No 73029.

Local railway workers had adorned its smokebox door with the words 'FAREWELL TO STEAM' and 'PLAY UP POMPEY' chalked in large letters. For those train-spotters and rail workers who witnessed the departure it was hard to believe that this really was the last steam train to leave Portsmouth . . . or was there to be another working?

The 5.20 pm Eastleigh to Portsmouth 'workmen's' train, as previously mentioned, was a steam working until the end, as shown by this photograph that I took on Wednesday 5 July 1967. The locomotive is Standard Class '4' 2-6-4 tank No 80016 and its train consists of four carriages, one blue and grey and three in SR green livery, of which one contained 1st class accommodation.

The photograph was taken from Kingston Cemetery wall, with Copnor Bridge forming the background. Behind the trees on left is a genuine railway cottage that is still there today - it was formerly part of a now long-removed level crossing and signal box at this point. It has shuttered windows, still retains its own garden and at one time had a very sizeable vegetable plot. Unsuccessful attempts were made to build a station at this location as far back as the 1870s. The signal box survived until the mid-1930s.

As No 73029 steamed through Guildford, it passed the depot semi-roundhouse where that shed's last two steam engines were being prepared to run to Eastleigh for withdrawal; these were Nos 34018 *Axminster*, a 'West Country' 4-6-2, and 'USA' 0-6-0 tank No 30072. The 'Pacific' ran via Woking and Basingstoke while the small tank engine, which had served as shed pilot at Guildford, having neither the speed nor the coal and water of the 'Pacific', was routed down the Portsmouth 'direct' line to Fratton, where it replenished its tanks for its final run to Eastleigh. Thus Portsmouth did have another *last* steam locomotive working, but this time it was for real - it *was* the last.

Although I was not personally present to witness this latter working, I gather that No 30072 steamed out of Fratton shed yard amidst exploding detonators and a display of non-stop whistle blowing! In fact, this working contained many 'lasts' - 'USA' 0-6-0 tank No 30072 was

- the last BR steam locomotive to leave Guildford,
- the last to travel down the 'direct' line,
- the last to steam out of Portsmouth through Cosham, Portchester, Fareham and Botley to Eastleigh, and
- the last steam engine at Fratton, and possibly the *first* appearance of a 'USA' at this depot.

As a final twist in its tale, after being destined for the breaker's yard, No 30072 was eventually secured from Salisbury shed yard and taken into preservation, and now operates in Yorkshire on the Keighley & Worth Valley Railway.

ROCK, POP, BLUES, FOLK AND A 'POMPEY' RECORD FEE!

The Birdcage at Eastney, Portsmouth, was the venue on numerous visits to see such bands as Jimmy James and the Vagabonds and Long John Baldry with Julie Driscoll, while pop artists like Gene Pitney and The Ronettes appeared elsewhere in the city. Blues and folk music was beginning to gain popularity, and one of my best remembered venues for this music was at the former music hall pub, the 'Cobden Arms', in Arundel Street.

At this date I both played football (Sunday League) and still supported Portsmouth FC. I recollect the then record fee of £40,000 paid by Portsmouth to Everton for the services of a certain Mike Trebilcock!

FOOTBALL EXCURSIONS

By the end of 1967 rail football excursions had in the main been replaced by coaches. For example, on Saturday 30 September I and a party of football supporters travelled to Derby by coach to see the Derby County v Portsmouth League Division 2 match. The party included David Copus, Roger Emptage and several others. I recall the 'Pompey' mascot, Barry Harris, parading around the pitch prior to the kick-off in a sailor's uniform and carrying a banner displaying the words 'PLAY UP POMPEY'. George Smith scored the goal in Portsmouth's 1-0 win.

Portsmouth attack the Derby County goal. Numbers 11 and 10 on the right are Nicky Jennings and Bobby Kellard, while Ray Pointer is involved in the action.

Programmes were on sale at 9d, and it is interesting to note that admission charges to League Football grounds at this date ranged from about 4 shillings for the terraces up to 15 shillings for a grandstand seat.

THE GHOST TRAIN!

For us train-spotters the 1960s also proved to be a varied decade of other leisure-time activities. Billy Manning's amusement park at Clarence Pier, Southsea, was one of those venues where we would retreat when not involved in railways. At this date we could save 6d by virtue of purchasing five sixpenny ride tickets for 2 shillings, which we often did.

On many occasions a party of us would travel on the Ghost Train, but the operator must have dreaded our visits as on more than one occasion, after paying our fares and making sure that we were the only passengers, we would wait until the slow-moving train had entered the darkness, then alight! The train would then continue its circuit, and when it returned to its starting point minus its passengers, the cursing operator would have to travel in on it with his torch looking for us. We would also have torches and would shine them at him as we bundled into the end carriage! The train would then continue back into the daylight, where we would make an extremely smart exit and disperse into the fun-fair crowds!

1968

A DIARY EMERGES

With the ending of steam-hauled trains on the Southern Region in July 1967, it was no surprise that the majority of my train-spotting companions who had always gathered on Fratton station footbridge had now gone elsewhere. I therefore witnessed the final months of British Rail steam working in the Portsmouth area with just a few of my friends, and no doubt it was the thought that we would see an occasional steam locomotive 'live' that had kept us together until their final demise.

British Railways standard gauge steam locomotives in general held a very special fascination, not only for me but for all my railway enthusiast friends who had accompanied me on railway visits since the mid-1950s. The very thought of railways without steam and a future of diesel and electric unit trains was too much to digest for many of my train-spotting pals, and as a result many of them disposed of their beloved Ian Allan ABCs, their spotters notebooks, shed books, and many their photographs too! Consequently, all their records of 'on shed' and engine notings were gone forever, leaving them with just their memories.

However, at the start of 1968 I had decided to retain all my spotting books, together with photographs, tickets, permits and an assortment of other miscellaneous items that I had kept from my train-spotting escapades; these included a 1926 box camera, a pair of brown 'Tuf' shoes, an old cloth haversack and of course the Pompey 'gong'.

At the same time I realised that my railway trips and all the stories that emanated from them would be best remembered if they could be published in book form. The suggested title was *Depart 1955* Arrive 1968: a 13-year railway adventure.

It took me two or three years to gather up all my trips and photographs and put them in some sort of diary order, as obviously they were all dated. I had no previous experience of using a typewriter, but I purchased a second-hand 'Olivetti 22' from a friend of my aunt in London and it proved, over the years, to be worth every penny of the £5 that I paid for it.

My original manuscript totalled over 840 typed pages, but this was obviously too much for a book, so I and my close friend Eddie Rooke, realising that a publisher was very interested in my unique compilation, got together and condensed the copy down to less than 300 pages, and from this - after being let down by the original publisher - Volume 1 of *Diary of a Train-spotter* was born. Published by Silver Link, it went on sale to the general public in April 1993 - an ambition had been achieved!

BARRY

TUESDAY 5 MARCH

This was a photographic visit to Dai Woodham's scrapyard at Barry, South Wales. I travelled with Eddie Rooke and we departed from Portsmouth & Southsea (High Level) on the 7.27 am through train, a DMU to Cardiff General. The return fare to Cardiff was 49 shillings (£2 9s), and I took 5 shillings spending money with me.

Plans for the day were to visit the scrapyard, pay a brief visit to the beach at Barry, then return to Cardiff city centre for some food and drink before catching the return train to Portsmouth at 6.35 pm.

Four redundant steam engines were noted as we passed Salisbury depot yard, Nos 34060, 35008, 35023 and 73085. Of note in sidings at the approach to Newport (High Street) station were four ex-British Rail steam locomotive tenders; three of them appeared to be in quite good condition.

We arrived at Cardiff General at 11.25 am and departed by DMU to Barry at 11.40 am, arriving at 12.08 pm; the return fare was 3 shillings. We made the 5-minute walk to the scrapyard; as we did not have an official permit for the visit, I asked permission of a railway worker to view the engines.

Steam locomotives totalled 204, 87 being Western Region, 41 Southern Region, 33 London Midland Region and 34 'Standards' - a further nine were unidentified. Although not known at the date of this visit, many of these engines were to be subsequently rescued for preservation; just a few that eventually 'came back to life' were Nos 3738, 3822, 4566, 5900, 6619, 6998, 7325, 7714, 7808, 30506, 30828, 31874,

34016, 34072, 35018, 42968, 43924, 45690, 53808, 71000, 73096, 75014, 76017, 80079 and 92240.

Numerous locomotives still had their connecting rods in place, some had coal in their tenders and some even in their fireboxes, and several had their former shedplates still fixed to their smokebox doors. In fact, many locomotives had literally been 'dumped', having come direct from their home

shed - they were left at the scrapyard to rust away.

My first ever visit to Woodham's scrapyard had taken place during the Western Region Railrover of May 1961, and it is of note that just 20 redundant steam locomotives, all tanks, had been noted then, compared to the 204 on this visit.

As mentioned above, in the years following this trip many of the steam locomotives were saved

from the blowtorch and purchased at considerable sums of money by various preservation societies. Woodhams then concentrated on the scrapping of wagons and vans, as the scrapyard owners realised that money could be made by *selling* the redundant locomotives. Many preservation societies were being set up in the late 1960s and Barry became their 'shop window' whenever a steam locomotive was needed for preservation.

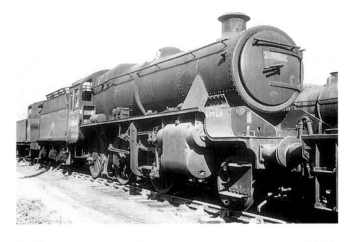

Top left A view of Woodham Brothers scrapyard at Barry Island. When I took this photograph there were over 200 ex-BR steam locomotives at this location.

Top right Class '6P5F' 2-6-0 No 42968 amongst the lines of redundant locomotives at Barry.

Above left 'Hall' Class 4-6-0s Nos 4979 *Wootton Hall* and 4942 *Maindy Hall*.

Above Class '7F' 2-8-0 No 53808, a former S&D locomotive. Behind is 'Manor' Class 4-6-0 No 7802 *Bradley Manor*. E. C. Rooke

Left '5700' Class pannier tanks Nos 4612 and 3738.

CORRALL'S WHARF

SATURDAY 30 MARCH

This location was probably better known as Dibles Wharf and was located about half a mile south of St Denys station, Southampton. I travelled as a passenger in Eddie Rooke's car for this visit. It was known that this location had two small tank locomotives in use and we intended to photograph them, although we did not have permission to enter the area. Prior to my visit I had purchased several reels of colour slide film from the Co-op, Fratton Road - at this date 36 exposures cost £1 3s 11d, including processing.

While at Southampton, Eddie and I decided to visit the Dell to see the Southampton v Sheffield Wednesday football match; the home team won 2-0. Returning home to Portsmouth, I had a social function to attend in the evening at Grosvenor Press works

canteen, Cosham. Being on the committee of the Sports and Social Club, I helped to organise many functions and this particular evening saw the group The Metros 'live' and female singer Maureen, who, according to my records, were booked for a 30-minute spot for £10. About 130 Club members and their guests attended and the bar was open. From my notes, I downed a pint of

Ex-SR Class 'B4' 0-4-0 tank No 30096, then named *Corrall Queen*. It was used solely for light shunting duties in Corrall's Fuel Supplies Wharf. This diminutive tank was an Adams LSWR design of 1891 vintage. Also at this location was Robert Stephenson & Hawthorn 0-4-0 saddle-tank *Bonnie Prince Charlie*. It was noted 'out of use' at the quayside, in a faded green livery. *E. C. Rooke*

bitter in 10 seconds to win a bet of 5 shillings!

ISLE OF WIGHT: RECORDING THE REMAINS

SUNDAY 14 APRIL

This was Easter Sunday. The return fare on the Portsmouth to Ryde ferry was 9 shillings. I visited the locations using Southern Vectis buses.

British Rail's final steam pas-

senger train on the Isle of Wight had run between Ryde and Shanklin on 31 December 1966, and the island's system had now been reduced to a mere 8½ miles (Ryde to Shanklin). It had also been electrified by the addition of a third rail and services recommenced in March 1967 using ex-London Transport tube stock.

These photographs show the very run-down and deteriorating state in April 1968, but, with the tracks still in situ, there was a possibility that preservationists could move in and re-open these locations with the added interest of steam-hauled trains.

Ryde depot (70H): Class 'O2' 0-4-4 tank No 24 *Calbourne* waits in the depot yard for preservation by the WLS and eventual continued use on the island at Haven Street.

Above left A general view of the closed Newport station; the carriages are being restored. The depot, ex-70G, with its water tower is visible on the right.

Above Whippingham station on the Ryde to Newport line.

Left Cowes (Mill Hill) station.

WALLINGFORD BRANCH 'STEAM-UP'

MONDAY 15 APRIL

On this Easter Monday I travelled as a passenger in Eddie Rooke's car to the small station of Cholsey & Moulsford on the Reading-Didcot line, where the Great Western Society, in conjunction with an 'open day' at Didcot, were running a steam-hauled train on the branch line to Wallingford. I paid Eddie 12 shillings petrol money.

This 2½-mile branch line serving the town of Wallingford, Oxfordshire, was at this date still used by trains to collect malt from the sidings of the extensive ABM Maltings Ltd factory in the town; the malt was mostly for export.

We made a return journey to Wallingford, steam-hauled by GWS preserved '1400' Class 0-4-2 tank No 1466. Originally known as the '4800' Class, introduced in 1932 and designed for light branch workings, these locomotives were push-pull fitted and over 90 were built between 1932 and 1933.

The other locomotive in use was 'Modified Hall' Class 4-6-0 No 6998 *Burton Agnes Hall*. Both were based at Didcot Railway Centre.

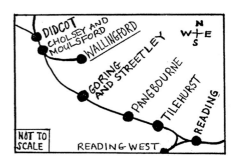

MANCHESTER & CARNFORTH STEAM FAREWELL

FRIDAY 19 TO SUNDAY 21 APRIL

I went on this trip on my own from Portsmouth, but met up with others at Euston, to make up a party of 18.

This was my *final* trip - we would see the very last of British Rail standard gauge steam locomotives in action before their complete withdrawal from active service. The final steam-hauled BR train was to be run on 11 August. The locomotives that were 'in steam' and those that were redundant at the date of this visit were to be the last of British Rail's standard gauge steam before complete take-over by diesel and electric types.

FRIDAY 19 APRIL (Day 1)

Departure from Portsmouth & Southsea (High Level) station was

THE THAMES VALLEY RAIL ENTHUSIASTS ASSOCIATION

Inc: The Thames Valley Steam Locomotive Club
     The Vectis Steam Enthusiasts Club
     The Solent Railway Society.

TOUR No. 2 D 8. - SATURDAY, APRIL 20th 1968

Travel will be by rail between Southampton, Portsmouth and London to Manchester and return. Travel will be overnight in BOTH directions. The depots to be visited (by coach from Manchester) are as follows:- Patricroft, Heaton Mersey, Stockport, Newton Heath, Bolton, Rose Grove, Lostock Hall, Carnforth and Wigan Yard. Participants joining at Southampton (Central Station) should meet in the ticket hall (UP Side) at 21.15 hrs, if joining at Portsmouth to meet by the enquiry office at Portsmouth & S'sea Station at 21.00 hrs, if joining at London to meet in the waiting room at Euston Station between 23.00 & 23.30 hrs - Friday evening, April 19th. Travel outward from Euston at 01.00 hrs; return early Sunday morning, connections arrive Southampton Central 09.33, Portsmouth arrive 09.45 hrs.

FARES: From London EUSTON; Juveniles, under eighteen - £2.18.0., Adults - £4.16.0.
From SOUTHAMPTON *}
or PORTSMOUTH} Juveniles, under eighteen - £3.14.0., Adults - £6.8.0.

DEPOSIT: 15/-.
* - Fare does not include travel to & from Euston and Waterloo on L.T.B. Underground. Participants may join en route, i.e. Eastleigh, Havant, etc, by prior arrangement with me.
* * * * * *

All monies sent for the above tour must be accompanied by a S.A.E. All cheques, P/O's, etc, should be crossed and must be made payable to A. Shepperd. All bookings must be made and fully paid for by Wednesday, April 17th. Should you wish to participate please complete and forward the form below, together with necessary remittance, to:- A. Shepperd, Secretary, T.V.R.E.A., 27, Albert Street, Ventnor, Isle of Wight.

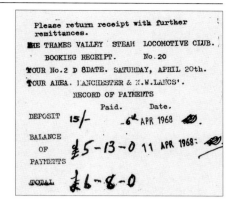

Please return receipt with further remittances.
THE THAMES VALLEY STEAM LOCOMOTIVE CLUB.
BOOKING RECEIPT.   No. 20
TOUR No.2 D 8 DATE. SATURDAY, APRIL 20th.
TOUR AREA. MANCHESTER & N.W.LANCS'.
RECORD OF PAYMENTS
                Paid.   Date.
DEPOSIT   15/-   6th APR 1968
BALANCE
OF   £5-13-0   11 APR 1968
PAYMENTS
TOTAL   £6-8-0

Left A letter from Mr Shepperd giving details of this three-day trip.

Above The receipt from Mr Shepperd acknowledging receipt of the cash.

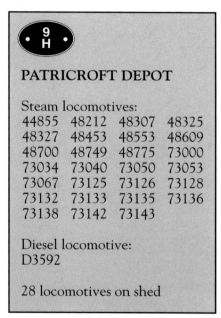

9H PATRICROFT DEPOT

Steam locomotives:
44855 48212 48307 48325
48327 48453 48553 48609
48700 48749 48775 73000
73034 73040 73050 73053
73067 73125 73126 73128
73132 73133 73135 73136
73138 73142 73143

Diesel locomotive:
D3592

28 locomotives on shed

on the 9.20 pm electric unit train to London (Waterloo). This three-day trip to photograph and list steam locomotives would actually centre on Saturday 20 April, the preceding and the final day being used for overnight travel to and from Manchester.

On the train I met up with several other enthusiasts from the Portsmouth area who were going on the trip. No locomotive numbers were recorded on the way to Waterloo and on our arrival we travelled by tube train to Euston where we met up with the remainder of the party in the waiting room.

SATURDAY 20 APRIL (Day 2)

Two early-morning sightings of freight trains were Class '8F' 2-8-0s Nos 48170 and 48465 actively employed in the Stockport area. Our train had just crossed the very impressive 19th-century railway viaduct; its 27 arches are reputed to contain 11 million bricks!

The train from Euston arrived at Manchester (Piccadilly) at 4.10 am and we stayed on the train until 6.15 am, when we left and

walked to the taxi rank and boarded the coach (Holts of Manchester). This departed 15 minutes later and was the start of a mammoth road tour that was to take in visits to nine depots and eventually return to Manchester some 13 hours later!

Our first visit was to Patricroft depot. We then continued on the coach to our second depot, Heaton Mersey.

Patricroft depot: Part of the yard, viewed from the footbridge. The coaling plant is prominent and the depot building is on the far left. Class '8F' 2-8-0 No 44855 is on right.

· 9 F ·

HEATON MERSEY DEPOT

Steam locomotives:
44903	45065	45114	45190
45253	45279	45392	48063
48107	48115	48117	48182
48191	48192	48193	48197
48201	48224	48252	48292
48317	48322	48323	48344
48356	48503	48507	48677
48683	48723		

30 locomotives on shed

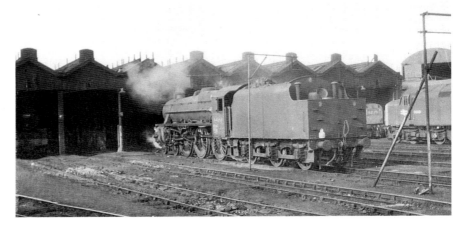

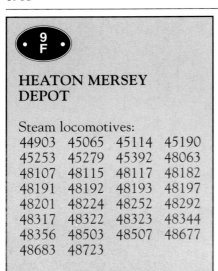

Heaton Mersey depot: A large coaling plant is prominent as Class '8F' 2-8-0 No 48182 noisily lets of steam - truly a 'live' scene.

· 9 B ·

STOCKPORT (EDGELEY) DEPOT

Steam locomotives:
44868	44871	44888	44940
45013	45027	45038	45269
45312	48170	48437	48745

Diesel locomotive:
D202

13 locomotives noted

Above Stockport (Edgeley) depot: A general view from the yard, looking towards the depot building, which was in a run-down state. The locomotive is 'Black Five' 4-6-0 No 44868; D202 lurks in the background.

Below Newton Heath depot: Steam rules, but not for much longer! London Midland steam is 'alive' in the depot yard; although only a few months remained for these Stanier-designed locomotives, all the usual menial tasks such as this - the fireman clearing ash from the buffer footplate of 'Black Five' 4-6-0 No 44910 - still had to be maintained. Two other railwaymen stand nearby awaiting their respective duties. In the background, simmering ready for its next job, is Class '8F' 2-8-0 No 48533. A grimy, dusty shed scene, with the locomotives in a run-down state - typical of all the depots visited on this trip.

The third depot was Stockport (Edgeley), which was a very grimy and neglected eight-road straight shed. On a siding, waiting to be taken away for scrap, were Nos 44940, 45038 and 48437. There were other diesels 'on shed', but their numbers were not recorded. The depot was due for closure on Monday 6 May.

The coach then took us to our fourth depot, Newton Heath. There was a large diesel depot in the vicinity of the steam shed, but we did not visit it.

We then travelled for nearly 10 miles to our fifth depot, Bolton.

The sixth depot was Rose Grove, Burnley, about 13 miles

Newton Heath depot: A trio of 'live' Class '5' 4-6-0s in the depot yard. This photograph could be titled 'Ready for the off', as they appear to be lined up ready for a race. Left to right, they are Nos 44845, 44878 and 45382.

NEWTON HEATH DEPOT

Steam locomotives:

44735	44780	44803	44809
44818	44845	44851	44878
44884	44891	44910	45101
45202	45206	45254	45255
45268	45330	45382	45420
48321	48368	48369	48373
48533	48612	48620	48678
70023	73069	73134	

31 locomotives noted

BOLTON DEPOT

Steam locomotives:

44664	44829	44947	44965
45073	45104	45260	45290
45294	45381	45394	48090
48332	48340	48392	48465
48467	48652	48702	48740
48744	48773		

22 locomotives noted

ROSE GROVE DEPOT

Steam locomotives:

44690	44848	44899	45350
45397	45435	48062	48081
48167	48247	48257	48310
48323	48348	48384	48400
48410	48441	48448	48451
48468	48476	48519	48544
48666	48727	48730	75032
75048			

29 locomotives noted

LOSTOCK HALL DEPOT

Steam locomotives:

43006	43008	43019	43027
43033	43106	44672	44683
44713	44761	44800	44816
44878	44942	44971	45227
45353	45391	45421	45436
45444	48077	48253	48335
48423	48445	48492	48510
48646	48763	92054	92069

32 locomotives noted

Rose Grove depot: The yard is scattered with parts from scrapped engines. Keeping 'alive' is Class '8F' 2-8-0 No 48727.

from Bolton. It was a six-road, block-ended straight shed with a turntable, and was one of the last three steam depots on BR. Locomotives were being cut up in the depot yard, and on the 'dead line' were Nos 44848 and 48544. Several 0-6-0 diesel shunters were 'on shed', but their numbers were not recorded.

We continued on the coach to our seventh depot, Lostock Hall, which was located near Preston. We travelled west via Blackburn,

the distance being about 18 miles. Lostock Hall was another of the last three steam depots on BR and

Above Lostock Hall depot: Class '9F' 2-10-0 freight locomotive No 92069 near the coaling plant. Its front number and shed-plate have been removed.

Above right A general view of the depot yard, with the shed in the background. All locomotives in this view were 'in steam'.

covered a large area. The building consisted of a straight shed and extensive yard, and sidings adjacent to the depot were used to store locomotives, although there was much evidence that many sidings in the vicinity of the withdrawn engines had been 'lifted'. A small number of diesels were also present at the depot.

We continued on the coach, heading north along the M6 motorway to our eighth depot, Carnforth. It was roughly 25 miles from Preston to Carnforth via Lancaster. Carnforth was a six-road through straight shed with a turntable. This was the third of

the last three steam depots on BR - later known as 'Steamtown'. Taking a brief look at the northern end of the depot yard we noted

Below Carnforth depot: Preserved Class '2' 2-6-0 No 6441, an Ivatt design of 1946, splendid in maroon livery. Note the tarpaulin over its chimney, denoting that it was 'temporarily out of use'.

Bottom Another preserved locomotive, Class '4' 2-6-4 tank No 42073, a Fairburn design introduced in 1945, under restoration in the yard at the rear of the depot. A sign on buffer beam reads 'THE LAKE-SIDE RAILWAY SOCIETY'.

that a 70-foot mechanical turntable was in use; other items of interest included a carriage painted bright red (part of a breakdown unit) and a siding full of well-filled coal wagons.

We next headed south on the coach along the motorway for nearly 40 miles, bringing us to our final visit of the day, Springs Branch (Wigan). Our visit to this location was to the 'yard only' - the depot building was either closed or being made into a diesel depot.

10 A

CARNFORTH DEPOT

Steam locomotives:

6441	42073	44709	44758
44874	44889	44894	44897
44963	45001	45017	45054
45095	45134	45209	45212
45390	45424	45445	48124
75009	75019	75020	75021
75024	75034	75041	75062
92004	92009	92077	92088
92167	92212	92223	

35 locomotives noted

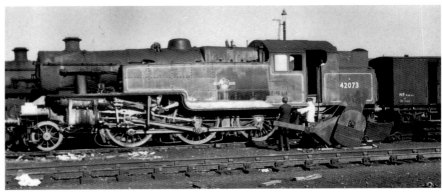

SPRINGS BRANCH (WIGAN) DEPOT

Steam locomotives:
44678 45198 45226 45281
45331 45368 45431 48061
48637 48675

Diesel locomotives:
12003 12004 12013 12020
12031 12032 D7556

17 locomotives noted

All the steam and diesel locomotives were 'dead', waiting to be towed away for scrapping. This yard being solely used for storage of engines, vans and wagons.

Leaving this location, we travelled on the coach to Manchester city centre, our final visit having been completed. The party of 18 were very tired and hungry, so we decided to visit cafes in the city centre and purchase dinner. The time was 7.30 pm.

After our meal we had about 3 hours to spare before our return train was due to depart from Piccadilly station. After splitting up into groups we walked around Manchester viewing the city centre and having a few drinks in a pub to pass the time. At Manchester (Exchange) station we saw two steam locomotives, Nos 44910 and 73133.

SUNDAY 21 APRIL (Day 3)

Our departure from Manchester (Piccadilly) station on a London (Euston) train was on time at 12.10 am. No locomotive numbers were recorded on the return journey, as sleep overcame the majority of us for most of the journey. I said goodbye to the party on arrival at Euston; some travelled by tube and others by bus to Waterloo to catch the Portsmouth line train. Realising after the others had gone that I had only a few pennies remaining, I was left to walk from Euston to Waterloo! I walked at a brisk pace and caught the 7.24 am electric unit train from Waterloo to Portsmouth & Southsea.

THE PORTSMOUTH AREA DURING 1968

LIFE AFTER STEAM

Although I had now resigned myself to the fact that BR standard gauge steam had finally ended, I was finding new interest in other avenues. I joined the Wight Locomotive Society and the Merchant Navy Locomotive Preservation Society, helping to restore SR carriages at Newport station and contributing to the preservation of Class 'O2' 0-4-4 tank No 24 Calbourne and 'Merchant Navy' Class 4-6-2 No 35028 Clan Line, then based at the Longmoor Military Railway, Hampshire.

A day trip in Mike Yerbury's car took in visits to the Bluebell Railway; Preston Park, Brighton (National Railway Collection); Longmoor and Droxford. Some of the steam locomotives noted at Longmoor were Nos 34023 Blackmoor Vale, 35028 Clan Line, 41298 and 92203. A special rail-

tour was noted behind diesel-electrics Nos 10201 and 10202, hauled by Class '9F' 2-10-0 No 92203 Black Prince on the Longmoor Military Railway. Class 'USA' 0-6-0 tank No 30064 was noted at Droxford station, partially covered with a tarpaulin.

Following my successful 1967 visit to North Wales, I decided to

---

An ex-Portsmouth train-spotter and old friend of mine, John Harris, was inspired to put together this poem:

'Just the start of another day'

As day dawns she's awaitin' there;
Simmering inside the shed without a care.

Driver and fireman climb into the cab;
The roster is viewed and they're glad.

They shovel the coal, they sound the whistle;
Their move off shed is without hassle.

A set of carriages are picked up on the way,
And soon they arrive in the station bay.

The time is eight o'clock - the whistle blows,
The regulator's open and off they go.

A slip and a hiss as it takes the strain;
The steam engine departs with its train.

18—EVENING NEWS, THURSDAY, MAY 9, 1968

STEAM NEARS END OF LINE

RAILWAY enthusiasts everywhere have mourned the passing of steam locomotives and, but for a few survivors, mostly industrial locomotives or those owned by preservation societies, the South of England will never again see anything but electric or diesel public trains.

There are but a handful of steam engines around southern Hampshire and these will be the subject of an increasing number of enthusiasts' pilgrimages as the years pass, writes Chris Wood.

Only one is in regular revenue-earning use at present, although earmarked for replacement by a diesel in the near future.

Of those that preservation-minded groups have happily saved from the breaker's torch, perhaps the most travelled is the little ex-London, Brighton and South Coast Railway class "A1X," 0-6-0T number 46 "Newington," built at Brighton in December 1876, and owned successively by five different railway companies and one development group before her final sale and display in front of a Hayling Island public house, (named appropriately enough "The Hayling Billy").

Inn sign

Her grand total of 87 years accredited public service (which included 36 years in the Isle of Wight), were rewarded with complete restoration to her original L.B.S.C. condition in May 1966, prior to her being unveiled as a most unique inn sign on an island where she had pushed and pulled countless trains between 1949 and 1963.

One of the class of "02" 0-4-4T London and South Western Railway engines that replaced number 46 in the Isle of Wight's picturesque system, has survived the scrappings that followed the change-over there from steam to electric power in early 1967.

This is W24 Calbourne, built at Nine Elms in December, 1891 as L.S.W.R. 209, transferred by the Southern Railway to the Isle of Wight in 1925 and purchased from British Rail by the Wight Locomotive Society last year for restoration to Southern Railway green livery and work on the Cowes—Newport line.

Presently stored at Ryde, Calbourne will eventually journey to Newport station by road as the connexion with the old Cowes line at Smallbrook Junction has been lifted.

The characteristic "pant" of the Westinghouse brake donkey pump fitted to the boilers of all the "02" engines in the Isle of Wight will therefore be heard again when the locomotive is restored and the Cowes line re-opened privately, as is hoped.

At Beaulieu rests an express engine of the famous Southern Railway "V" or "Schools" class of 4-4-0, once described as the most powerful locomotives of this wheel arrangement in Europe.

Lord Montagu of Beaulieu purchased this engine with three pullman coaches and a "Bournemouth Belle" headboard from British Rail in December, 1963, and restored the locomotive as 928 Stowe, repainted in malachite green livery with black and white edging.

Express

Introduced between 1930-5, the "Schools" class were highly successful lightweight express engines, designed mainly for use on the weight-restricted eastern section of the Southern, and were frequently used on the most important services between London and Dover until ousted by the Bulleid Pacifics 12 years later.

A dock shunter built for the London and South Western Railway in 1893 is still in daily use at Dibles Wharf, Southampton, shunting coal wagons.

Now the last of the once 25-strong "B4" 0-4-0T class initially introduced by William Adams, the locomotive—now named Corrall Queen—was, in company with 13 of her sister engines, sent to work in Southampton docks when new as L.S.W.R. 96 Normandy.

From 1893 until 1947, when American-built 0-6-0 tank locos began to replace the little 33-ton "dock-tanks," 96 spent most of her time in Southampton and still found employment there up to the time when British Rail withdrew her in 1963.

She was purchased a few weeks later for her present job, but now Corrall Queen may be going to the breakers yard, unless a preservation group intervenes to save her when she is replaced by diesel power.

This locomotive is believed to be the last L.S.W.R. engine working daily anywhere in the country. The only other known survivor from this company's motive power still active being "0415" class 4-4-2T, 488, built in March, 1885, and in occasional employ on the privately owned "Bluebell Railway" at Sheffield Park, Sussex.

£850 buy

Parked on a siding next to the single track line that once connected Alton and Fareham, is one of the U.S.A. Transportation Corps 0-6-0 tank locos that the Southern Railway purchased in 1946 for replacing the "B4" dock-tanks in Southampton.

This engine, the latest acquisition of the Southern Locomotive Preservation Company, was bought from British Rail for £850 in January and towed from Salisbury locomotive depot complete with several irreplaceable and essential spare parts from some of her scrapyard bound sister engines.

Built by the Vulcan Ironworks in 1942, this locomotive was shipped to Europe with hundreds of similar engines and used here by the U.S. Army shunting war materials as WD.1388 until the Southern Railway purchased her and 13 others at the end of hostilities and gave her a new number—64.

Two years later the 46½ ton shunter became B.R. 30064 and as such worked mainly in Southampton Docks and Eastleigh Railway Works until the Southern Region's remaining steam stock was entirely withdrawn last year.

When towed from Salisbury (one of the common muster points for redundant locomotives), 30064 was accompanied by a full engineer's report stating her to be sound of boiler and mechanically in first-rate condition, easily the best example of the ten U.S.A.-class engines withdrawn in July, 1967.

This in itself was quite a compliment for both her builders and the fitters who had maintained and serviced her in her 25 years, for Vulcan's themselves only gave the type an estimated life expectancy of five years from new.

The Southern Locomotive Preservation Company, whose small but dynamically energetic membership of 24 has already accumulated £3,500 worth of preservable railway relics, intends to restore its latest charge to full working order and eventually transfer it together with their total rolling stock, which also includes two small diesel locomotives, to a permanent home in Longmoor Military Railway.

Left and below left An article by Chris Woods that appeared in the Portsmouth *Evening News* on Thursday 9 May 1968. It was no doubt of interest not only to local railway enthusiasts, but also to the general public, of whom many had fond memories of steam railways in the south Hampshire area. *Reproduced by kind permission of* The News, Portsmouth, *formerly* Evening News

railway was visited, as was the electric railway and a ride on the unique horse-drawn trams at Douglas. My holiday ended with a visit to Chester, taking in the cathedral.

My interest in steam, other than railway locomotives, took a new turn when I made my first visit to a traction engine rally at Liphook in Hampshire. The sight of 'live' traction engines, road rollers, steam vehicles and other preserved transport tempted me to pursue this hobby with some enthusiasm in later years.

STEAM TRAINS NO MORE, BUT SPORT AND MUSIC PLAY ON . . .

During 1968 it eventually 'sank in' that steam-hauled trains on BR had finally *ended* - and this would mean that we had more leisure-time to fill. Visits to football matches, both home and away continued, as did our interest in the local music scene.

Our support for Portsmouth FC continued as always. We attended every home game possible; the exceptions at this date were usually when Eddie Rooke and I had decided to visit a railway centre or a former steam site. I remember one visit where we achieved both a railway visit and a football match on the same day. It was on Easter Monday when Eddie and I motored up to Oxfordshire in the morning to visit the steam-operated Wallingford branch (see page 120), returning home for the 3 pm kick-off against Aston Villa. The match ended 2-2.

take a similar holiday in 1968 based at Llandudno. Notes taken from my spotting book record that the train fare from Portsmouth via Waterloo and Euston was £8. I caught the 09.05 Euston to Llandudno train, arriving at 13.33.

I took £18 cash spending money. My aim was to visit narrow gauge steam railways in North Wales, and I also included a ferry trip from Llandudno to Douglas on the Isle of Man, the return fare being 30 shillings. The Isle of Man steam

As mentioned earlier, one of my sporting highlights in the summer months was to visit Burnaby Road to see Hampshire Cricket Club in action. During 1968 I had the satisfaction of seeing the great Barry Richards score a brilliant 206 against Notts - magic!

Attending shows at Portsmouth Guildhall and other large venues proved to be as popular as ever. Many local pubs and clubs were visited and there was a new venue on the club scene, The Tricorn Club, which I remember had a televised opening featuring Dicky Valentine.

One of my favourite pubs at this date was the 'Parade Hotel', Southsea, where once a week DJ Steve Kingsley played all the latest sounds. It was in a small room and I still wonder to this day how so many young people could fit into such a small area; it certainly helped us to converse with the females!

I had begun to type what was to become *Diary of a Train-spotter*, and the early stages of its compilation certainly kept me busy - I did not realise it at the time, but this would continue to be part of my life for the next 25 years!

Having taken a keen interest in art when I was at school, I decided to try and reproduce some of my favourite railway photographs as oil paintings and water colours. I completed one in that year depicting the scene at Southampton Central railway station in 1963 (see page 84), and ironically both of the steam locomotives featured - 'West Country' Class 4-6-2 No 34105 *Swanage* and Standard Class '4'

2-6-0 No 76017 - were at a later date preserved.

Finally, to end 1968 on a musical note, I recollect seeing on the local folk scene Jon Isherwood and Pat Nelson 'in concert' at the Portsmouth Guildhall. On the 'pub scene' the place to be for an evening of traditional folk and blues music was the 'Star Inn', Lake Road, Portsmouth, where I recall USA blues singer 'Champion' Jack Dupree 'live' on stage.

A TRAIN-SPOTTER'S HONEYMOON

Perhaps it was the dreadful thought of a lifetime of diesels and electric units following the demise of BR steam that led my close friend Eddie Rooke to a moment of madness in August 1968 - he decided to get married!

They honeymooned in Aberystwyth. He was obviously influenced by the location, as their hotel just happened to be a few yards away from the sole remaining steam-hauled train service on BR, albeit narrow gauge - the Vale of Rheidol!

Both the hotel and the weather turned out to be a disaster, so they decided to motor south to Torquay, hoping to take in the Dart Valley Railway (which, at this date, was just starting up). On the way Eddie was quite surprised to come across preserved '1400' Class 0-4-2 tank No 1442 'static' on a plinth in Tiverton town centre.

By now, Eddie's other half had no doubt realised that steam railways would continue to be a part of their lives!

Preserved GWR Class '1400' No 1442 in Tiverton town centre. *E. C. Rooke*

INDEX OF LOCATIONS